Michael Basseler
An Organon of Life Knowledge

American Culture Studies | Volume 24

Michael Basseler (Dr. habil.), born in 1976, works as Academic Manager at the International Graduate Centre for the Study of Culture at the University of Gießen. His research focuses on US-American literature and culture as well as literary and cultural theory, especially the study of narrative, African American literature, and the short story. His current project deals with the concept of resilience from a literary and cultural perspective.

Michael Basseler

An Organon of Life Knowledge

Genres and Functions of the Short Story in North America

[transcript]

Bibliographic information published by the Deutsche Nationalbibliothek
The Deutsche Nationalbibliothek lists this publication in the Deutsche Nationalbibliografie; detailed bibliographic data are available in the Internet at http://dnb.d-nb.de

Cover layout: Maria Arndt, Bielefeld
Printed by Majuskel Medienproduktion GmbH, Wetzlar
Print-ISBN 978-3-8376-4642-9
PDF-ISBN 978-3-8394-4642-3
https://doi.org/10.14361/9783839446423

What are those times? Times, perhaps, when someone is feeling the need for a science of life.
(Martha Nussbaum, *Love's Knowledge*, 283)

You ask "What is life?" That is the same as asking "What is a carrot?" A carrot is a carrot and we know nothing more.
(Anton Chekhov in a letter to his wife, Olga Knipper Chekhov, 1904)

Contents

Preface and Acknowledgements

The past few years have witnessed a renewed interest in the interrelation between literature and knowledge. The variety of approaches dealing with this relationship, and thus also the scope of their respective theoretical frameworks, are remarkable. They range, broadly, from literature and science studies to discourse analysis to the New Historicism and similar approaches dealing with the poetics or 'poetology' of knowledge, and draw on a number of diverse disciplines such as philosophy, anthropology, psychology, history, and sociology. As a basic assumption, however, all these approaches share the notion that literary texts, in one way or another, engage with knowledge and knowledge formations in the sense that they reflect, negotiate, play with, disseminate, store or produce knowledge. Literature is regarded as a medium in and through which knowledge is constituted.

After some decades of relative demise short story criticism and theory have also resurfaced lately. While at the end of the last century short story criticism found itself at a crossroads (see Lohafer/Clarey 1989) between its somewhat inhibiting structuralist-formalist legacy and new, still to be developed approaches, in the 1990s and early 2000s the crossroads looked more like a cheerless dead-end street, with fewer and fewer scholars willing to go there. Short story theory got stuck between the sober recognition that there are no essential differences between the short story form and its neighboring genres, and its insular, almost hermetic position within literary theory that was the result of sustained efforts to provide exactly those essential answers to the question of what a short story is. Recently, however, attempts have been made to re-conceptualize the short story form, either by applying a cultural studies perspective that takes into account, for instance, how questions of race, ethnicity, gender, and class play out in the generic setup of short fiction, or by addressing new genre developments such as the short story composite, flash fiction, and so forth. Although there still might be some tendency within the field to shut off short story theory and criticism from other narrative theory (see Copland 2014), there is also reason to believe that short story theory and criticism will eventually move from a rather unfortunate insularity to more dialogic approaches, connecting their insights to the larger fields of narrative, literary, and cultural inquiry.

Asking how the short story form, particularly in the last one hundred years or so, has engaged in the production and circulation of 'life knowledge' this study wishes to contribute to both the growing field of literature and knowledge studies and to the resurgence of short story scholarship. Drawing particularly on Ottmar Ette's (2010) programmatic notion of 'literature as knowledge for living' and 'literary studies as science for living', the focus is on the ways in which the texts under scrutiny, individually and as members of the short story genre, serve as concrete manifestations of life knowledge, that is a knowledge of and about human life. Like autobiography, narrative fiction presents exemplary lives, yet it is not to the same degree obligated to the 'reality' or verisimilitude of these lives. The lives presented in literary fiction need not have a footing in the real world – they are by no means restricted to lives that have actually been led –, yet they are always in some way or another related to it. Dealing in imagined stories about life, literary fiction invites the reader to identify with, imitate or reject these imagined lives, thus serving as a medium in which life knowledge – a knowledge about what life is, and how to live it – is negotiated and given an aesthetic form that contributes in important ways to our very understanding of what we actually mean by this ludicrously abstract term 'life'.

With its focus on the short story, this book is also a contribution to genre theory and history at large, since it is interested in how individual genres and subgenres produce and circulate knowledge in particular historical, social, and cultural contexts. The overall approach may thus be labeled as a "wissenspoetologisch interessierte Gattungstheorie und Gattungsgeschichte" (Bies/Gamper/Kleeberg 2013: 9), that is a particular form of genre theory and history centering on how 'knowledge' is generically constituted and, *vice versa*, how genres such as the short story are inscribed in larger cultural frameworks of knowledge production. Genres are not merely neutral containers of preexisting notions of human life (or other fields of knowledge), but they rather construe particular perspectives on and knowledge about life, which are entwined with the formal-aesthetic conditions of the respective genre. Genres are powerful tools in the production, circulation, and reflection of culturally sanctioned life knowledge, and they are always closely connected to the conceptions and knowledge of life prevalent in society.

* * *

The circumstances under which this book was written and revised deserve some elaboration, as this will only reveal the massive extent to which its very existence is indebted to a number of colleagues, friends, and family members. I started the research for this book almost ten years ago after finishing my PhD in 2008. I am grateful to Justus Liebig University Gießen for providing me with a two-year post-doctoral scholarship in their (at the time new) program *Junior Science and Teaching Units (Just'us)*. This scholarship gave me the opportunity to pursue this project while also entering a new phase in my life that involved the balancing act between academic work and 'career-building' on the one hand, and the joys and challenges of 'family-building' (i.e., parenthood) on the other. It also allowed me to spread out intellectually after the strenuous PhD work (everybody knows the certain fatigue that makes one want to shift one's academic attention to just about *any* other subject than one's current project) and to lay the foundation for this book, while it enabled me to develop some strategies for the impossible limbo commonly known as 'work-life-balance'. Other life events, however, have proven to be even more formative in the process of this work. Much of the writing of the manuscript for this book, submitted in February 2012 as my *Habilitationsschrift*, was overshadowed by the unexpected diagnosis, fierce illness and untimely death of my father-in-law, Frank-Peter Schulzke. His admirable strength and courage were a great source of inspiration for me, even if it was at times difficult to think and write about the 'life knowledge' of literature in the face of his impending death. For me this book will always be entangled with my memories of him.

Over the decade in which this book was conceived, researched, written and – in a painfully slow process – revised, many people have taken their part in its progression. First of all, I would like to thank my teacher, colleague and friend, Ansgar Nünning, whose immense intellectual generosity, critical feedback, and support of my work and 'career' (a concept he finds utterly suspicious) over all these years exceeds all descriptions. I owe to him countless ideas, concepts, and practical advice, many of which I have internalized to the degree that I believe them to be my own. Moreover, I'm thankful to Ottmar Ette, not only for providing me with the key idea and concept for this study, but also for inviting me to Potsdam to present my work in his colloquium during the very early phase of the project. Thanks also to Ingo Berensmeyer and Wolfgang Hochbruck for their valuable feedback on my manuscript. To my former colleagues and friends at the English Department in Giessen, especially René Dietrich, Wolfgang Hallet, Roger Dale Jones, Rose Lawson, Greta Olson, Andrea Rummel, Alexander Scherr, and Robert Vogt, I am grateful for various conversations on and off topic. A special thank you goes to Simon Cooke, whom I owe the idea of structuring this book along the life phases depicted by the respective stories/subgenres. Lothar Bredella, with whom

I had many thought-provoking conversations on the project and who has read several parts of my work in progress, sadly passed away too soon for me to thank him properly. Moreover, I'm thankful to Angela Locatelli and Heta Pyrhönen for reading my manuscript and for the many valuable comments and suggestions I received as a result; and to Jochen Achilles, Ina Bergmann, Jeff Birkenstein, Renate Brosch, Philip Coleman, Ailsa Cox, Elke D'Hoker, Steve Gronert Ellerhoff, Adrian Hunter, Susan Lohafer, Maria Löschnigg, Rob Luscher, Christine Reynier, Michelle Ryan-Sautour, Oliver Scheiding, Emmanuel Vernadakis and all colleagues and friends from the European Network of Short Fiction Research (ENSFR) for sharing with me their love for, and insights into, the short story form at various occasions around the globe throughout the last ten years. I would also like to thank my students in Giessen and at the University of Wisconsin-Milwaukee, particularly those who attended my classes on "Literature and Knowledge" on both sides of the Atlantic between 2010 and 2011. Kudos also to my wonderful colleagues at the International Graduate Centre for the Study of Culture (GCSC), you're such a fun bunch to work with (and now you know what I've been mostly doing on the occasional Friday mornings when I snuck out of my office to do some quiet work). A special thank you to Franziska Eick for helping me with the formatting of the manuscript; as well as to Dagmar Buchwald and Annika Linnemann at transcript for smoothly and efficiently guiding me through the production process.

My biggest thanks, however, go to my family, especially to Tanja, Ella, and Frieda, for lovingly enduring my professional and personal neuroses, and for keeping reminding me of all the things that count in life beyond academic concerns.

Introduction

> Organon, n.: *tool*, an instrument for acquiring knowledge; a body of principles of scientific or philosophic investigation; a means of reasoning, discovery, etc.; *esp.* a system of rules or principles of demonstration or investigation.
> (*Oxford English Dictionary*)

> Literature is not only the continual recurrence of the world in which we live, but it is also the reflection of what we are.
> (Iser 1989: 228)

> What does the text in question seem to say, or show, *about* human life, *about* knowledge, about personality, about how to live? And how are these claims related to the claims made in and by the form itself?
> (Nussbaum 1990: 35)

In the afterword to the 2008 edition of the *O. Henry Prize Stories* the American writer David Leavitt, member of that year's jury, picks Alice Munro's "What Do You Want to Know For?" as his favorite story from the annual collection. Munro's quite overtly autobiographical story centers on the narrator's coping strategies in reaction to a cancer diagnosis, unfolding an immensely deep and multi-layered view on life in rural Ontario that includes the region's geographic and colonial history as well as the narrator's family history. Leavitt praises Munro for her unequaled narrative style and her mastery of the short story form, but the major reason for his choice seems to lie beyond the mere literary refinement of the story and the technical virtuosity of its author. Munro's piece is "strangely helpful,"

Leavitt (2008: 321) writes, and relates how "in the course of reading the story, I had learned a great deal not only about the cemeteries of western Ontario, but about – there is no better way to say this – how to live." He thus grounds his choice not primarily in the aesthetic qualities of Munro's story but in the way in which it responds to a cognitive concern, particularly the desire to *learn* something about life itself.

As such, Leavitt's comment is arguably not much more than a rather personal and probably even idiosyncratic (note the almost paradoxical combination 'strangely helpful') response to the story. What it implies, however, is a common expectation shared by many readers of fictional literary texts, namely the notion that they "function for human subjects as vehicles of partial and provisional recoveries of meaningfulness," as Richard Eldridge (2009: 4) aptly puts it. Among many other reasons – entertainment, distraction, education, understanding other people's motivations,[1] and so forth –, people turn to fictional literature in order to find their own lives illuminated. Literature is replete with imaginative experiences that can have an impact on a reader's life, i.e. on his or her beliefs, values and norms, or life practices. As a rich repository of such 'life knowledge' literature creates an experimental space that is continuous with, rather than detached from, our lived lives and has the potential to retroact on them (cf. Scheffer 1992). At the same time, it offers possibilities for emotional and cognitive experiences that would otherwise be inaccessible. It is in this sense that "literature is a privileged speaking which readers come to hungry for what life cannot usually provide" (Ford 2007: xx). This is also the kind of understanding of literature that fuels Leavitt's appreciation of Munro's story as a 'strangely helpful' medium in which we can come to terms with the most existential aspects of human life, imparting answers to the very question of how to live.

1 That literary fiction enhances our mind-reading capacity has been repeatedly propagated recently, for instance in Lisa Zunshine's *Why We Read Fiction* (2006), in which she applies the Theory of Mind to the study of novels.

Conceptually speaking, Leavitt's quote ties in with recent theorizing and critical discussions about the ethics,[2] uses,[3] values,[4] and cognitive significance[5] of literature, which have gained remarkable momentum in recent years. Trying to establish a counterweight to the "hermeneutics of suspicion" as the default of literary and cultural theory during the reign of postmodernism and poststructuralism,[6] there is an increasing effort to come up with alternative ways of reading and interpreting literature not primarily characterized by suspicion and negativity, as Rita Felski explains: "More and more critics are venturing to ask what is lost when a dialogue with literature gives way to a permanent diagnosis, when the remedial reading of texts loses all sight of why we are drawn to such texts in the first place." (2008: 1) Although quite diverse in their respective theoretical underpinnings and methodological paradigms, what unites these approaches is a general interest in the ways in which the literary imagination works on our understanding of the 'real world' – an alien notion to much of structuralist and poststructuralist thinking. They are therefore *con*textual in the sense that the primary interest lies in the cul-

2 Cf., for example, Adamson/Freadman/Parker (1998), Carroll (2002), the special issue of *Poetics Today* on "Literature and Ethics" (2004), George (2005), Erll/Grabes/Nünning (2008) as well as Brie/Rossiter (2011). Regarding the intersection of narrative and ethics, Norbert Meuter summarizes the major interest in recent discussions as follows, linking it to the concept of narrative identity: "The stories of the literary canon provide a rich source of alternative forms of the 'good life.' But there is an even deeper structural interrelation between narrative identity formation and the moral dimension of human existence. The formation of a narrative identity is identical with the development of a set of values that are independent of any given situation and which lend a whole life – or at least certain stages of a life – moral meaning and stability." (2009: 251)

3 Cf., e.g., Calvino (1986) and Felski (2008). Kenneth Burke's work, especially his seminal essay on "Literature as Equipment for Living" (1973), could also be subsumed under this category.

4 Cf., e.g., Easthope (1990), Rorty (1998), Hunter (2001), Conolly/Haydar (2007), Pettersson (2008), Eldridge (2009), Baumbach/Grabes/Nünning (2009), and Brown/Luzzi (2011).

5 Cf., e.g., Huemer (2007), Köppe (2008), and Gabriel (2010).

6 Bruno Latour has importantly helped to pave the way for a shift towards an understanding of critique that is associated "with *more*, not with *less*, with *multiplication*, not *subtraction*" in his provocative, self-critical essay "Why Has Critique Run out of Steam?" (2004: 248).

tural work of literature and its "real-world consequences" (ibid.: 5), reconceptualizing the ways in which our critical engagement with literature can heighten our "awareness of the density and distinctiveness of particular life-worlds" (ibid.: 46).

In her seminal book *Love's Knowledge*, Martha Nussbaum addresses similar questions, asking what certain literary texts 'know' (and show) *about* human life. Nussbaum's focus is thus on the extra-literary meaning in, or import of, literary texts, connecting literature not only to 'real life' but also to other discourses concerned with ethical and epistemological questions, especially philosophy. What happens if people read literature 'as if for life', that is if they ask what a particular literary work may teach them about life, human relationships, moral values etc.? How can literary texts enlighten and deepen our understanding of (certain aspects of) human life itself?

Far from talking only about the themes of literary texts and instead highlighting the importance of form, however, Nussbaum goes beyond a mere 'aboutness' or 'contentism'. She importantly claims that form and content are always already interrelated, and that the very choice of a certain form carries certain epistemological, ideological, and other implications. Hence, literary representations of life are never separable from the formal peculiarities of the genre in which they are expressed:

> A view of life is *told*. The telling itself – the <u>selection of a genre</u>, formal structures, sentences, vocabulary, of the whole manner of addressing the reader's sense of life – all of this <u>expresses a sense of life</u> and of value, a sense of relations and connections. Life is never simply *presented* by a text; it is always *represented as* something. This 'as' can, and must, be seen not only in the paraphrasable content, but also in the style, which itself expresses choices of selections, and <u>sets up, in the reader, certain activities and transactions rather than others</u>. (Nussbaum 1990: 5; italics in the original, underscore added, M.B.)

What Nussbaum describes here is, in its essence, also what this book is about, namely the rich potential of literary texts to work on a reader's 'sense of life', the complexity of thematic, formal, stylistic, and generic choices through which literary texts are tightly interwoven with the reader's view of what life is and how it can or cannot be understood.

Taking its cues from both the notion of literature as a medium that reflects on as well as actively shapes our understanding of life itself *and* the important addition that this representation is inextricably intertwined with formal and especially generic specificities, this study attempts to explore the ways in which literature in general, and the North American short story in particular, may relate to 'real life', and how it may even produce and disseminate a certain knowledge about and of life. I am thus decidedly arguing against what John Gibson (2007a: 36) has called "literary isolationism," i.e. the tendency in (Western) literary theory and criticism to deny literature its potential of having to say something significant about ourselves and our lives. As a consequence of this tendency that prevailed in critical discourse for many decades, "the informational transfer between real life and narrative make-believe, and the cognitive mechanisms behind such a transfer, remain under-investigated and not fully understood" (Swirski 2007: 5).

This study is thus a – necessarily provisional and inconclusive – attempt to further investigate the complex interrelationship between real life and narrative make-believe. It rather baldly – and maybe boldly – asks how the genre of the North American short story has functioned and continues to function as what I would like to call an *organon of life knowledge*, i.e. an "instrument of thought or knowledge" that contributes to a culturally modeled notion of life. Very basically, the organon metaphor is meant to point to the fact that knowledge is never pure or innocent of the *forms* of its representation.[7] There is no such thing as immediate (or un*mediated*) knowledge. On the contrary, knowledge is always necessarily bound to the discursive, symbolic, and cultural specificities of its concrete manifestation. To regard the short story as an instrument or tool for acquiring knowledge of and about life has at least two important implications: First, it moves the interrelationship between literature and life center stage, and second, it stresses the claim that knowledge is inescapably a matter of representation, including all the choices of selection in terms of genre, style, vocabulary etc. pointed at in the above quote by Nussbaum. Thus, the term 'organon' already serves to emphasize the active, poietic function of literature in general, and the short story in particular, in reflecting and generating 'life knowledge'.

7 My use of the organon metaphor is only indirectly, if at all, indebted to Aristotle's works on logic, or the critique thereof by Francis Bacon in his *Novum Organum*. Perhaps it loosely and quite broadly shares with these texts an interest in how, i.e., by what methods and epistemological assumptions, systems of knowledge are constituted. With Karl Bühler's (1999 [1934]) semiotic 'organon model' – whose influence was Plato rather than Aristotle – it shares a functionalist approach. If for Bühler the central question was how words and language serve as 'tools' in the communication of meaning, then I am mainly interested in how literary genres and particularly the short story fulfills similar functions in the communication and construction of knowledge or meaning of 'life'.

NARRATIVE LITERATURE AND (LIFE) KNOWLEDGE

The 'knowledge of literature' has been established in recent literary critical discourse as an umbrella term to refer to the complex ways in which literature, both as a symbolic and social system, is entangled with the production of knowledge.[8] Applied to narrative fiction in particular, the phrase 'knowledge of literature' implies slightly different, if interrelated, meanings. First, it may point toward knowledge as the subject of a narrative literary text and subsequently ask how this knowledge is represented or referred to, or storied and stored in, that particular text or texts. Second, narratives can be understood as media or mental representations in and through which individuals, but also societies negotiate what actually constitutes knowledge and what should (or should not) be known. In this second sense narration endows knowledge by constructing certain causalities and connections, which can lead both the producer and recipient of a narrative to new findings or insights (Klein 2013: 18-21).[9]

This study's notion of literature as life knowledge entails both of these uses of the phrase, and is strongly indebted to Ottmar Ette's programmatic approach of literary studies as a form of 'science for living'. Ette outlined and advanced this concept in several of his publications, most importantly perhaps his monograph *ÜberLebenswissen: Die Aufgabe der Philologie* (2005), his spirited manifesto "Literaturwissenschaft als Lebenswissenschaft" (2007/2009),[10] and an essay published in *PMLA* in 2010. Taking his departure from the diagnosis of the current predominance of the self-proclaimed 'life sciences' – i.e., first and foremost the biological, biomedical, and biotechnological disciplines – in describing and defining what life is, Ette argues for a reconceptualization of the relation between literature and life, as well as a self-confident re-appropriation of the term 'life' within the humanities. This would create or rather re-create an important space for phil-

8 Cf., e.g., Locatelli (2002-2010), Liska (2004), Hörisch (2007), Köppe (2008; 2011), Valenza (2009). Also cf. Deleuze (1997).

9 On the double notion of 'knowledge of life' that entails both the genitivus objectivus (life as the object of knowledge) and genitivus subjectivus (life producing knowledge), also cf. Canguilhem (2008).

10 Originally published in the official 'year of the humanities' in Germany (2007) in the journal *Lendemains* alongside a number of critical responses, the article has been republished in Wolfgang Asholt/Ottmar Ette (eds.), *Literaturwissenschaft als Lebenswissenschaft* (2010), a collection that includes the original debate from *Lendemains* as well as further responses to, and perspectives on, such an approach.

osophical and philological as well as cultural theoretical reflection in which notions of life and models for living together can be negotiated, both in addition to and in critical interdisciplinary engagement with the life sciences. In this context, literature represents a primary source for inquiry, since it "never misses an opportunity to tell us about life and to show us the paradoxes and aporias of knowledge for living" (Ette 2010a: 984-5). Allowing incoherence, multiperspectivity, and polyvalence, literature has important and very distinctive perspectives to contribute to our understanding and knowledge of life and living together, providing us with an incredibly large and multi-faceted stock of life-models, life-styles, and forms of life (see Basseler/Hartley/Nünning 2015).

To further unpack the phrase 'the (life) knowledge of literature', there are at least two distinct dimensions or levels at which such literary life knowledge can be located, an intratextual dimension and an extratextual one (see Ette 2010a: 987-8). On an intratextual level, literary texts present different events, narrators, and characters who often possess, articulate or represent (explicitly or implicitly) particular forms of life, ways of living and thus different kinds of life knowledge. The challenge, as Ette explicates, is "to understand the dynamic modeling of characters as complex choreographies of individuals who possess different kinds of life knowledge" (ibid.: 988). Thinking of literary characters as choreographies of life knowledge, the short story has produced some of the most powerful and memorable examples in American literature, including Rip van Winkle (historical transformation and life knowledge between the colonial period and Early Republic, see chapter 7), Bartleby (urbanization and life knowledge), and Nick Adams (adolescence and life knowledge). In Flannery O'Connor's masterpiece "A Good Man Is Hard to Find" (1955), for instance, the grandmother's life knowledge sharply contrasts with that of her murderer, the Misfit. In the killing scene at the end of the story the grandmother clings to certainties rooted in Christian religion, her belief in "nice people" and the conservative values of the old South, trying to appeal to the Misfit's humanity. The Misfit's knowledge of life, however, is shaped by his experience as a social outsider, who was punished for a crime he does not even know or understand. The life he has known has nothing to do with the grandmother's notion of what a good life – or a good man, for that matter – is, and so her pleas to honesty, forgiveness, and morality remain unintelligible to him. Though the meaning of the story ultimately remains contested, complicated by O'Connor's own claim that the Misfit is the 'good man' referred to in the title, the story can be read as a clash of divergent life knowledges, acted out in the most existential of situations, and finding its climactic expression in the condensed form of the short story.

The extratextual level of literary life knowledge refers to the ways in which literary texts create spaces of experimentation in which the reader can experience or 'live through' certain situations that she could not, or rather would not, experience in real life. The 'extratextual level' in Ette's terminology bears a close semblance to what Swirski (2007: 5) has called the "informational transfer" between literature and life, and hence to the question as to how literature could produce knowledge and equip readers with a 'knowledge for living'. This knowledge may differ greatly according to the respective cultural and historical conventions of literary discourse, but it always centers around the question of "how intratextual knowledge for living might be transformed into extratextual life practice" (Ette 2010a: 988). Any reader of "A Good Man is Hard to Find" would arguably be well advised to neither adopt the grandmother's nor the Misfit's life knowledge; the informational transfer would instead have to abstract from the characters' knowledge and life practices, perhaps by rejecting their perspectives or by reflecting on the socio-economic conditions of the 1950s American South that have created these perspectives in the first place. Although intratextual and extratextual life knowledge can and should be differentiated analytically, however, there is of course a reciprocal relation between them, since the reader's response to a certain text is always necessarily bound to the level of representation.

But Ette is, of course, not the first or only literary critic to address the interrelationship between literature, life, and knowledge. In fact, the discussion of 'the knowledge of literature' has been led across national and disciplinary boundaries for several decades. Particularly in the last fifteen years or so, there has been a remarkable resurgence of interest in the cognitive values of literature. How do literary texts and especially fictional works relate to our knowledge of and about the world? What kind of knowledge do literary texts impart? Does this knowledge differ from other kinds and discourses of knowledge? And if so, how? Whereas questions like these were at best marginalized in academic discussions of literature for the biggest part of the second half of the 20th century, it seems that they are now more urgent than ever before for a discipline that faces substantial budget cuts and – in some places more than in others – a severe existential crisis. As William Paulson warned us as early as in 1993, "if literature remains cut off from contemporary communication and discourses of knowledge it will die out, slowly but surely" (1993: 35).[11]

11 What Paulson fails to recognize in this statement, though, is the fact that literature itself has arguably never been cut off from contemporary discourses. What seems to be cut off, however, is literature in an academic sense, i.e. the professional discipline that deals

With this scenario in view, it comes as little or no surprise that at least some literary scholars seek solutions and fresh input in the re-establishment of the interrelationship between literature and knowledge. Consequently, 'literature and knowledge' has become a flourishing field in literary studies in the last few years, yet it is probably one of the most diverse, contested, and theoretically heterogeneous fields of research.[12] Among the most fruitful and widespread approaches in this area are those that focus on the discursive connections between literature and particular disciplines such as medicine (cf. Hörisch 2007: 113-30), law (cf. ibid.: 75-112), religion, and the sciences. The articles in the collection *Literatur, Wissenschaft und Wissen seit der Epochenschwelle um 1800* (Klinkert/Neuhofer 2008a), for instance, examine what literature 'knows' *about* schizophrenia, evolutionary theory, or human consciousness, how literary texts engage with other forms or systems of knowledge production, and what epistemological functions literature might fulfill. Taking their cues from systems theory (cf. Pethes 2003), Foucauldian discourse analysis (cf. Moser 1993), cultural poetics (cf. Höcker et al., 2006 Basseler 2010), and other theoretical paradigms, studies in the field of 'literature and science' are mostly interested in the dynamic exchange processes involved in the intersections between literature and other discourses.[13]

Another dominant approach to literature and knowledge can be subsumed under the label 'philosophy of literature', or 'literary cognitivism', and these works usually focus on the question of how fictional discourse and literary language relate to the non-fictional discourse of an empirical reality, i.e. how something that is explicitly marked as fictional and therefore not true can nevertheless contain or produce reliable knowledge about the extra-literary reality. The major challenge for literary cognitivism is summed up by John Gibson: "[T]he prospects of literary cognitivism ultimately hang on whether we will be able to explain just how it can be that a text that speaks about fictions might nonetheless be able to say something

with literature – and particularly literary theory – which has, especially since postmodernism, continuously eradicated the ties between literature and 'real life.'

12 See the excellent surveys in Klausnitzer (2008), Köppe (2011b) as well as Pethes (2003).

13 Studies in this field analyse, for instance, how certain writers appropriate specific knowledge from various scientific disciplines in their literary works: John Milton's use of Ptolemaic cosmogony, Marcel Proust's medical knowledge in *A la récherche du temps perdu*, or Thomas Pynchon's transferences of the physical law of entropy to the realm of literature are all cases in point. See, e.g., Slade/Lee (1990); Bruce/Purdy (1994); Shusterman (2007); Schmitz-Emans (2008); Klinkert/Neuhofer (2008a); Breger et al. (2008).

of cognitive consequence about reality" (2007a: 2). On a very general level, the central problems for any approach to literature and knowledge is thus the 'representational gap', i.e., the question of how to reconcile the discrepancy between the supposed autonomy, singularity or 'otherness' of literature (or literary language) and its complicated relations to our day-to-day lives and the real world, but also to other fields and forms of knowledge production. Discourse analysis and neohistorical approaches generally tend to elide this problem by leveling the differences between literary sign production and other discursive formations. What they emphasize are the topical overlappings, the discursive fabric running through all texts in a given culture and the 'social energy' that circulates freely regardless of such categories as fictional and non-fictional, literary and non-literary, narrative and visual. Approaches of this variety are less interested in the differences than in the similarities and the interplay of literary and non-literary discourses. The 'knowledge of literature', from this point of view, can therefore never be a unique or specific knowledge, but always inevitably links up with other discourses and the social fabric of knowledge, beliefs, and social practices.

At the other end of the spectrum of approaches that are concerned with this representational gap, critics lay claim to the otherness of literature and therefore also the uniqueness of literary knowledge, while at the same time insisting on its relations to, and consequences in, 'the real world'. Due to its aesthetic structure and the exemption from the obligation to speak the truth or stick to empirical facts, literary discourse serves to fulfill important functions with regard to our systems of knowledge: from this angle the knowledge of literature is not the same kind of knowledge found in other, non-fictional discourses like science, law or religion. As Michael Wood argues in *Literature and the Taste of Knowledge*, literature often unsettles the 'direct' knowledge of those other discourses, suspending it in a playful "entertainment of possibilities" (2005: 4) and thereby challenging, debunking or enlarging it.[14] Hence, in contrast to the approaches referred to in the above paragraph, such conceptions of literary knowledge insist on both the epistemic dissimilarity of literary and non-literary discourses, and the cognitive and epistemological value of literature.

As these brief examples already serve to demonstrate, the study of literature and knowledge has gained a significant momentum in recent debates within literary and cultural studies, if admittedly with often extremely heterogeneous prem-

14 Also see Bühler/Eder's (2015) notion of the 'uselessness' of literary knowledge as well as Gamper's (2010) notion of the nesience or non-knowledge (*Nicht-Wissen*) of literature.

ises, epistemic goals, and heuristic values. What connects these approaches despite the varied basic assumptions as well as the extensive theoretical and methodological differences is that they emphasize the interrelations between literary discourse and the 'real world' over the autonomy and separateness of literary communication. It seems that this realization is an achievement of the late 20th and early 21st century, in which it has become possible to claim the 'best of both worlds' without necessarily earning raised eyebrows from literary theorists: Literature may be a self-contained symbolic and social system with its very own particular rules and logic, but at the same time it bears numerous connections to other social systems and discourses – and to our lives.

GENERIC KNOWLEDGE: THE AMERICAN SHORT STORY AS AN ORGANON OF LIFE KNOWLEDGE

Although much ink has been spilled on the question of what characterizes 'the knowledge of literature', works in this field of research are marked by a conspicuous trend towards great abstraction. Tellingly the very phrase – 'the knowledge of literature' – contains two of the most abstract terms in the English language. What we mean by 'knowledge' is arguably as contested, multifarious, and ambiguous as our notion of 'literature', a concept so large as to be almost unfathomable (as philosophers and critics from Jean-Paul Sartre to Jonathan Culler have taught us). This conundrum, however, has not prevented scholars from coming up, time and again, with rather grand claims such as the following: "In essence, literature functions fundamentally as a cognitive, conceptual medium that creates knowledge related to and useable in nonliterary experience." (Herring 1986: 171) Although I share the general belief that literature can fulfill these cognitive-conceptual functions and provide us with 'knowledge for living', the present study sets out to unpack this claim by exploring how a specific literary genre, the short story, is entangled on various levels – formally, structurally, thematically as well as with respect to its reading effects – with culturally prevalent notions and knowledge of life.

Conceptualizing the short story genre in North America as an organon of life knowledge – a literary space in which knowledge of and about life is enacted through certain formal affordances and constraints (see Levine 2015) –, the present study zeroes in on the cultural-cognitive functions of short stories. Historically, the short story (and its many predecessors in magazine fiction, ghost stories, captivity narratives etc.) arguably played a vital role in the process of 'worlding

America', serving as textual commodities for daily use that not only provided entertainment but ultimately allowed Americans to make meaning of their lives and surroundings, drawing on a great variety of cultural, linguistic, religious, and geographic frameworks (Scheiding/Seidl 2015: 8). As these narratives merged into what today we call the American short story, they not only advanced the formation of 'American Literature' but also contributed significantly to culturally sanctioned notions of 'life' and how to live a good and worthwhile life. Psychologist Dan P. McAdams has convincingly argued that there "are indeed certain universals in human development, but they do not generally extend to the kinds of life stories that people tell to provide their lives with identity. In fact, it is in the realm of life narrative where some of the most interesting differences in cultures can be observed" (2006: 116). From this angle, the formation and development of the short story in North America appears as a tradition that serves as a narrative source of life knowledge, explaining, defining, and inventing the constitutive ingredients of 'American lives' (see Hornung 2013). At the heart of what life means, and particularly of what 'American lives' mean, are "stories that Americans have traditionally told about themselves and about their nation" (McAdams 2006: 10).

Expanding McAdams's focus on autobiographical texts (or life-writing) as the main source for stories Americans live by, I will address the question as to how short stories, from the early 20th century onward, have projected values and meanings that have been at the center of cultural conceptualizations of life in an American context. Far from merely erecting and affirming hegemonic notions of life, however, short stories often serve to function as a critical, imaginative counter-discourse (Zapf 2016: 108-14) through which certain socio-cultural tendencies and developments are rendered as problematic, alternative positions and culturally excluded forms of life are articulated, and hegemonic life knowledge is undermined. This counter-discursive quality manifests itself, for example, in the disruptive moments that short stories frequently center around; we may think here, for example, of Bartleby's "I would prefer not to" as a response to the individual's increasing alienation and anonymization in modern work life. Whereas the dominant narrative genres – the novel, but also autobiography – traditionally present life as a coherent, chronological narrative and thereby purport to mimetically reflect life, short stories often dwell on the episodic and fragmentary and thus highlight the "open and discontinuous quality of life" (Löschnigg 2011: 110). As Martin Löschnigg states with regard to contemporary Canadian short story cycles: "The emphasis on individual episodes rather than on the continuity of a life in short story cycles [and short stories, M.B.] reflects the growing skepticism about rendering lives as consistent wholes which has characterised life-writing since the beginning of the twentieth century." (ibid.: 112) In my conceptualization of the short story as an organon of life knowledge, these complex and sometimes contradictory processes of the cultural reflection, critique, production, and dissemination of 'life knowledge' take center stage. In so doing, the study aims to provide a fresh look at the genre of the North American short story that takes seriously the expectations that many readers bring to it – i.e., the pre-theoretical idea that a short story may illuminate one's own understanding of life –, and grounds this idea in an aesthetico-epistemological as well as a cultural-historical framework which allows one to describe how literary discourse produces something like 'life knowledge'.[15]

The most general assumption of the present study is perhaps that literary scholars not only need to take into account the "medium-specific forms of attention to life" (Eldridge 2009: 1), but also the genre-specific forms of representation if they want to come to terms with the (life) knowledge that literature provides. Instead of focusing on literature as a coherent, monolithic entity, it is arguably wise to differentiate between not only the different kinds of literature (Fowler 1982), but also the various ways in which these kinds of literature generate knowledge and produce certain truth effects. This does not mean, however, that genres should be viewed as stable essentialist categories or even 'natural forms'. On the contrary, recent genre theory has moved away from such ontological notions of genre and instead highlighted the functions that genres fulfill in the transfer of knowledge: "Genre is a framework for processing information and for allowing us to move between knowledge given directly in a text and other sets of knowledge that are relevant to understanding it." (Frow 2010: 80) Understanding genres as "fields of knowledge" (Dimock 2007), this study aims to contribute to a genre-sensitive approach to the literature and knowledge debate. Despite their flexibility and elusive or fluid nature, genres function as vehicles, which already shape and even generate knowledge of the world. Genres are not neutral containers of meaning (or

15 It may go without saying that such questions by far exceed the mere personal response of a particular reader (e.g., Leavitt's response to Munro). For an empirically grounded approach that addresses the question as to "How Literature Enters Life", see the essays in the special issue of *Poetics Today* 25.2 (2004). As people's notions of life are never merely individual, but already shaped by, and embedded in, collectively shared forms, practices, and models of life, this study is not and in fact cannot be an empirical study that investigates how real empirical readers 'make sense' of literary texts and relate them to their own lives. Instead, it seeks to explore the ways in which the short story genre has contributed to the reflection and formation of 'American lives' (see Hornung 2013) especially since the mid-19th century, i.e. in that historical period in which the short story has become one of the major genres in American literature.

knowledge) but, as John Frow (2010: 2) argues, serve to "create effects of reality and truth, authority and plausibility, which are central to the different ways the world is understood in the writing of history or of philosophy or of science, or in painting, or in everyday talk." If, for example, a poem 'knows' anything at all, or contains some specific kind of knowledge, for that matter, this knowledge arguably differs significantly from the knowledge presented in a scientific paper or a philosophical essay.[16] But it probably also knows something different than a novel does, and it surely *knows it differently*, i.e., employing the formal affordances of poetry.

And yet, one might object, why should the short story be a particularly relevant or especially revealing genre to pursue these questions? What makes the short story a privileged literary *form* of life knowledge or, in Ette's terms, knowledge for living? On the one hand, the knowledge of the short story is not opposed to but rather representative of the knowledge of literature in general. One can conceive of the short story as a condensed literary form (*Verdichtungsform*) that represents the mechanisms and representational practices of literature per se (see also Ette 2008b: 1; 2008a). On the other hand, however, the generic setup of the short story – its brevity, compression, and the resultant reading experience – has led to its perception as a genre in which some specific knowledge about life is revealed, a kind of knowledge that "may be in some way at odds with the 'story' of dominant culture" (Hanson 1989: 6). One of the great challenges of this study will therefore be to account for the generic specificities of the life knowledge of the short story, while at the same time regarding it as a model and representative example of literary knowledge production in general. To qualify my hypothesis that the short story as a genre is closely connected to life knowledge, let me articulate a number of ideas that, to a greater or lesser extent, have been prevalent in critical discussions of the form.

First, part of what makes the short story an especially intriguing genre to study the relationship between literature and (life) knowledge lies in its truncated narrative form. Narrative is commonly regarded as a privileged discourse of human experience (see Fludernik 1996). People make sense of their lives by telling, hearing, and reading stories about it. Mark Turner even regards story as a "basic principle of the mind" (1996: v), a fundamental form of knowledge that is "indispensable to human cognition generally" (ibid.: 5). Other scholars as diverse as Paul Ricœur, Arthur Danto, Jerome Bruner, and Donald Polkinghorne have also highlighted the vital role of storytelling for human meaning-making and have described 'life as narrative', i.e. they have stressed the role of narrative as a central

16 Cf. Zymner's (2013) thought-provoking essay on the knowledge of poetry.

mode of knowing. In a sense, storytelling can be conceived as a process that makes the very idea of 'life' possible in the first place, allowing us to relate and combine the huge diversity of biological or physical, psychological, emotional, social, and other aspects we subsume under this term. As Jerome Bruner notes with regard to the psychological and philosophical implications of the term 'life': "There is no such thing psychologically as 'life itself'. At the very least, it is a selective achievement of memory recall; beyond that, recounting one's life is an interpretive feat. Philosophically speaking, it is hard to imagine being a naïve realist about 'life itself.'" (2004: 693) In this sense, the stories people tell about (their) life are representations of the prevailing concepts of life in a given historical and cultural situation: "Given their constructed nature and their dependence upon cultural contentions and language usage, life narratives obviously reflect the prevailing theories about 'possible lives' that are part of one's culture." (ibid.: 694) Short stories, then, arguably take part in the 'storying' of human life, both recurring to and shaping culturally available life models:

> The sense of storyness, whether derived from neurological patterns, perceptual gestalts, or cultural models, is a cognitive integer – and that accounts for the primacy of the short story as a narrative form. [...The short story] activates, in order to modulate [...] the sense of storyness. (Lohafer 1994: 310)

Second, the American short story's origins in earlier short narrative forms further underscore its cultural-cognitive function as a repository – or better, because less passive: organon – of life knowledge. It has often been argued the short story derives from primordial short narrative forms, particularly the fable, exemplum, parable, riddle, hoax, and conundrum (cf., for instance, March-Russell 2009: 1-21). What these genres, which exist in similar forms in virtually all cultures, have in common is that they serve to function as media of ethical reflection. By imagining and narrativizing particular ethical, religious, and other problems, these forms serve as literary thought experiments, triggering cognitive processes that are immediately linked to the question of how to live. Similarly, the early predecessors of the (American) short story, such as moral tales, conversion narratives, and sentimental stories, had the explicit function to convey certain life knowledge and instruct their readers in 'how to live'. As Martin Seidl and Oliver Scheiding point out: "In conjunction with moral tales, the sentimental story provides the reader with virtuous examples that are considered worth of imitation [sic], offering individualized stories that serve as generalized modes of life." (2011: 69) These early narrative forms served to ascribe meaning to the often puzzling and startling reality of life on the North American continent, for instance the contact with the indigenous people and the question of cultural identity that fuel the genre of the captivity narrative.

Third, moral disquisition and questions of what constitutes a good and desirable life have arguably played a role throughout the history of the genre, from Nathaniel Hawthorne's allegorical tales to Flannery O'Connor's grotesques. The notion of the short story as a medium of ethical reflection and practical self-help is still visible in contemporary discourses about the genre. Some writers have speculated that the short story – in its suddenness and narrative compression – is a particularly moral or ethical genre that through its aesthetics of compression cautions the reader to pay attention to their life:

> You! You're not paying enough attention to your life, parceled out as it is in increments smaller and more significant than you seem aware of. Here's a form which invites more detailed notice – displaying life not as it is, admittedly, but in flashbacks, in hyper-reality, with epiphanies and without, with closures, time foreshortenings, beauties of all sorts to please you and keep you interested. (Ford 2007: xvii-xviii)

Through its formal qualities – the careful handling of narrative time, epiphanies, and so on – as well as the reading experience that results from these qualities, the short story genre is an example *par excellence* for the cognitive function that Nancy Easterlin ascribes to imaginative literature at large in her 'biocultural' approach to literary studies: Short stories "reawaken" us to our human "sense of meaning-making", thereby "bring[ing] back into consciousness some of what, for purposes of expediency, has been pushed out of conscious thought" (Easterlin 2012: 24).

Fourth, since the 19th century the short story has held a particularly prominent role in American culture, and has thus arguably played an important part in devising culturally specific notions about life and its representation. It has often been pointed out that the emergence of the short story genre in America was directly connected to the socio-historical life-world and the experience of Americans in the late 19th and early 20th centuries. As Ruth Suckow argued:

> It was the chaos, the unevenness, the diversity of American life that made short stories such a natural artistic expression in the first place. Roving, unsettled, restless, unassimilated, here and gone again – a chaos so huge, a life so varied and so multitudinous that its meaning could be caught only in fragments, perceived only by will-o'-the-wisp gleams, preserved only in tiny pieces of perfection. It was the first eager, hasty way of snatching little treasures

> of art from the great abundance of unused, uncomprehended material. Short stories were a way of making America intelligible to itself. (1927: 318)

Hence, particularly in an American cultural context the idea of life knowledge – presented in fragments and "will-o-the-wisp gleams" – seems to be 'built into' the very genre of the short story. From this angle, short stories can be regarded as cognitive devices that contributed, and continue to contribute, to a comprehension of the vast diversity and unevenness of 'American life'. At least with the short story's transition from romanticism to realism (see May 2002: 42-61), writers and critics alike have frequently attested to the genre's pronounced 'closeness to life', a notion that becomes especially apparent in one of the most influential subgenres of the modern short story, the so-called slice-of-life story. Many short stories present themselves as "scenes from the life of the common man or woman, episodes and crises which are typical of those of ordinary life" (Scofield 2006: 8).

Fifth, and also at the topical level, the short story has the reputation of being a genre that is apt to provide new material, i.e. new subject matters, and to "introduce new regions or groups into an established national literature, or into an emerging national literature in the process of decolonization" (Pratt 1994: 104). In so doing, the genre does important cultural work by expanding and questioning what are considered to be collectively acceptable forms of life. Whether one thinks of Bret Harte's stories about social outsiders (e.g. in "The Outcasts of Poker Flat"), about the feminist voices of Kate Chopin, Charlotte Perkins Gilman or Edith Wharton (see, e.g., Rippl 2011) or about the flowering of ethnic short story writing since the 1980s, the short story genre has lent itself to the presentation of marginalized forms of life, and thus contributed to their inclusion into the hegemonic discourse. Short stories in this sense constitute what Deleuze and Guattari have referred to as 'minor literature' (Deleuze/Guattari 1986), connecting the individual to a "political immediacy" (ibid.: 18) and subversively abusing, defamiliarizing, and pluralizing "the discursive structures of the 'major' language" (Hunter 2007: 138).

Sixth, the short story can be described as what Mary Louise Pratt calls a "productive genre" (1994: 93), i.e. a thriving genre that has produced and continues to produce works that reach a comparatively broad readership. This circumstance seems crucial to my argument of the short story as an organon of life knowledge: Literary texts, as well as genres, can only be expected to have a lasting impact on people's conceptions of life if they are widely read, and if they remain relatively stable across time and space. As a fixed institution in the cultural economy of the United States and Canada (see, e.g., Levy 1993), the short story genre has the potential to engage in the social discussion and proliferation of collectively shared notions of life and living together, as well as to critically respond to other, for example scientific or philosophical, discourses about life. This becomes especially apparent when stories deal with pressing ethical questions like euthanasia (e.g. James Salter's "Last Night") or with epochal diseases that alter a society's very conception of human life, such as cancer, AIDS or Alzheimer's. In "The Way We Live Now," published in the *New Yorker* in 1986, for instance, Susan Sontag explored how the HIV virus not only affected the biological or medical conception of life, but also irrecoverably changed the way people actually lived in personal relationships, thus probing into the very mundane, tangible social consequences of the bioscientific 'discovery' of the virus.

Seventh, the short story's closeness to the day-to-day lives of Americans does not only manifest itself on a thematic level, but also in its particular position in an American literary economy. Short stories can be easily integrated into the reader's day-to-day routines without forcing her to sacrifice large portions of her time for the perusal. Historically, this quality helped the short story to its immense popularity since the mid-19th-century, as Andrew Levy points out: "[f]rom the time of Poe, the short story has been designed as a culturally disposable artifact – a thing to be read once and enjoyed" (1993: 2). During the late 19th and early 20th century, short stories were primarily published in numerous magazines, periodicals, newspapers and supplements, and those magazines were most successful that had the best short stories in them (see ibid.: 33). Built into the fabric of everyday life and communication, the short story was not only more readily available than other literary forms such as novels or poems,[17] it was also closer to the everyday life of its readers than most other genres, thanks to its wide proliferation in the mass media of print culture.

Finally, various scholars have commented on the particular reading experience of short stories that endows the genre with a special potential to work on our imagination and retroact on our sense of life. From this vantage, "[f]iction is a way towards action in the real world," and although the reader's own "action cannot be included in the tale, [...] there is a sense in which his story begins too. The story leaves the reader with a sense of heightened awareness towards living which the fictional immersion in other selves can bring" (Scofield 2001: 107). Following Renate Brosch (2007), one may refer to this as "projective reading": In a projective

17 The enormous popularity of the short story in magazines and newspapers during the later 19th and early 20th century also explains why the genre was so enthusiastically embraced as a 'national art form'; see Levy (1993: 34): "The genre-fication of the short story was an informal declaration of independence from an economic subservience to European literature."

reading, we constantly transgress the material boundaries of the text and extend its meanings by projecting it onto our own lives (this argument will be examined more closely in chapter 5). This idea nicely resonates with Walter Benjamin's remarks in his famous essay "Der Erzähler", in which he points to the meaning or sense of life (*Lebenssinn*) inherent in stories:

> Actually, there is no story for which the question as to how it is continued would not be legitimate. The novelist, on the other hand, cannot hope to take the smallest step beyond that limit at which he invites the reader to a divinatory realization of the meaning of life by writing 'Finis'. (Benjamin 2006 [1936]: 372)

ON THE AIMS AND STRUCTURE OF THIS STUDY, OR: WHAT ISN'T 'LIFE KNOWLEDGE'?

The first and foremost goal of this book is to provide a fresh approach to the study of the (North American) short story that is at once grounded in the theorizing of the form (as well as of narrative in general) and goes beyond such theorizing by addressing the short story as a narrative genre that reflects, negotiates, shapes, and produces life knowledge. It is my contention that short story criticism continues to be too much involved with taxonomic questions ("What is a short story?") rooted in the formalist-structuralist tradition of short story theory, whereas questions about the cultural and epistemological functions of the form remain at best marginalized. At the same time, as an intervention in the discussion around 'the knowledge of literature', this study aims to de-generalize this discussion by focusing on the genre-specificity of literary life knowledge, manifested in the American short story. The following aims and research questions derive from this major goal.

First, I wish to frame my argument about the short story as an organon of life knowledge in the context of recent theorizing with regard to the relationship between literature and knowledge. Taking my cue from Ottmar Ette's works, his notion of 'literature as knowledge for living' needs to be expanded by addressing the very processes and epistemological underpinnings that enable – or, potentially also restrain – the 'informational transfer' between literary texts on the one hand, and the reader's non-literary experience and knowledge on the other. As a genre that has regularly been associated with notions of sudden recognition and insight, or epiphany, the short story provides an intriguing case study for this.

In close conjunction with the above, I wish to foreground the category of genre in the discussion of literary (life) knowledge by examining how the short story may produce *particular* kinds of life knowledge and how it shapes the reader's life knowledge in particular ways. So far, most contributions to the debates surrounding the question of the knowledge of literature have short-circuited the genre-question, making virtually no distinctions between the forms and functions of different genres with regard to the reflection and dissemination of knowledge.[18] Whereas some literary genres are rather closely and obviously associated with the way in which they shape our cultural knowledge of human life (e.g. the *Bildungsroman* as the literary form in which the humanistic ideal of human perfectibility is expressed), this has not yet produced any systematic interest in the generic constitution of literary life knowledge. The second aim of this book is thus to redress the literature and knowledge debate by developing analytical models and a terminology with which to approach the short story as an epistemological form.

Moreover, I want to introduce and contextualize such an approach within American literary studies as a contribution to current conceptual and methodological developments in the discipline. As of recently, there is evidence that the study of 'life' (or lives), manifested in literary artifacts and other cultural representations, is (re-)gaining importance in American studies. In a recent collection entitled *Living American Studies* (2010), the editors point out that "American Studies has insisted, from its beginnings, on the inseparability of 'art' (or the academic study of art, literature, and culture at large) and life," (Banerjee et al. 2010: ix), thus emphasizing the continuum of life and cultural production.[19] The present study wants to contribute to these discussions by shedding some light on how literature and life interrelate, how literature may impart a certain knowledge of and about life, as well as by looking at a particular genre that is currently neglected in the larger field of 'life writing', viz. the short story.

By highlighting the ways in which the short story genre may serve as a medium in which notions, models, and practices of life are negotiated, I also aim to make a modest contribution to short story theory and criticism in general. After the somewhat sobering phase of formalist approaches to the short story in the 1960s to 1990s, which led short story theory to a crossroads at best (see Lohafer/Clarey 1989), and a dead-end at worst, there has been a remarkable resurgence of academic interest in the short story in the past few years.[20] Numerous publications of

18 A rare but notable exception is the volume *Gattungs-Wissen* (Bies et al. 2013a).

19 Cf. Kucharzewski (2011) for an intriguing exploration of the many (re-)engagements of literary and scientific life knowledge.

20 See my own survey of short story theories and typologies in Basseler (2011a).

the past five years or so attest to this renewed interest in the genre in both English and American studies,[21] and one chief intention behind many of these publications is to develop new approaches to the study of the short story that jettison the formalist legacy and essentialist tendencies of short story theory. In a similar, but slightly different vein, the present study attempts to go beyond traditional short story criticism and theory by zooming in on the cognitive-cultural functions of the short story as an organon of life knowledge.

Last but certainly not least, I would like to provide a new and fresh take on the history of the North American short story by looking at a number of canonical as well as recent, less well-researched texts. My aim here is to offer new interpretations of these stories by addressing the question of what kind of life knowledge they may comprise and how this knowledge is related to the formal characteristics of the genre. In so doing, I am proposing a new approach to the history of the American short story that centers not so much around authors, periods, writing-styles or topics but around the cultural-cognitive functions of the short story form, its ability to act on the readers' 'sense of life'.

* * *

The discussion of concepts like 'life knowledge' or 'knowledge for living' inevitably entails one central caveat that results from the high level of abstraction of the two central terms, 'life' and 'knowledge'. The basic problem with the term life and its definitions, whether in science or the humanities, is that we can never examine life as such. Life is a semantically open, suggestive, and highly ambiguous term that denotes something we cannot directly observe, yet have a certain idea of. Hence, the question 'What is life?' remains an abstract one, at least if it is not further specified (cf. Böhme 2000). Furthermore, since life "is not a quality that is demonstrable in itself, it tends to be identified with secondary qualities and effects" (Connor 2006: 4). Consequently, different disciplines – from biology to philosophy, medicine to psychology – tend to identify life with a whole plethora

21 For example, see the two *Cambridge Introductions* to the American (Scofield 2006) and English (Hunter 2007) short story, Bendixen and Nagel's *Companion to the American Short Story* (2010), the *Edinburgh Companion to the Short Story in English* (Delaney/Hunter 2018), the *History of the American Short Story* edited by Basseler and Nünning (2011a), the newly founded journal *Short Fiction in Theory and Practice* as well as the monographs and collections by Iftekharuddin et al. (2003), Korte (2003), Buchholz (2003), Löffler/Späth (2005), Ibánez et al. (2007), Brosch (2007), March-Russell (2009), and Boddy (2010).

of highly diverse qualities and effects (see Zapf 2016: 131), so that life "has been defined by many different, though allegedly essential features" (Connor 2006: 4). "What we call life," Terry Eagleton therefore aptly remarks, "is just a necessary fiction" (2007: 15). It is a working fiction, a "grand signifier" (Bogdal 2010: 86), or highly elusive factual fiction, we rely on in order to refer to a reality that we all experience and share, yet cannot satisfactorily pin down to any coherent and comprehensive definition, let alone theory.

Similarly, 'knowledge' is also anything but a clear-cut and easily definable term, but one that allows for almost endless definitions, subcategories and variations. On a very general level, the noun knowledge refers to three related yet different aspects: 1) "the fact or condition of knowing something with familiarity gained through experience or association" (*Merriam-Webster Online*); 2) "the circumstance or condition of apprehending truth or fact through reasoning" (ibid.); and 3) "the sum of what is known," i.e. "the body of truth, information, and principles acquired by humankind" (ibid.). We can further distinguish, for example, between theoretical and practical knowledge, procedural knowledge (i.e. the usually implicit knowledge that allows us to exercise certain tasks), knowledge by acquaintance and knowledge by description, unconscious or tacit knowledge (Polanyi 2009 [1966]), incremental knowledge (Stehr 2000), everyday knowledge, narrative knowledge, body knowledge, local or indigenous knowledge, or even metaknowledge. All of these terms not only imply, to greater or lesser degree, certain (often contrasting or even conflicting) theories of knowledge, they also show that we are a far cry away from any universal or generally accepted notion of knowledge.

As a consequence, any notion of 'life knowledge' cannot possibly be about neutral or objective qualities of life 'as such', but must necessarily and inevitably be a matter of highly selective, culturally and historically specific as well as disciplinarily determined attributions. Rather critically, then, one may just as well ask: 'What *isn't* life knowledge?' If life is just a working fiction we rely on to refer to our shared experience in and of this world, and if knowledge is 'the sum of what we know', then the very term 'life knowledge' seems so ludicrously vast and all-embracing that it loses all conceptual and pragmatic value. At the same time, however, it is precisely this notion of life knowledge as a working fiction which invites the perspective of literature as one of humankind's preeminent tools for making (the) meaning of life (cf. Köppe 2005; also see Wilson 2009).

To conceive of literature as a medium of life knowledge thus means to examine one dimension of how 'life' as a working fiction is construed: What does literature, what do the various genres of literature contribute to our understanding (or knowledge) of this vast phenomenon we tend to call 'life'? How does literature take part in the formation and negotiation of our cultural notions and models of life? If one accepts the pragmatist credo that we should talk about our exposure to, or interaction with, things we cannot directly observe, then literature in general and the short story in particular could be conceptualized as a very specific and highly specialized discourse dealing with the production of knowledge of life (see Basseler 2009). We may not be able to define 'life' as such because we cannot observe it, and therefore the term necessarily remains a rather vague umbrella term or a grand signifier for an almost infinitely large number of vastly diverse phenomena. What we can observe and therefore also analyze, however, is how literature treats such a phenomenon as life and how it engages in the reflection, production, and dissemination of life models, lifestyles, life practices, notions of the good life, and so forth.

* * *

In Part I, I will develop a theoretical framework that allows us to conceptualize the complex and dynamic relationship between the three major components in this study's central equation: literature, life, and knowledge. While the thrust of the argument in this part is already towards the formal characteristics of the short story and the aesthetic experience it provides, this chapter is also concerned with more general questions about the (life) knowledge of literature. The goal in this part, hence, is to introduce a terminology as well as a model for the analysis of short stories that takes its departure from the assumption that literature is a pertinent vehicle for the construction and dissemination of life knowledge.

Part II, then, will be more explicitly concerned with the particular kinds of life knowledge that the short story imparts, as well as the ways in which these kinds of life knowledge correspond to the formal features of the genre. Against the backdrop of existing theorizing of the short story form, as well as in light of the genre's literary history, the short story's life knowledge will be described with regard to thematic and formal aspects as well as the result of what might be called the specific reading experience of short stories. While chapter 4 deals with the widespread notion that short stories possess a certain 'life-likeness' that resides, for example, in the genre's preference for moments which reveal some essential truths about life ('epiphany'), chapter 5 is concerned with how this quality of revelation (at a formal and thematic level) also determines the reading experience of short stories. Chapter 6 explores how the short story is frequently associated with notions of crisis and turning point, a trait of the genre that has often been pointed out yet rarely explored in detail. It is especially the temporal characteristics of the short story, its sense of time and specific handling of life's rhythms and sequences that equips it as a medium of life knowledge, recording and shaping notions about the time-related dimension of human life. To illustrate this, chapter 7 employs two examples (Irving's "Rip Van Winkle" and Fitzgerald's "Benjamin Button") to analyze how short stories have responded to the 'temporalization of life' – that is, the increasing temporal patterning, regulation, and governing of forms of life – that characterizes the project of modernity in America.

The temporal patterning of life most evidently plays out on the level of the various phases or stages in which we tend to portion our lives, from infancy to old age. This patterning is not merely a consequence of our biological nature, but is essentially based on storytelling:

> Our own life stories draw on the stories we learn as active participants in culture – stories about childhood, adolescence, adulthood, and aging. Stories distinguish between what culture glorifies as good characters and vilifies as bad characters, and they present the many varieties that fall in between. Stories depict full and fragmented lives that are exciting, frightening, infuriating, enlightening, admirable, heroic, dignified, ignoble, disgusting, wise, foolish, and boring. Stories teach us how to live and what our lives mean. (McAdams 2006: 288-9)

Instead of viewing life as one coherent, comprehensive story, short stories tend to tell life as a series of fragmented episodes, thus providing a life knowledge that – thematically, but even more important, formally – differs significantly from longer narrative forms. Accordingly, the exemplary readings in part III are arranged according to the different stages or ages of life, from childhood and youth to maturity to old age, identifying typical themes frequently associated with these phases. This organizing principle is not a random decision, but already implies a central argument of this study: By either focusing on brief episodes and the different stages of life or by telling 'a whole life' in an extremely condensed manner, short stories contribute to our 'life knowledge' insofar as they inscribe a certain structure onto our lives. If narrative texts both privilege and model certain aspects of life and the human life course (see Malcolm 2011: 97), then the short story arguably tends to favor a fragmented model of life over the concluded model that the novel presents. This preference already results from the formal peculiarities of the genre, especially its brevity as the main structuring principle (Zumthor 2016: 74). As David Malcolm (ibid.: 100) maintains in a recent essay:

> The short story's modelling of human life as a fragment can be (and is, frequently) contrasted with the *longue durée* of the novel. The novel is seen as expansive, substantial, complex, offering broad perspectives, and a vision of life made up of multiple interlacing

> strands. […] The short story offers a model of the human life-course which privileges the single moment, rather than the longer term.

Thus, focusing on life phases rather than comprehensive and coherent biographies, short stories tend to emphasize the situational quality of human life and identity, while de-emphasizing the teleological life-model that underlies the traditional novel. But even if, as in Fitzgerald's "The Curious Case of Benjamin Button," for example, a whole life is presented in the fast-forward (or in this case fast-rewind) mode of a short story, this often serves to highlight the narrative sequencing of life and the constructive nature of the life-course model. Though not the main focus, age and aging as important categories of cultural analysis thus influence the critical perspective and structure of this study. Despite the work that has already been done in recent years, aging – along with phenomena such as ageism or age consciousness – is still an undertheorized and somewhat marginal concept or "site of difference" (DeFalco 2010: xv) in literary and cultural studies. Arranging the text analyses along the dominant life-course model of Western and particularly American culture, I want to both reflect on and critique this model as a social construct that depends on cultural representations in order to exert its influence on people's lives.

The literary-historical scope of this study can be loosely defined as the 'long 20th century' – that is roughly the time between 1890 and the early 2000s, with a few forays into the earlier 19th century –, based on the assumption that the short story is an essentially *modern* literary form (see Allen 1981: 3). Flourishing for a number of decades in the magazine culture of the 19th century, around 1900 the (North) American short story had been definitively established as a distinct literary form (by then also carrying the generic name 'short story') and defined by various writers and critics, most importantly perhaps Brander Matthews's *Philosophy of the Short-Story* (1901, first published anonymously in *Lippincott's Magazine* in 1885). It was also around 1900 that the short story was increasingly associated with notions of a certain 'lifelikeness' as well as epistemological functions. Through the realist interventions of writers like Henry James and Stephen Crane, the short story was gradually removed from the allegorical mode of romance in which characters embodied basic human fears and desires, and focusing more and more on everyday life and social reality (cf. May 2002: 45). Ever since, short stories have been linked to ideas like 'slice of life' and the notion that they present brief, ephemeral yet representative moments and events in people's lives and thus grant the reader a "glimpse through" (see Beachcroft 1968: 263). Even the radical experiments with the short story form, the anti-stories of postmodern writers like

John Barth or Robert Coover, are closely entwined with such notions as they ridicule and subvert them (as in Barth's *Lost in the Funhouse*).

As a modern literary genre, the short story is inseparably interconnected with an epistemological uncertainty and a fragmentation of 'life' that is considered to be a central characteristic of (post-)modernity. As philosopher Wilhelm Schmid suggests, the process of modernity can be understood as the gradual loss of practical life knowledge: "In modernity, practical life knowledge is no longer passed on from person to person, from generation to generation; the progressive liberation [of the individual from tradition, convention, religion, etc.] has broken this chain." (Schmid 2014: 40, transl. M.B.) The emergence of the short story form, as well as of other modern forms of literature, not only coincides with the process Schmid describes, but may even point to the function of the short story as a literary space in which such a loss of practical life knowledge is reflected and, perhaps, even compensated and produced. As Frank Farrell argues:

> The space of the literary text remains one where that life of the self, its fundamental way of setting itself in relation with the universe, its relations to fate and chance, to grief, death, and loss, are being enacted in a particular fashion, not only in the lives of the characters but also in the very processes of writing and reading. (2004: 10)

As a literary and cultural "space," the North American short story of the late 19th to early 21st century can be understood as a repository as well as a vehicle for the negotiation and recovery of meaning and a non-reductive sense of human life that includes phenomenological, metaphysical, linguistic, metaphoric, aesthetic, psychological, historical, and social dimensions (cf. ibid.) (this argument will be examined in greater detail in chapters 3-7). This study is thus an attempt to explore the particular "affordances of form" (Levine 2015: 6), that is the potentialities residing in its generic structure and conventions, that enable the short story to *do* so many different and even contradictory things with regard to presenting, organizing and shaping life knowledge.

Part One: Life, Literature, and Knowledge: Theoretical Premises

1. Literature, Life Knowledge, and 'Science for Living'

In 2007, the 'year of the humanities' in Germany,[1] Ottmar Ette, a scholar of Romance literature, sparked a lively discussion about the role of literary studies within the context of what has become known as the 'life sciences', i.e. a group of loosely connected medical and biotechnological disciplines engaged in research on living organisms and especially human (but also nonhuman) life. The term 'life science' dates back at least to the mid-19th century, and according to the *Oxford English Dictionary* its first recorded use was in an article in the medical journal *The Lancet* in 1861. Today the term essentially denominates an interdisciplinary project in contemporary scientific research, and thus a phenomenon of the late 20th and early 21st century. The list of disciplines considered to be part of the illustrious circle of life sciences include such diverse fields as anatomy, biochemistry, agrotechnology, cognitive and computational neuroscience, molecular biology, and tissue engineering. As an interdisciplinary conglomerate the life sciences imply the rise of a new "culture of life" (Knorr Cetina 2005: 76). Abandoning the Enlightenment ideas that until today constitute the backbone for the humanities and social sciences, the life sciences move towards the perfectibility and enhancement of life in biological and economic terms (cf. ibid.). It is hardly surprising, then, that disciplines interested in the historical, social or cultural dimensions of (human) life are conspicuously missing from the list of the so-called life sciences. Consequently, it is by the very term 'life sciences' that "a constellation of biotechnological disciplines has appropriated the term *life* in an effective, deceptively self-evident way, increasingly robbing the humanities of any authority to produce knowledge about life" (Ette 2010a: 983).

1 The 'year of the humanities' (*Jahr der Geisteswissenschaften*) was the eighth motto of the so-called *Wissenschaftsjahr*, initiated by the Federal Ministry of Education and Research to advance the exchange between academia and the public.

In his programmatic essay published in the journal *Lendemains*, Ette (2007) introduced his ideas of literary studies as a form of life science or "science for living" to a broader public; ideas, which he had already addressed in his monograph *ÜberLebenswissen: Die Aufgabe der Philologie* (2004). Ette's main concern in this essay, his book-length study and numerous other publications (see, for instance, Ette 2009, 2010a, 2010b) was to challenge the predominance of the life sciences in defining and limiting the public notion of life to material and technological aspects, but also, as a consequence, to rethink the role and methods of the humanities in this context. In asking meaningful questions about the contribution of literary studies for our understanding of life, the aim of Ette's approach is to undercut the "semantic reductionism of a bioscientifically formulated notion of life" (Ette 2007: 11, transl. M.B.).

According to Ette, the idea of literary studies as a science for living (*Lebens-Wissenschaft*) is not only crucial for a multidimensional, holistic understanding of 'life' itself, but also an important, or, as it were, *vital* strategic move for the entire discipline. "For the humanities to survive in our present and future societies it is vital that they conceive of themselves as *sciences for living*." (2010a: 983) Instead of surrendering to the predominance of the life sciences and their concept of life, scholars in literary studies should decidedly "develop an open concept of life and of knowledge *about* and *for* living." (ibid.) Literature is replete with such configurations of knowledge in a vast amount of social, historical, and cultural constellations, thus rendering the 'life knowledge' of literature as multifarious, complex, and highly relevant as those phenomena scrutinized by the bio-sciences. As Ette puts it, there simply is no good reason why the philologies should dispense with the concept of 'life' and thus relinquish it entirely to other disciplines, especially those in the 'hard' sciences. Instead, he argues, it is about time that literary studies and literary theory also returned to the long-shunned questions of how literature and life interconnect, and how literary and cultural studies may contribute to our societies' notions and discourses of life (cf. Ette 2004: 19).

But how can the humanities regain some of their authority to produce 'knowledge of life', and why is this even necessary or desirable? What *kind* of knowledge about and of life does literature contain, generate or impart? And in connection with these questions, what is the role of literary *studies* in the critical engagement with literature and literary (life) knowledge? What, in other words, should literary studies as 'science for living' (Ette 2010a) look like? Moreover, to what extent could or should this life knowledge or knowledge for living be evaluated in interdisciplinary terms, i.e. how can we conceptualize literary life knowledge in such a way that it corresponds to and complements other (scientific) discourses about life?

In order to further elaborate on the concept of literature as 'knowledge for living' as well as the approach of literary studies as 'science for living' it is worth quoting Ette at some length here:

> I want to use the concept of knowledge for living to suggest new perspectives on the relevance of literature and literary scholarship to human societies and their histories. Terminologically, *knowledge for living* opens our view onto the complex relation between the semantic poles of the compound phrase. This relation is multilayered or multidimensional. To combine *living* with *knowledge* implies knowledge *about* or *of* life. It also implies knowledge for the purpose or benefit of living. Further, these different aspects of knowledge exist *in* life and are inseparable for a living (and knowing) subject. Knowledge is a fundamental characteristic of life processes and the practice of living. From this vantage, knowledge for living appears as a specific way of living one's life, which includes reflecting on how one lives. Knowledge for living can be gained through concrete experiences in immediate life contexts *and* through the production and reception of symbolic goods. In this way, knowledge for living can be understood as an *imagined* form of living and as a process of imagining life (and lives), in which self-referentiality and self-reflexivity are critically important. In other words, knowledge for living is bound up in life experiences but never tied to a single logic. (2010: 986, emphasis in the original)

This passage nicely sums up the main constituents of Ette's notion of literary 'knowledge for living', combining programmatic claims with theoretical considerations (even if these are mostly implicit). The programmatic aspect of Ette's approach hinges on the notion of 'relevance'. Given the predominance, prestige, and economic as well as social capital of the life sciences, literature and literary scholarship in the early 21st century are not immediately considered to contribute to knowledge of or about life. Reconnecting literature with life (and life knowledge), however, means more than correcting the public understanding of literary studies. It also means to 'suggest new perspectives' for a discipline that has gradually and often radically moved away from any notions of a connection between literature and 'real life'. Literature is not separated from everyday life experiences, and so literary knowledge is not restricted by any boundaries between "immediated life contexts" and such that are mediated, e.g. through literature. Instead, literary life knowledge is always connected to, and part of, the life-world (*Lebenswelt*) of both authors and readers. The close relation of literature to life may immediately strike many lay readers: What else does one read a work of literary fiction for, if not to gain a glimpse into the lives of other (real or fictitious) people, to escape from one's own life for a little while, or even to learn something from these literary lives? This is, as John Gibson phrases it, the "*humanist intuition*," i.e. the idea that "literature presents the reader with an intimate and intellectually significant engagement with social and cultural reality." Literature is "the textual form to which we turn when we want to read the story of our shared form of life: our moral and emotional, social and sexual – and so on for what ever aspects of life we think literature brings to view – *ways of being human*" (Gibson 2007a: 2, emphasis in the original).

However, it seems that for the majority of professional readers – i.e. literary critics and scholars – the notion that literature is the textual form of our shared form of life does no longer have much valence. In the context of some of the most influential literary-theoretical paradigms of the 20th century (formalism, new criticism, structuralism, poststructuralism etc.), literature is first and foremost conceptualized as a more or less autonomous symbolic system in which signs do not relate to an extra-textual reality, but only to other signs (see Herring's (1986) critique of Paul de Man and Murray Krieger). This is arguably one of the major reasons why especially in the course of the 20th century, "the term *life* has almost entirely disappeared from methodological and ideological debates" (Ette 2010a: 983) within the humanities, and especially within literary studies.[2] In *The Meaning of Life*, Terry Eagleton makes a similar point, identifying postmodern theory as the peak of an academic hostility toward the term 'life' (and the humanist ideas behind it):

> Post-structuralism, and then postmodernism, dismissed all attempts to reflect on human life as a whole as disreputably 'humanist' – or indeed as the kind of 'totalizing' theory which led straight to the death camps of the totalitarian state. There was no such thing as humanity or human life to be contemplated. There were simply differences, specific cultures, local situations. (Eagleton 2007: 35)

Against the backdrop of the poststructuralist and deconstructivist paradigms of decentering and *différance*, it was no longer acceptable or even possible to conceptualize 'life' as a metaphysical entity or super-concept. Consequently, 'life'

2 See also Asholt (2010: 67): "Wenn Hans Ulrich Gumbrecht und Henning Ritter in der Woche der Buchmesse 2009 in einer ‚Zur Sache' Kolumne mit dem Titel ‚Philosophische Derivate' der Philosophie der letzten Jahrzehnte vorhalten, ‚den als Metaphysik verteufelten Bezug auf die Welt als Referenz ‚durchzustreichen,' so gilt diese ‚Verteufelung' in vieler Hinsicht auch für die Literaturwissenschaft."

became "one among a whole series of discredited totalities" (Eagleton 2007: 28), one among several unwanted 'grand narratives'.[3]

The problematization of the concept of life in (post-)modern theory and philosophy may have led to the widespread suspicion within literary studies with regard to such approaches that regarded literature as a more or less direct expression of humanist ideas. With the mainstream of literary theory assuming that it is a pretheoretical naiveté that we learn from stories, the "paucity of research into *how* we learn from literary fictions has, in turn, impoverished our understanding of *what* we may learn from them" (Swirski 2007: 5). But the discomfort of literary critics with regard to the relationship between life and literature has also other, and earlier, contexts. In her seminal study *Love's Knowledge*, Martha Nussbaum outlines how the mainstream positions in literary studies ever since the New Criticism have rejected any notion of literature as an expression of human life:

> It was assumed that any work that attempts to ask of a literary text questions about how we might live, treating the work as addressed to the reader's practical interests and needs, and as being in some sense about our lives, must be hopelessly naive, reactionary, and insensitive to the complexities of literary form and intertextual reference. (Nussbaum 1990: 21)

It is this strong tendency within literary criticism and theory to marginalize or even outright discredit the term 'life' as well as the relation between literature and life against which the project of literary studies as science for living is set up. Rather than abandoning or exiling life from literary theory and literary criticism, it would arguably be wise to reconsider the role of literary life knowledge within our contemporary societies. Against this background, literary studies as science for living decidedly aims to reinvigorate a kind of research that takes seriously again the connection between literary texts and readers' sense of life, and thus to rethink the broader relevance of literature and literary scholarship, particularly in the face of the new 'culture of life' that the rise of the life sciences imply.

Though postmodern theorizing may thus have contributed to the discipline's withdrawal from any authority to produce knowledge for living, literary theory is indispensable to fully understand the ways in which literature partakes in the social construction of knowledge, and how it is embedded in the practice of living.

3 While Eagleton certainly has a point, one needs to consider, however, that many of the so-called poststructuralists and postmodernists Eagleton implicitly refers to – thinkers like Barthes, Deleuze, Foucault, and Derrida – were in fact well aware of, and even emphasized, the complex interrelations of literature, philosophy, and life. See also Asholt (2010: 66).

To understand how literature 'enters life' (see Andringa/Schreier 2004) and how it imparts knowledge, one needs to start from the "production and reception of symbolic goods" (Ette 2010a: 987) which are at the core of such knowledge. What is also needed, however, is to redirect and expand literary theorizing in order to take into account how the specific discursive rules and conventions, the symbolic forms and structures with which literature engages in the production of the meaning of 'life'. Literary studies as science for living must therefore not collapse on pre-theoretical, naïve concepts of a (however conceived) mimetic relationship between literature and life but maintain its complexity, which is essentially the result of the project of literary theory. In order to be able to live up to widely accepted scientific standards, literary studies as science for living has to manage a delicate balancing act: on the one hand, it must reconsider the complex relations of literature and life dismissed by a great part of literary theory of the 20th century, while on the other hand it must retain and reflect the valuable insights into the intrinsic logic of literature that this discourse has furnished.

Theoretically as well as methodologically, the approach of literary studies as a form of life science as proposed by Ette poses a number of questions and challenges. Jörg Dünne has succinctly pointed out that Ette's approach tends to dehistoricize life, making life appear as an anthropological given rather than a historically formed discourse (as, for instance, in Foucault). This anthropological, corporeal perspectivization of the concept of life – or "re-anthropologization", as Dünne (2011: 75) calls it – makes it difficult to connect it to historical approaches, and therefore to grasp the historicity of any understanding or knowledge of 'life'. Moreover, Ette's emphasis on the moral function of literature, that is his claim that literature has a particular relation to life and that it can and does make the world better by transforming life's burdens, atrocities, and traumas into pleasure (in the sense of Roland Barthes's notion of *plaisir du texte*), and by imaginatively creating positive forms of human cohabitation limits and morally overburdens literature at the same time (see ibid.: 77). Interestingly, Nancy Easterlin's "biocultural approach" to literary theory and interpretation similarly emphasizes the role of literature to respond to, and potentially transform, the dysfunctional, destructive, and traumatic of life (e.g. in a colonial context) (Easterlin 2012). It is, however, questionable whether literature is morally superior to other discourses (or even to immediate life experience), and whether it always performs such positive transformative power. What literary texts do, however, is to create another layer of meaning through which life's burdens (as well as pleasures) are held up for the reader's examination in a self-reflexive, semantically open manner that findings from the life sciences usually do not possess.

From a methodological point of view, it remains largely open to debate what 'literary studies as a form of life science' would or should look like, and how literary life knowledge (given that it always presents itself in symbolic form) may be 'decoded' by literary scholars. As Ansgar Nünning (2007: 214) therefore reminds us, literary studies as science for living first of all would have to take into consideration the paradigmatic axis of selection (which aspects of life are represented in literary discourse and concrete texts?), the syntagmatic axis of combination or configuration of life knowledge (how, i.e. with which formal strategies and structural patterns, are certain notions and forms of life staged in a literary text?) as well as the discursive axis of communication, including the question of the perspectivity of any kind of life knowledge. What literary narratives show, after all, is not life itself, but an aestheticized – and to a certain degree conventionalized – interpretation of life. "Life has no story teller. Life is an amorphous, interweaving, inchoate and chaotic flow of events, out of which any narrative selects, occludes, and elides." (Malcolm 2011: 97) Thus, far from a naïve reading of literary narratives that looks for a text's mimetic 'representation of life' a strong disciplinary and theoretical foundation is needed to explore the forms of life and ways of living implied in literary discourse (see also Basseler/Hartley/Nünning 2015).

Despite the somewhat problematic claims about the moral value of literature, the project of literary studies as a form of life science or science for living inevitably alludes to the functions of literature within a broader cultural and social context. Ette conceives of literary knowledge for living as "an imagined form of living and as a process of imagining life (and lives)" (2010a: 986). In this sense, he regards literature as an "ever-changing and interactive storehouse of knowledge for living" (ibid.).[4] Important as this notion of literature as a storehouse or repository of life knowledge may be, this metaphor does not seem to fully account for the various functions that literature – potentially or actually – serves to fulfill.[5] Of course, literature constitutes a medium or archive in which a great variety of forms of life, ways of living etc. are recorded and remain at the disposal of readers in entirely different historical or cultural situations. Literary texts can become collective texts in Astrid Erll's (2004) terms, shaping individual and collective

4 Ette, in his *Lendemains* essay, speaks about literature as an interactive storage medium of life knowledge ("Literatur als interaktives Speichermedium von Lebenswissen," Ette 2007: 24) and as a dynamic and highly regenerative repository of life knowledge ("dynamischer und hochrückgekoppelter Speicher von Lebenswissen," ibid.: 28).

5 For an illuminating discussion of the 'storehouse' metaphor and the conservational functions of literature, see Moser (1993); for a similar critique of Ette's metaphor, cf. A. Nünning (2010).

memory and thus cultural identity models. Sometimes, as in authors like Shakespeare, these forms of life and ways of living may even be regarded as a universal knowledge of life and the 'human condition' (cf. Bloom 1999) that translates across historical, cultural and social boundaries (though especially postcolonial criticism seems to have eradicated this notion for good).[6]

However important this retaining, archival function of literature may therefore be, there are several strong reasons for sharing Ansgar Nünning's (2010: 56-57) view that literature is much more than just a container medium for the storage of life knowledge or knowledge for living. In addition to this rather passive function of storing and conserving knowledge, literary texts potentially fulfill a number of more active functions within specific historical and cultural situations:

> yes, literature is in fact a discursive locus where knowledge can be stored. And no, literature is not only a storehouse. In other words, in order to properly understand the relations that literature maintains with its surrounding discourses, we need to go beyond the metaphor of storage, which only takes into account one moment, one specific operation within a complex process. (Moser 1993: 135)

Literature should not be conceived as a mere 'storehouse', but as an "eminently productive medium for generating life knowledge as well as a meta-knowledge about the limitations, range, and validity of different forms of knowledge" (Nünning 2010: 56, my translation, M.B.). Therefore, my discussion of the North American short story as an organon of life knowledge will not be limited by how the individual stories discussed in Part III serve to store a particular, historically and culturally situated life knowledge, but instead discuss how these stories actually engage(d) in the cultural negotiation and production of cultural knowledge of life.

Literature, and particularly the various kinds of imaginative literature such as the short story, thus potentially fulfil functions within our knowledge societies that go beyond a mere storage of knowledge. Hubert Zapf's concept of "literature as cultural ecology", and particularly his triadic functional model of literature, provides a useful framework for such a notion of literature as a productive medium for generating, instead of merely representing or storing, life knowledge. As a

---

6 Cf. Ette's claim that the reception or appropriation of literature in different cultural environments can create new connections between cultures and influence the behavior and conduct of life on a global scale ("neue Verbindungen zwischen diesen Kulturen schaffen und weltweit Einfluß auf das Verhalten, ja auf die Lebensführung unterschiedlicher Lesergruppen nehmen," 2007: 25).

transformative rather than conservative medium, literature serves to fulfill three major discursive functions (Zapf 2002; 2003; 2016: 95-124): 1) As a culture-critical metadiscourse literary texts can respond critically to "hegemonic discursive regimes" (Zapf 2016: 104) that shape collectively shared notions about life. 2) As an imaginative counter-discourse", literary texts can articulate and semiotically empower alternative forms of life and thereby valorize otherwise marginalized and excluded life knowledge. 3) As a reintegrative interdiscourse, "literature brings together the civilizational system and its exclusions in new, both conflictive and transformative ways" (ibid.: 114) and thus has the capacity to reconnect otherwise dissociated knowledge of life. In this dynamic, literary *Lebenswissen* unfolds in the tension-field between discursive formations, socio-political power relations, and literature's capacity to imaginatively project alternative knowledge. "In the view of cultural ecology, and in the light of the nonreductionist adaptation of the contemporary life sciences [...], literature can be seen as a multiperspectival form of writing that potentially encompasses and participates in all of these different meanings and manifestations of life." (ibid.: 131-2)

Accordingly, the (life) knowledge of literature is by no means limited to a mere reflection or thematization of other forms and discourses of knowledge, even if this is an integral part of the functions of literature described in Zapf's model. Literature, it is often stressed, is not confined to prevalent notions of knowledge or truth, and thus to the discursive rules of other, e.g. scientific fields of knowledge. In fact, more often than not literature deliberately flouts such categories and willfully blurs the lines between fact and fiction, 'objective truth', and imagination and thus forces us to rethink these very categories. Any approach to 'literature as life knowledge' must therefore consider the challenge that literature poses with regard to the production and even the very nature of knowledge: the way in which literary works correspond with our knowledge about the world, ourselves, and life, sometimes playfully undercutting its own claims to knowledge, yet sometimes leaving it up to the reader to decide whether it is just playing or not (cf. Wood 2005: 37).

This brief discussion and contextualization of Ette's manifesto of literary studies as a form of 'life science' and the various debates that it touches upon has served to emphasize the necessity to reconceptualize the complex, dynamic interrelationship between literature, life, and knowledge. As the various responses to Ette indicate, such an approach poses a great challenge to the field of literary studies, including central questions of methodology, terminology, analytic frameworks, as well as the very concept of literature. Yet it also promises valuable insights into the "indispensable cultural dimension" (Ette 2010a: 991) of life that is arguably lacking in the life sciences, but also in all other fields of knowledge:

"Literary scholars need to rise to the challenge of using their analytic frameworks to emphasize the 'abundance of life' that literature holds in store for its readers, to augment it, and to carry the results of their critical analyses out into our various societies." (ibid.)

The remainder of this study will be dedicated to further unfold and elaborate the approach of 'literary studies as life science' at a theoretical, literary-historical, and practical-analytical level. Before I will address the question of how generic structures, conventions, and expectations shape the 'life knowledge' of the genre under scrutiny here (i.e. the North American short story), and how such an approach may provide a fresh take on the study of the short story, however, some further light needs to be shed on the cognitive and epistemological status of literary fiction. While Ette, in his otherwise wide-ranging, provocative, and insightful considerations, conspicuously shuns the question of what literary knowledge can actually mean and how it relates to other kinds of knowledge, these questions have been tackled and answered quite conflictingly by a variety of scholars and over many decades. Constituting one branch of research in what is frequently labeled as 'philosophy of literature' (see John/Lopes 2004; Davies/Matheson 2008; Lamarque 2009), the discussion of the epistemological status of literary fictions has a very long history that reaches back to antiquity. Before claiming a distinctive, cultural life knowledge of literature in general, and of the short story in particular, then, it seems necessary to investigate the epistemological underpinnings of this claim by looking at how the relationship between literature and knowledge has been conceptualized from a philosophical, i.e. cognitive and aesthetic, point of view.

2. The Knowledge of Literature:

Positions, Debates, and Approaches

The phrase 'the knowledge of literature' can mean quite different things. Understood as a *genitivus obiectivus*, it refers to the knowledge that we can have *about* literature, for instance: What is the narrative perspective in Hemingway's "The Killers"? What are the generic features of a 'story of initiation'? Who are the characters in Flannery O'Connor's "Good Country People"? What is a short story? What is considered as 'literary'? Some answers seem to be pretty straightforward, whereas others (what is 'literary'?) point to the very foundations and methodological underpinnings of literary studies as an institution. Despite their divergent levels of complexity and difficulty, however, all the possible answers to these questions imply a certain knowledge about literature that is not merely subjective or contingent, but grounded in the institutional organization of literature and consolidated by an 'interpretive community'. The knowledge of literature, in this sense, thus refers to the cumulative knowledge *about* literature that the institution of literature has brought about.

As a *genitivus subiectivus*, on the other hand, the phrase relates to knowledge that is *represented in*, *disseminated through*, or *produced by* literature. This second meaning assumes that literature itself 'knows' something, that it contains, conveys or constructs (a special kind of) knowledge, and maybe even that this particular knowledge cannot be found in other areas or discourses. Whereas the first meaning of literature's knowledge is hardly controversial – who would deny that we can know, for instance, what the major conflict in Shakespeare's *Othello* is, or how his sonnets are structured? – the second meaning of 'the knowledge of literature' has been debated vigorously and controversially. Can literature really 'know' anything? Or should we not rather refrain from attributing any cognitive value to literature and from claiming that it is connected with something like knowledge? Is it not precisely the self-sufficiency and aesthetic autonomy we appreciate most about literature, its divergence from, and resistance to, "the meek submissiveness characteristic of linguistic discourse faithfully serving some end beyond itself" (Walsh 1969: 44)? The major aim of this chapter is to discuss and ultimately defend the idea of 'the knowledge of literature' in the second sense (*genitivus subiectivus*), thereby providing the conceptual basis for the more genre-specific considerations that follow in part II and III.

Answers to the question of what qualifies or disqualifies literature as a source of knowledge have of course been far too numerous and diverse to be comprehensively discussed within the confines of this chapter.[1] Being one of the oldest questions in Western literary criticism, it has resurfaced regularly, bringing to the fore the respective notions of 'literature' and 'knowledge' held in different historical periods, as well as the notions of related concepts such as 'fiction',[2] 'imagination', 'aesthetics', 'belief', and 'cognition'. Despite, or probably because of the longevity of this discussion, the "question of literature's relationship to knowledge remains open; much will depend, of course, on how we define the act of knowing," as Rita Felski succinctly remarks (2008: 83). And, one might add, it will also depend on how we define the institution and the practice of literature.

Recent discussions of the knowledge of literature have honed in on the very nature of such knowledge as well as its relation to the aesthetic configuration of literature. Jochen Hörisch, in a book-length study entitled *Das Wissen der Literatur* (2007) defends the thesis that fictional literature contains a specific kind of knowledge, which might not fulfill the usual criteria for knowledge as intersubjective truth, but nevertheless deserves to be taken seriously. Precisely because literature does not operate on the same guiding distinction (what Luhmann would call the system specific *Leitunterscheidung*) as science – i.e. true vs. false –, but has a fundamentally different epistemic structure based on aesthetic principles, it constitutes an important societal counter-discourse in which alternative, marginal, contended, and 'dissident' positions are being articulated. Such alternative knowledge ("Alternativ-Wissen", ibid: 10) is the actual domain of literature. For Hörisch, then, the question of whether literature contains 'real' knowledge is, eventually, irrelevant. What is more important are the ways in which literary texts, as articulations of specific historical and discursive formations, give voice to particular ideas and conceptions of human life and society, including a variety of

1 See Klausnitzer (2008), Köppe (2011a), Wübben (2013), Borgards (2013) for such overviews. Also see the impressive multi-volume work on 'the knowledge of literature' edited by Angela Locatelli (2002-10).

2 Cf. Lamarque/Olsen's (1996) meticulous discussion of the relationship between truth and fiction in literature.

topics such as epochal diseases, memory and forgetting, friendship and love, and the human experience of time.[3]

At the other end of the spectrum are those positions who argue that it does in fact matter a great deal how we conceptualize the epistemic status of literature. Drawing on the formal logic of analytic philosophy, such approaches insist that we need to clarify whether a literary text can really contain knowledge in a formal sense or whether we should rather speak of certain notions or opinions manifested in a given text. Recently, this discussion has been led quite extensively and passionately in response to an essay by Tilmann Köppe (2007a), published in the journal *Zeitschrift für Germanistik*. In it, Köppe outright rejected any notion of knowledge in literature as misleading, arguing that knowledge necessarily requires a *relation* between a person and a proposition (ibid.: 402-9). As the ensuing discussion of Köppe's essay has shown, however, much will ultimately depend on how we define 'knowledge', and whether or not literary critics are really well-advised to adopt the formal logic prevalent in analytic philosophy (see Borgards 2007, Dittrich 2007, Köppe 2007b, Jannidis 2008).

Given the historicity, cultural specificity, and theoretical frameworks that shape our notions of the knowledge of literature, it seems not only impossible but also futile to even try to provide a comprehensive historical overview of this debate, partly since the literary 'objects' in focus here – North American short stories of the 19th to the 21st century – already help to delimit and delineate the relevant positions and theoretical conceptions the question evokes. Whereas the problem of 'truth' and the 'truthfulness of representation' were major concerns for the poets of ancient Greece, for instance, the dawn of modernist literature has brought forth new notions of literary mimesis. With the increasing functional differentiation of Western societies that is usually dated around 1800 (the so-called *Sattelzeit* or *Epochenschwelle*),[4] literature has been less and less concerned with, or at least less obligated to, concepts like 'truth' or 'referentiality', leading to the (relative) autonomy of the literary system we now treasure and defend. Arguably, no contemporary reader of a short story like Fitzgerald's "The Curious Case of Benjamin Button" (see chapter 7) would disqualify it solely on the basis of its lack of representational truthfulness, i.e. because it depicts an entirely unbelievable biography

3 For a similar approach – similar in so far as it also emphasizes the role of the aesthetic in literary communication – see Schlaffer (1990).

4 The term *Sattelzeit*, of course, is borrowed from Reinhard Koselleck (1979: XV), and describes the transition from the early modern to the modern period. Cf. also Klinkert/Neuhofer (2008b: 1), who discuss how during this period literature gained its status as an autonomous, self-referential (or autopoietic) system in Niklas Luhmann's sense.

that inverts the fundamental biological reality (i.e. aging) of human beings. We know and accept that imaginative literature is not necessarily true in any referential sense. Yet we can still regard it as a source of knowledge which, to stay with the previous example, may tell us something about how our lives are all similar in their temporal organization and synchronization within the society – precisely because literature is exempted from the liability to 'stick to the facts'. As a result, Plato's problem is arguably no longer our problem,[5] and therefore his answers to the question of the knowledge of literature cannot or at least should not be ours (cf. also Wood 2005: 3). However, in order to identify some of the most important and persistent questions that emerged in the controversial and multifaceted discussion of literature and knowledge, it may be useful to begin with a very brief survey of the central questions as well as the literary-theoretical and philosophical positions attached to them.

Unsurprisingly, critical discourse on the question of the knowledge of literature has been dominated by philosophical approaches (sometimes also called the 'philosophy of literature'). This philosophically centered debate around the epistemological status of literature is usually said to have its origins in ancient Greek philosophy, or more precisely in the works of Plato, and it is still a common reference point in contemporary discussions. In what is probably his most famous work, Plato – through his mouthpiece Socrates – reflects on the order of the ideal city-state (*polis*) ruled by truth-loving philosopher-kings and identifies an 'ancient quarrel' between poetry and philosophy with regard to the question of which *genre* (i.e. philosophy or poetry) could better explain the world. As Martha Nussbaum reminds us, "the quarrel was a quarrel about literary form as well as about ethical content, about literary forms understood as committed to certain ethical priorities, certain choices and evaluations, rather than others. Forms of writing were not seen as vessels into which different contents could be indifferently poured; form was itself a statement, a content" (1990: 15). Plato's position in this quarrel is quite clear: According to him, poets should not have a say (and place) in his ideal society since they distract its citizens from truth.[6] Merely imitating the objective world (*mimesis*), the poets are twice removed from the Platonic ideal of a metaphysical

5 For a discussion of 'Plato's Problem', see Walsh (1969); see also Schlaffer (1990), Davies (2007: 143-44) and Klausnitzer (2008: 64-68).

6 See also Felski, who summarizes the Platonic tradition of condemning literature as a discourse of truth vs. 'un-truth': "The work of art, in this line of thought, is essentially a sham, a shameless un-truth, this failure of knowledge drawing all kinds of calamitous consequences in its wake, from the pollution of the polis to the creation of countless apologias for the inequities of capitalism." (2008: 78)

truth. Socrates illustrates this problem of *mimesis* by introducing the famous 'three-beds' metaphor, which differentiates between the conception, instantiation, and representation of truth: Whereas the ideal *conception* of a bed constitutes an ultimate, divine truth and the actual *instantiation* of a bed made by a carpenter only imitates this ideal, the poet's *representation* of a bed via language is an imitation of the carpenter's bed, and thus at one further remove from the Platonic ideal. Moreover, Plato believed that poetry was the art of 'divine madness'. For Plato, then, the poets did not speak the truth, but deliberately deceived and manipulated the people. The 'knowledge' of literature, thus, is regarded as a perilous threat to society: "It is fair to say that since Plato's famous decision there has been an implicit but consistent association of the poetic art with a peculiar, mysterious, and even dangerous sort of knowledge." (Gourgouris 2003: 2)

The legacy of the three-beds metaphor and the attached problem of *mimesis* is still important in philosophically oriented discussions about the knowledge of literature. Ever since Plato first described the quarrel between poetry and philosophy as a major epistemological problem, arguments about the cognitive status of literature – its relation to the realm of knowledge and cognition – have covered the whole range from complete rejection to emphatic affirmation. Recently, 'literary cognitivism' has become a more or less common term for the idea that literature has a cognitive value;[7] accordingly, positions that argue against this idea are referred to as 'anti-cognitivist'.

Literary cognitivists usually regard the cognitive efficacy of literature not as a mere bonus or padding to the aesthetic pleasures provided by *belle lettres*, but deem it relevant or even constitutive for the aesthetic value of literature. In other words, the epistemic work that literature serves to fulfill is part and parcel of every meaningful approach to literature: Literature "is valuable because it is a source of knowledge [...] bearing upon the extra-fictional world" (Davies 2007: 143). The key premise of literary cognitivism is that the knowledge created through literary texts in the act of reading is transferrable and "useable in nonliterary experience" (Herring 1986: 171).[8] How exactly literature 'bears upon' the extra-fictional reality and how it informs, challenges, and expands our knowledge of the world and

---

7 Literary cognitivism is not to be confused with cognitive approaches to literature, which usually work on the interdisciplinary intersections of literary studies and cognitive science. For this latter branch see, for instance, the issue of *Poetics Today* 23.1 (2002).

8 Cf. also Gibson (2007a: 10), who argues that the "question of the cognitive value of literature is the central challenge in the development of a serviceable model of humanism [i.e. an approach to literature that accounts for the potential of literary works to reveal truths about, and provide insights in, the world and human life, M.B.], and it is

our lives is the central question and the bone of contention for studies in literary cognitivism. Its major task is therefore to "explain why we turn to literature with the expectation of having our understanding of the world refined, augmented, even shocked; to give support to the perhaps vague but nonetheless pervasive belief that in literary experience we often come to know ourselves and the world better" (Gibson 2007b: 1).

Positions toward literary cognitivism can be further separated into two cardinal attitudes or stances, a "dismissive stance" and a "permissive stance" (Swirski 1998: 7-12). Generally speaking, proponents of the dismissive stance hold that literature cannot and/or should not be regarded as a legitimate source of knowledge and that, consequently, a cognitive or epistemological approach to literature is neither allowable nor desirable. The reasons for the dismissal of the idea of literary knowledge, however, vary to a great extent (cf. ibid.). In a first version of the dismissive stance, the epistemic or cognitive value of literature is not entirely repudiated, but the epistemologically freighted term 'knowledge' is replaced by other, less vigorous notions such as 'understanding', 'acknowledgement' or 'rightness'.[9]

In keeping with this position, literature is sometimes regarded as a medium that can provide readers "with an *understanding of general principles*" (Davies 2007: 145) of the real world, rendering (oftentimes implicit and ambiguous or 'oblique', cf. Wood 2005) insights into certain moral, psychological, or metaphysical aspects of human life. Moreover, literature can be conceptualized as a source of "*categorical understanding*" (Davies 2007: 146), imparting conceptual frameworks and thus functioning as a 'way of worldmaking' (Goodman 1978). According to such a notion of categorical understanding through literature, what "we acquire are new ways of classifying and categorizing things and situations" (Davies 2007: 146), leading to a "kind of practical knowledge" (ibid.). (I will come back to the differentiation between theoretical and practical knowledge later).

---

also the most difficult to answer." Unsurprisingly, this aspect of the relevancy of a literary work's cognitive value for its overall aesthetic value *as a piece of literature* is fervently discussed. Cf. also Lamarque (2007) and Köppe (2008, especially 222-5).

9 In *Of Literature and Knowledge* (2007), Swirski presents a slightly revised version of his distinction between the permissive and dismissive stances, splitting up the dismissive faction into 'revisionists' and 'abolitionists.'

Examples of this "weaker strain" (Swirski 1998: 7) of the dismissive stance arguably include Catherine Elgin and Nelson Goodman's concept of 'understanding'[10] (Elgin/Goodman 1988; see also Swirski 1998: 7), Stanley Cavell's (1996) notion of "acknowledgement" or Richard Rorty's idea of the "*inspirational value* of great works of literature" (1998: 140, emphasis added, M.B.). These approaches, then, circumnavigate the problems attached to the idea that literature contains or produces knowledge in the narrow, philosophical sense of the term – usually defined as *justified true belief* –, by granting literature a different kind of epistemic and/or cognitive value. Even if literature does not qualify as a source of knowledge in a philosophical or scientific sense, it still helps us to make meaning of our lives and the world. Another example of a weaker version of the 'dismissive stance' would be Michael Wood's (2005) notion of literature as a "taste of knowledge". Wood replaces the rigid philosophical and scientific notion of knowledge with a more modest epistemic claim: rather than profound and self-contained knowledge, literature only provides a non-satiable *taste* of knowledge: "We are going to have to go elsewhere for the continuous main course." (ibid.: 10)

While all these examples are still indebted to Western philosophy's traditional concept of knowledge and particularly Plato, a second version of the dismissive stance breaks with "the classical theory of knowledge" (Swirski 1998: 8). Proponents of this position 'abolish' the traditional epistemology of *justified true belief* altogether by displacing all notions of truth, objectivity or rationality and negating the very possibility of systematic, universal knowledge. This stance is usually associated with postmodernism, and especially with social constructivist and radical relativist theories.[11] On the premise of an absolute denial of any claim to 'knowledge', literature is believed to "free us from the shackles of a pedestrian reason chained to facts, consistency, evidence, justification" (Livingston 1992: 498). Hence, literature is privileged in these approaches as the manifestation of

10 In *Reconceptions in Philosophy and Other Arts and Sciences*, Nelson Goodman and Catherine Z. Elgin suggest an alternative epistemology that "comprehends understanding of cognition in all of its modes – including perception, depiction, and emotion, as well as description" (1988: 4-5).

11 The argument Swirski criticizes here relies heavily on poststructural thought, especially the idea of the instability of language and the infinite deferral of meaning. Cf. John Gibson (2007a: 37), who refers to this as the "poststructural drift." For a highly readable if sometimes generalizing critique of social constructivism and relativism and its role in shaping the epistemic project of the humanities and social sciences, see Slingerland (2008: 74-150).

the very impossibility of something like 'objective' knowledge as claimed by the sciences or traditional epistemology. However, as Swirski persuasively argues, these radical skepticist displacements of knowledge in general, and of 'the knowledge of literature' in particular, "do not and cannot achieve what they set out to do" (1998: 9), simply because their arguments are often "incoherent and self-refuting" (ibid.): By asking us to believe that our beliefs "cannot be evaluated in terms of truth" (ibid.) – and therefore cannot be regarded as knowledge – such a radical relativism undermines its own argumentative and epistemological foundations.[12]

The permissive stance toward the knowledge of literature, on the contrary, generally defends the idea that literature has a significant cognitive or epistemic value, even if this value is not necessarily desirable. Swirski (ibid.: 10-19) further subdivides the permissive stance into three distinct positions, a negative, a dualist, and an affirmative one. Although it may seem counter-intuitive on a first thought, Plato's expulsion of the poets from his republic would thus be subsumed under the permissive stance, or more precisely, it serves as an example of the negative variant of the permissive stance. It is important to keep in mind that Plato did not reject the idea of literary knowledge altogether, but regarded it as "dangerous because it can be cognitively persuasive without being cognitively reliable" (Walsh 1969: 23). In other words, Plato admits that literature has a cognitive content, but contends that it can never be the medium of *reliable* or *desirable* knowledge.

The dualist version of the permissive stance, by contrast, assumes a fundamental "difference between cognition in science and cognition in literature" (Swirski 1998: 10), thus stressing and securing their "mutual autonomy" (ibid.). This position can be traced back to the neo-Kantian differentiation between *nomothetic* and *idiographic* knowledge, between knowledge based on the supposedly 'objective phenomena' of nature and knowledge based on the 'subjective phenomena' of culture. As such it largely conflates with the 'two cultures' argument that emphasizes the allegedly fundamental difference between the "cognitive goals and praxes" (ibid.: 10) in the humanities and the (natural) sciences.[13] In the history of literary theory, the dualist version of the permissive stance can be found in Roman Ingarden's *The Cognition of the Literary Work of Art* (1973), in which Ingarden

12 Also see Swirski (2007: 23): "Indeed, postmodern principles are all refuted in practice. What's the point of arguing, and what is the argument about in the first place, if discourse is all ideology, the world unknowable, facts non-existent, meanings unstable, and reality socially constructed?".

13 On the history of the two-cultures controversy, see Pethes (2003) and especially Ortolano (2009).

stresses the essential role of literature's aesthetic qualities (e.g. in the use of metaphors, figurative language, etc.), the multilayered meaning and the resulting polysemy of literary works. Dualist positions are still widespread, and it would be easy to list a whole number of approaches which insist on the 'otherness' or 'singularity' (cf. Attridge 2004) of literature and literary knowledge as opposed to empirically verifiable scientific knowledge.[14]

Despite its lasting popularity and influence, the dualist stance is built upon a methodological dilemma that arises from the problem of translating literary knowledge into non-literary, critical discourse. If, as some critics argue, literary knowledge cannot be paraphrased in non-literary terms – precisely because its knowledge is tightly interwoven with, and thus inseparable from, literary language and forms, and because the specific logic of literary knowledge is therefore irreducible –, then it seems impossible to explain, at least in non-literary terms, what exactly this knowledge is.[15] If it is possible, on the other hand, to paraphrase literary knowledge in propositional form, "the argument for the demarcation between the two modes of cognition loses its *raison d'être*" (Swirski 1998: 11). Thus, in the dualist version of the permissive stance the epistemic status of literature is rather shaky, since it "turns literature into an epistemic curiosum, one which, apparently, can be accessed and assessed by neither a 'literary' nor a propositional form of knowledge" (ibid.).

The affirmative version of the permissive stance, finally, "adhere[s] to a classical definition of propositional knowledge and assess[es] literature's epistemic status in terms of its (in-)ability to further this type of knowledge" (ibid.: 14). Accordingly, proponents of the affirmative stance generally believe that the knowledge of literature can also be expressed (or paraphrased) in non-literary terms. However, the audacity of these approaches varies significantly: Whereas some scholars claim that literary works can express all different sorts of coherent,

14 Recently, the dualist stance has been taken by Nancy Easterlin. Arguing that it is literature's instable, immaterial "core feature" of meaning that separates literary studies from science, Easterlin claims that "because of fundamental differences in the objects of inquiry, the kind of knowledge produced by literary inquiry will continue to differ from that produced by scientific inquiry" (2012: 24).

15 On the problem of 'translating' literary knowledge into a scientific discourse about literature, cf. also Kohlroß (2007) and Köppe (2008). As Kohlroß (2007: 244) argues, any attempt to translate the language of a literary text into the language of literary criticism requires the recourse to a theory, and thus to the respective meta-language. His proposal of a 'radical interpretation' thus aims at the consolidation of the language of literature and the language of literary theory and criticism (ibid.: 245).

rational and empirically verifiable knowledge and thus can serve as a heuristic medium that contributes to the formation of *new* knowledge, others hold more modest claims, e.g. that literature merely serves to 'popularize' and disseminate knowledge from other areas and disciplines: "Literary works, on this view, can offer fictive substantiations of abstract theses researched elsewhere" (ibid.: 16).

What this brief and necessarily piecemeal overview reveals is the philosophical fervor with which this debate around 'the knowledge of literature' has been led. Despite the heuristic benefits of a coherent conceptualization of the relationship between literature and knowledge based on philosophical methodology and formal logic, the problems with, and limitations of, a strictly philosophically oriented approach to the knowledge of literature are also obvious. Literary discourse, it seems, simply does not work on the same principles as other, more explicitly systematic, mimetic or 'fact-oriented' fields and forms of knowledge production. As a part of these problems and limitations, John Gibson has identified an "analytic drift" (Gibson 2007a: 42), i.e. the notion that "whatever is outside the *literary* text is beyond the reach of the words of that text" (ibid.). Therefore, the analytic interest is primarily in "the nature of truth, reference, and correspondence" (ibid.):

> What we see in this drift is a palpable preoccupation with the philosophical and linguistic problems raised by the element of fictionality in literature; and the overriding interest becomes one of showing that, while we do not take literary texts' descriptions to be fact, we nevertheless do not […] read them as a continuous string of simply *false* claims. (ibid.: 43)

By clinging to such logically sound, but rather narrow definitions of 'knowledge' provided by analytic philosophy, literary critics are prone to lose sight of the cognitive potential and the value of literature. Whereas the methods for analyzing the formal logical coherence of language introduced by analytic philosophy make sense with regard to science and philosophy, however, this "approach is notoriously unapt […] to account for the language of literature" (Huemer 2007: 234). Drawing on the works of philosophers of language such as Bertrand Russell and Rudolf Carnap, Wolfgang Huemer states that by looking at literature from an analytic philosophical standpoint "we are easily drawn to the conclusion that in literary texts language is not used properly" – simply because most (or all) of the propositions in literary texts are false. However, it seems that literature (or broader: art) does not provide us with true propositions, but "forces us to reflect on our conceptual schemes" (ibid.: 235). Art does not deliver any literal or descriptive truths (as the sciences purport to do), but disrupts, disorients, challenges, and explores our conceptions of the world and thus our knowledge (see Elgin 2007).

The most central question – What is, beyond mere aesthetic pleasure and a Kantian 'uninterestedness', really valuable about reading literature? – seems to get lost in such an approach, and with it the place of literary works "in the educational curriculum" as well as "the importance of reading literature in the lives of so many people" (Davies 2007: 142). I therefore concur with Richard Rorty, who speculates that literary critics "may take philosophy a bit too seriously" (2008: 53), expecting philosophy to provide them with irrefutable theories of knowledge that can be applied across disciplinary boundaries. More than anything, the desire for such a theory of knowledge seems to stem from the attempt or at least the aspiration to be scientific (cf. ibid.: 54).

The problem with a general theory of knowledge and particularly the propositionalist approach, as pragmatists and neo-pragmatists like William James, John Dewey, Richard Rorty, and Richard Shusterman have tirelessly reminded us, is that it suggests a homogeneity and universality that simply does not do justice to a reality that is much more complex and less systemized than our formal systems make us believe. The very need for such a general theory of knowledge, Richard Rorty remarks, "is the sort of need which James and Dewey tried to put in perspective by insisting, with Hegel, that theory follows after, rather than being presupposed by, concrete accomplishment" (2008: 54).[16] An abstract, general theory of knowledge that does not take into account the content or substance of such knowledge risks to overlook how literature can affect a reader's life and how readers often – consciously or unconsciously – adapt their choices of literary texts as well as their reading strategies to their own life situation (cf. Andringa/Schreier 2004). Obviously, literary 'life knowledge' necessarily entails subjective, perhaps even idiosyncratic epistemic elements that cannot be generalized in a systematic way and thus cannot be tested and validated empirically: what life is or means to one person is not necessarily what it means to another one, despite the neuronal and biochemical processes that may be identical for both. Hence, an important dimension of the knowledge of literature involves the ways in which literature works at the intersections between people's (and characters') lives and their different conceptions of it.

While general theories of literary knowledge thus seem to be of rather limited use to do justice to the many ways in which literary texts actually contribute to

16 It is debatable, however, whether this conclusion should result in the kind of literary criticism championed by Rorty, a criticism which "simply proceed[s] to praise our heroes and damn our villains by making invidious comparisons." (Rorty 2008: 54) See Leypoldt (2008) for a concise discussion of Rorty's literary criticism.

cultural life knowledge, one may nevertheless differentiate between two distinct kinds of knowledge: theoretical and practical.

Put bluntly, theoretical knowledge is the knowledge that something *is the case*. It relates to particular facts or circumstances in the world. Theoretical knowledge about a particular phenomenon can be stated in declarative sentences. More specifically, theoretical knowledge refers to the true beliefs of a person, which pertain to what is actually the case and for which that person can offer adequate reasons or justifications (Köppe 2011: 56). Theoretical knowledge can include principally all kinds of contents and fields of knowledge, and it is thus impossible to narrow it down on a thematic basis. With regard to the short story, the reader of Edward P. Jones's "Bad Neighbors" (2006), for instance, may gain the theoretical knowledge that there exist vicious class conflicts between African American neighbors in Washington D.C.; a reader of Bharati Mukherjee's "The Management of Grief" (1988) obtains the theoretical knowledge that the Indian-Canadian community suffered from intra-ethnic division and identity crisis after the terrorist bombing of Air India Flight 182 in 1985.

Literary texts may be regarded a "source of *factual information* about the world" (Davies 2007: 145), and thus as a source of theoretical knowledge. In other words, by reading literary texts we can not only expand our theoretical knowledge about literature itself, but we can also create hypotheses about the 'extra-literary' reality, even when this reality is only represented indirectly in a work of literature (cf. Köppe 2011: 105-6). For example, literature is often granted the potential to serve as a source of theoretical knowledge with regard to the 'human condition' as well as to the question of what the reality 'feels like' from a certain perspective (ibid.: 131-50, Köppe calls this latter aspect "Anmutungsqualitäten"). The notion of literature as the foremost medium in which the *conditio humana* finds its expression has arguably formed the basis of the very institution of literature, at least in Western societies.[17] Similarly, the widespread notion of the singularity of literature, to use Derek Attridge's (2004) term, stems from the fact that literature provides us with unique possibilities to experience the perspectivity of our *being in the world*, enabling complex experiences of how situations are perceived from a

17 This does not necessarily mean that we should regard literary texts as storehouses of universal truths about human life, as certain humanists would claim. Quite to the contrary: "We do not glimpse aspects of ourselves in literary works because these works are repositories for unchanging truths about the human condition [...] Rather any flash of recognition arises from an interplay between texts and the fluctuating beliefs, hopes, and fears of readers, such that the insights gleaned from literary works will vary dramatically across space and time." (Felski 2008: 46)

variety of points of view. In fact, both qualities – the insights into a general 'human condition' and the perspective-bound nature of reality – often go hand in hand in literary texts: "We can learn from literary works what effects certain principles have on the experiential horizon of people – what a person regards as important, beautiful, repulsive, etc." (Köppe 2011: 149, transl. M.B.).

In contrast to propositional or theoretical knowledge, practical knowledge refers to the broad question of 'how to live'. Tilmann Köppe defines practical knowledge as "(sufficiently) well-founded attitudes, in which a person concedes that an action or way of life is good, advisable, or right for him- or herself" (2008: 168, transl. M.B.). More plainly than theoretical knowledge, practical knowledge *per se* might therefore be conceived as life knowledge, as it essentially relates to the question of how to live a good life. It is always formed in the process of successful practical considerations, resulting in the reasonable, well-founded attitudes and beliefs by which a person answers the question of how she should live (ibid.). Practical life knowledge is closely related to the Aristotelian concept of *eudaimonia*, and thus to virtue ethics. The ancient Greek word *eudaimonia* refers to "what makes life complete and worth the while" (O'Grady 2003: 5). It is an abstract term that is commonly translated as 'happiness', but only in so far as happiness is not considered as purely individual phenomenon but captures the idea of an "objectively desirable life" (ibid.), and thus a social phenomenon. The eudaimon, then, is the person who enjoys this state of happiness and spiritual wealth. Eudaimonia and practical knowledge not merely refer to individual lives but also consider how these lives are shaped by cultural notions about the good life. Literature at large, and the short story in particular, can be regarded as a source of practical life knowledge, or *eudaimonia*: "Literary works can have a substantial influence on what we consider as good, advisable, or right behavior." (Köppe 2011: 170, transl. M.B.)

While this notion of the eudaimonic, practical life knowledge of literature already becomes obvious in David Leavitt's response to Munro's "What Do You Want to Know For?" cited at the very beginning of this study, it needs to be stressed again, however, that literature usually allows for a variety of responses, also with regard to the offerings a text makes in terms of practical life knowledge. Literary texts are not so much a manual for good living but a repository of often indirect, refracted, contradictory and at times obscure practical knowledge. Whereas there might be some examples for eudaimonic characters in short stories, the most memorable examples are usually those stories in which a character's state of happiness and spiritual wealth is fractured and foreclosed by the wider cultural circumstances by which his life is framed: We may think of Melville's Bartleby, whose "I would prefer not to" becomes the formula for the discrepancy between an individual's ideal of a good life and the biophobic structures, rhythms, capitalist logic, and role expectations of the modern society as well as between the "human and nonhuman, anthropocentric and biocentric forces" (Zapf 2016: 135) dramatized in the story's cultural ecology; or of the nihilism of the old man in Hemingway's "A Clean, Well-Lighted Place" whose "nada"-soliloquy seems to deny the possibility of *eudaimonia* in the modern world outright.

If we accept the notion that literature can be a source of theoretical and practical life knowledge useable in the nonliterary reality, there is arguably not just one way in which literary texts work on our system of beliefs and thereby refine our understanding of the world. We might instead ascribe a whole number of epistemological functions to literary texts, including the expansion, transmission, illustration, popularization, problematization, and anticipation of knowledge as well as the entanglements of literary discourse with other areas of knowledge (see Köppe 2011b: 5-8).

Any attempt at coming to terms with literary life knowledge, therefore, must take its departure from the object of inquiry itself, i.e. literature, and not from some abstract, preconceptualized definition or theory of knowledge. What follows from the above considerations is that literary life knowledge (theoretical or practical) is always relational: It involves a variety of textual specificities (the content of a work, but also its formal characteristics, generic features, etc.), contextual constellations, as well as actors (and thus the intersubjective relation between author and reader). As such, literary life knowledge is thus not only inherently social, but also always necessarily provisional. It is a tentative knowledge contingent on historical contexts, the author's belief system, and the reader as interpreter and co-constructor of meaning. To further unpack this relationality of literary life knowledge, the next chapter will discuss the aesthetic dimension of literary experience which, in the case of the short story form, hinges upon the concept of fiction. Why, in other words, do we read (short) fiction, and how does it contribute to our system of theoretical and practical life knowledge? After the foregoing chapter has dealt with the more general questions of how we may define 'the knowledge of literature', it is the specific role of narrative fiction and the reading act that I will now turn to.

3. Why Fiction? Aesthetic Experience, Life, and Knowledge

Within the field of aesthetics, the term 'aesthetic experience' has served as a key concept since the 1960s, describing a general turn toward the processes of reception and appropriation of artistic objects (see Küpper/Menke 2003: 7). As an early proponent of the centrality of aesthetic experience in the reception of artworks, John Dewey, especially in his works *Experience and Nature* (1925) and *Art as Experience* (1934), has laid the foundation for an understanding of art and literature that departs from the traditional assumption of the material manifestation of a 'work of art' and instead highlights the unique experience it provides (also see Bredella 1999; 2002 and Balmer 2009). Later, especially since the 1970s, literary scholars like Wolfgang Iser and Winfried Fluck, by developing the approach known as reception aesthetics, have also focused on the aesthetic experience of literature, emphasizing the role of imagination in the process of literary reception. As their works have shown, imagination (or rather, "the imaginary") is an anthropological constant as well as a culturally formative process, and as such it is tied up with the aesthetic experience of literary fiction. Without imagination there would be no literature in the first place, while vice versa in its actualization the imaginary rests upon the concept of fiction.

So, the central question is whether and how the aesthetic experience of literature in general, and of the short story in particular, is essential for gauging its cognitive and conceptual impact and its function as an organon of life knowledge. With Richard Eldridge one may ask, for instance, how the "poetic configuration" of literature binds "together feeling and attention to subject matter imaginatively, in a way that is productive for life" (2009: 4)? As Eldridge (ibid.: 8) continues,

> the work of the literary imagination is that of reassurance and animation, of opening routes of fuller and more aptly felt interest in life, where fullness and aptness of felt interest are

threatened by general dullness, habit, inattentiveness, and the necessity of coping with the demands of material life.

Relying on the power of literary imagination (and hence aesthetic experience), Eldridge thus emphasizes the potential of literature to override the mundane, alert us to what is usually buried by day-to-day trivialities, and thereby change our worldview. In this sense, literary life knowledge would consist of 'self-intensification' and 'self-extension' (Eldridge borrows these terms from Rita Felski; one might also add 'self-implication', see Kuiken et al. 2004). But how exactly does literature do this? How can the aesthetic experience made possible by literary texts allow us to overcome the myopia and inattentiveness that pervade our lives and offer us alternative perspectives that, in turn, can alter the way we assess (and live) our lives? How, in other words, is aesthetic experience crucial for the life knowledge that literature offers?

In the post-Kantian Western tradition of literary theory and aesthetics, the cognitive (i.e. knowledge) and the aesthetic (pleasure) usually do not go together very well. It has been argued that in contrast to other, especially scientific disciplines and their respective practices, we usually do not read literature for its cognitive content, that means we do not read a novel or a poem in order to acquire some sort of specific knowledge.[1] Whereas in philosophy, for example, reading is necessarily connected with learning and is therefore "*constitutively cognitive*" (Lamarque 2007: 15), literary reading usually lacks this cognitive imperative or necessity.[2] Moreover, even in those instances in which literary works do contain "examples of highly particularised items of knowledge" (Conolly/Haydar 2007:

1 This argument could, for instance, be corroborated by Lubomir Dolezel's (1998: 24) distinction between the "world-constructing" quality of fictional (literary) texts and the "world-imaging" quality of non-fictional discourse. Whereas non-fictional texts purport to contain factual, i.e. empirically adequate statements about the 'real' world, literary texts do not lay the same claim on truth or factual knowledge. Instead of 'imaging' the world, literary texts 'construct' worlds that are relatively independent from the (f)actual world. See also Gibson (2007a: 29).

2 Moreover, even if a literary text had some cognitive import, one could still ask whether this has any relevance for its status within the literary value system, which is arguably not based upon the code of true vs. false, but on the differentiation between coherent vs. incoherent (see Hörisch 2007). Peter Lamarque therefore maintains that cognitive aspects are "contingent by-products of fiction or literature" (2007: 15), and that "there is nothing about fiction per se that requires it to be a vehicle for learning or the transmission of belief" (ibid.).

120; see also Klausnitzer 2008: 2) – say, about 19th-century whaling techniques or the topography of rural southern Ontario – literature is deemed not to be the "most suitably [sic] place" (Conolly/Haydar 2007: 120) to look for such information or knowledge (see also Davies 2007: 142; Walsh 1969: 81). If we want to find information about glacial landscapes in southeastern Canada, we would probably be better off looking for special maps and geo-historical publications than to read Alice Munro's short story "What Do You Want to Know For?".

Therefore, instead of an increase of knowledge, the activity of literary reading is first and foremost connected to the unique, singular pleasure it promises, and thus to aesthetic rather than cognitive aspects. Literature is beauty, not truth: "A work of imaginative literature trades aesthetic creation rather than factual representation." (Gibson 2007b: 2) Winfried Fluck (1999b: 227) also follows this line of argument when he claims that we turn to aesthetic objects such as literature "because they provide an experience that goes beyond the mere communication of meaning." He emphasizes, however, that this dimension of aesthetic experience is much more than a mere embellishment or "decorative wrapping of a core meaning to which we ought to penetrate as quickly as possible" (ibid.) Quite to the contrary, "[t]he term aesthetic denotes a distinct mode of communication and experience without which we would have no object in literary and cultural studies and no good reason for the existence of a separate field of study" (ibid.: 228).

However, one might also argue that the aesthetic is a central component of, or prerequisite for, the ways in which literature deals with knowledge. The literary work "only becomes manifest as an object of significance in the reading process, where interpretation necessarily *begins*" (Easterlin 2012: 22). Critical interpretation, in contrast to a merely "linguistic interpretation" (Gibson 2007a: 124) is the activity which literary critics are usually concerned when asking "what sense we can attribute to the literary object itself rather than to its constitutive sentences" (ibid.).[3] Critical interpretation must therefore take into account the aesthetic dimension of literary texts (rather than the mere 'literal' content). How can we, for instance, arrive at the interpretation that Melville's "Bartleby" is a story about alienation in a modern world if the text itself does not express any such idea explicitly? The answer, as many theorists have argued, obviously lies in the act of imagination that is so inextricably intertwined with literary discourse: "This imaginative act, which opens up to view the fictional world of a work, makes possible a form of literary experience and appreciation to which we have no access if we take a purely linguistic stance toward a literary work." (Gibson 2007a: 131) The

3 For theories of interpretation, see the articles in Jannidis (2003).

result of this act of interpretation that exceeds the mere linguistic level of the literary texts is what Gibson (ibid.: 132) calls "critical meaning". In this sense, "critical interpretation marks a process of articulating patterns of salience, value, and significance in the worlds literary works bring to view" (ibid.). If we want to use the example of "Bartleby" once more, this would mean that "it is part of the critic's task to devise an interpretative framework that can render explicit the meaning, the significance, of human life as configured in the world Melville created for us" (ibid.).

For Fluck, the aesthetic experience of literary texts is based upon the structural process of *doubling* (cf. Fluck 1999b; 2005).[4] On the one hand, fictional literature always harks back to an extra-textual reality (how else could we read and understand it?), on the other hand, this reality is always mediated or represented in the mode of the fictional, and thus restructured in a very specific way.[5] This restructuring and representation of reality within fictional discourse always involves a certain perspectivization: it is never neutral, but pursues particular political, ethical or epistemic goals (see Fluck 1999b: 237). Whereas fiction thus multiplies reality by constructing a new reality, this performative act of 'doubling' (*Verdopplungsakt*) constitutive for each and every work of fiction is then repeated in the act of reception: "In this reception, the recipient produces a second narrative that constitutes, in fact, a second text." (ibid.: 239) The fictional text in its material manifestation (as a written and published novel, short story, poem, etc.) produces or evokes a second text in the act of reading, the text of an individual reader at a given time and space. What is more, the very same material text may even potentially – and is in fact very likely to – produce a third, fourth, tenth, etc. text if read by the same reader in a different situation at another time: The reader's knowledge might have changed, she may be able to see intertextual relations that escaped her the first time, she may simply be in another mood that alters her affective response

4 Fluck follows Iser here, who also emphasizes the 'doubling' structure of fiction when he argues that "literary fiction offers the chance to be with oneself and simultaneously outside oneself, which may well mean that in such a state the human being enjoys what is never achieved in life, namely to be and to have oneself" (Iser 2000: 175).

5 See Kohlroß for similar ideas: "Was Dichter [...] machen, ist, dass sie mit Objekten, die uns über die Erfahrung, die wir mit ihnen gemacht haben, mehr oder weniger vertraut sind, eine zweite Welt erschaffen, die mit der ersten Welt, anhand derer wir die Erfahrungen gemacht haben, *verglichen* werden kann. Und je interessanter und aufschlussreicher für jene erste Welt dieser Vergleich ist, desto sicherer sind wir, dass wir es mit Poesie und nicht mit einem idiosynkratrischen Sprachgebrauch zu tun haben." (2007: 225)

to the text, and so on and so forth. Like reception aesthetics and reader response theory in general, Fluck thus valorizes the role of the individual reader not only in the process of interpretation and meaning-making, but in the very construction of literary texts.

Thus, meaning does neither reside exclusively in the text, as the New Critics would make us believe, nor 'in' the reader, as some proponents of reader response theory have argued. Rather, it seems that we have to account for literature's distinct 'doubling structure' in order to come to terms with the question of how we "inves[t] fiction with life," as John Gibson (2007a: 136) aptly puts it. In aesthetic experience, the two narratives – one cultural, one individual (see Fluck 1999b: 241) are cast against each other. For literary studies as a form of life science, this implies that the critic needs to articulate the "dependence without identity between these two sorts of meaning" (Gibson 2007a: 135), bringing to the fore the life knowledge that potentially springs from the aesthetic experience of a text. "Without this act of critical articulation, the passage from literature to life remains a mere potential in the literary work." (ibid.: 137)

The 'doubling structure' characteristic of the aesthetic experience of literary fiction also considers the phenomenon that as readers we tend to consume literary texts not only for entertainment, but also in order to reflect on our own lives. As Martha Nussbaum puts it with reference to Dickens's *David Copperfield*, we often "read 'as if for life', bringing to the text our hopes, fears, and conclusions, and allowing the text to impart a certain structure onto our hearts" (Nussbaum 1990: 22). Such ideas emphasize the way in which the literary text becomes important and meaningful *for* and *within* the life of the reader, namely by making it possible for her to enunciate her own wants and feelings. Within the larger literary anthropological framework of Fluck's argument, this also explains why we read fiction in the first place: "The prospect that other texts can enable us to articulate and authorize our own need for articulation drives us back, again and again, to fictional material. It also makes us interpret and redescribe these texts again and again in order to assess how plausible the analogy is and whether it can be shared." (Fluck 1999b: 240; also see Fluck 2009) Finally, then, this is the point where the anthropological significance of the argument of literary life knowledge comes to its full bloom: by enabling readers to produce a second narrative that entails their own feelings and ideas, literature responds to an anthropological basic need. In its "boundary-crossing capacity", literature functions as an "extension of man," as Wolfgang Iser (1989: 228) put it with a nod to McLuhan's catchy phrase. From this vantage, literature – or more precisely: literary fiction – "is nothing but a pointer towards something other than itself" (Iser 1989: 228).

Aesthetic experience, then, is fundamentally an experience of self-reflection and self-extension, a process of oscillation between the fictional narrative (the 'first' narrative) and the reader's realization of it (a 'second' narrative):

> if the two narratives are cast against each other in order to throw light upon one another, so that we retain a sense of their difference, then staging oneself as someone else can become an object of self-observation and self-reflection. An intense aesthetic experience means that a transfer has taken place, although it is part of the effectiveness of such an experience that it can make us forget this fact. (Fluck 1999b: 240)

Literary (life) knowledge may thus be said to emerge as the result of a transfer of meaning between two narratives, which takes place in an 'intense aesthetic experience'. The aesthetic surplus of fictional literature, then, is crucial for its boundary-crossing capacity, its potential to work on our theoretical and practical life knowledge. In addition to the aspects of self-observation and self-reflection Fluck highlights, however, literary life knowledge as an outcome of the doubling structure realized in an aesthetic experience also implies an observation and reflection of the (fictionalized) lives of *others*. Where Fluck's notion is in danger of a solipsistic notion of literature that only feeds the ego, we also need to take into account the potential of literary texts to make us feel compassion for others.[6] In the short stories of George Saunders, for example, the empathy-inducing capacity of narrative fiction takes center stage as his often surreal, satirical stories serve to trigger readerly responses that debunk the human being's innate tendency toward self-centeredness (see Basseler 2017).[7]

Interestingly enough, results from empirical tests in cognitive literary studies seem to support the idea that the 'second narrative' of a literary text (i.e. the narrative produced by the reader) becomes more and more important the longer the

---

6 Among several recent studies addressing the function of literary fiction in creating compassion for other people, see Keen (2007) and Zunshine (2006).

7 As Hubert Zapf maintains in a commentary on Evan Thompson's *Mind in Life:* "If imaginative literature is a cultural mode of communication that is based on 'empathy' in a broad sense, that is, on the generic potency of stepping outside oneself into an alternative world of fiction while yet remaining oneself as a reader; of taking ever new perspectives of strangers while never fully escaping one's own; of immersing oneself in the embodied minds of other human and nonhuman beings while depending on one's own previous experiences – then literature has indeed a special contribution to offer in terms of that more comprehensive knowledge of life envisioned by Thompson." (2016: 130-1)

reading experience dates back. There is a strong likelihood, even, that this 'second narrative' gets more or less fully adjusted to and incorporated in the reader's system of beliefs. Experiments have shown that readers, with increasing temporal distance to the reading experience, not only remember less and less of the text's actual words, but that they also tend to restructure the textual information in such a way that they match other knowledge structures in the reader's memory (Schneider 2004: 207). Whether or not literature fulfills all formal criteria one may set up for the category of knowledge, thus, empirical research seems to corroborate the very fact that literary texts can and do become part of our knowledge.

What apparently follows from the above is that aesthetic experience is crucial for the very kind of knowledge that literature contains, imparts, or generates. It is a well-established notion that literary experience allows readers to imaginatively 'live through' certain situations, to act in an 'as if' space, and to gain certain transferable insights as a result of that process. Literature, from this common point of view,

> provides knowledge in the form of realization: the realization of what anything might come to as a form of lived experience. The kind of knowledge, as well as the manner of knowing, is something familiar to us on the basis of life experience [...]. This is knowing by living through and it is something distinguishably different from knowing about. (Walsh 1969: 136-7)

Literary knowledge, or the process or ability of literary knowing, is a "knowing through imaginative participation" (ibid.: 138). This 'imaginary participation', in turn, is made possible by literature's specific aesthetic structure and the potential experience resulting from it. Even though it may be possible to obtain similar realizations in real life (or in other discourses) as well, art and especially literature have a particular potential to provide "occasions for such realizations," because they already impose a form and structure on them: "Life experience, as actual experience, is idiosyncratic, fragmentary, and fleeting; only virtual experience [i.e. literary experience, M.B.], structured and articulated, lifted out of the temporal flux of ongoing happening, provides something that can be fully realized and shared." (Walsh 1969: 139)

What Walsh calls 'realization' here – the cognitive and emotional upshot of imaginary participation (or 'living through') in an aesthetic experience – bears a close similarity to the concept of 'acknowledgement', which has also been employed to account for the specific cognitive potential of literature in contrast to science. "While scientific treatises (can) add to our knowledge of the world, literature is cognitively relevant by adding to our abilities to reply to the claims that concepts make on us, they add at the level of *acknowledgement*." (Huemer 2007: 238) Acknowledgement, of course, is not identical with knowledge. However, acknowledging may even go beyond knowing, particularly where a practical knowledge about how to live (and how to live together) is concerned. Stanley Cavell has elaborated on the relationship between knowing and acknowledging, using the example of what it means to 'know' the pain of another. Since the suffering of a person makes an ethical claim upon another person, Cavell argues, it is not enough to simply know that pain. Rather, "I must *acknowledge* it, otherwise I do not know what '(your or his) being in pain' means." (Cavell 1996: 68) Where the lack of knowledge can mean mere ignorance, a "blank" or an "absence of something", a failure to acknowledge "is the presence of something, a confusion, an indifference, a callousness, an exhaustion, a coldness" (ibid.: 69). For Cavell, therefore, acknowledgement goes beyond knowledge "in its requirement that I *do* something or reveal something on the basis of that knowledge" (ibid.: 63).

Such notions of knowledge and acknowledgement through literary texts have also been voiced in the concept of literature as thought experiment.[8] As a fictional thought experiment, literary texts allow the reader to act out or think through certain situations on a trial basis without having to fear direct consequences for their own lives. The advantage of literature, as has often been pointed out, is that as readers we are exempt from the pressure to act (*Befreiung vom Handlungsdruck*): confronting readers with the moral conflicts or other existential situations of fictional characters, literature opens up a space for a playful experimentation that would not be possible in 'real life'. The concept of literature as 'thought experiment' conducted in the "laboratory of the mind" (Elgin 2007) thus implies a high degree of participation and cognitive as well as affective involvement on the part of the reader without which the whole idea would be pointless: If there is no reader who is willing to get involved in the thought experiment offered by the text, then there is no such experiment in the first place. Like in any other form of meaning-making through interpretation, the knowledge that can be derived from literary

8 See Rescher, who emphasizes the 'fictional' (or hypothetical) dimension of thought experiments: "A 'thought experiment' is an attempt to draw instruction from a process of hypothetical reasoning that proceeds by eliciting the consequence of an hypothesis which, for aught that one actually knows to the contrary, may well be false. It consists in reasoning from a supposition that is not accepted as true – perhaps even known to be false – but is assumed provisionally in the interest of making a point or resolving a conclusion." (Rescher, qtd. from Gibson 2007a: 176). On the notion of literature as thought experiment, see also Devenport (1981), Gibson (2007a: 175-8), Swirski (2007), Cochran (2007), Ansgar Nünning (2008) and Vera Nünning (2010).

thought experiments is relational in that it requires at least two components: text and reader. Therefore, similar to test arrangements in science, literature can fruitfully be conceptualized as a field for experimentation.

This notion of literature as a field for experimentation and the testing of hypotheses could even be considered as a general understanding of the institution of literature, at least as far as Western societies since the 19th century are concerned. Since early modernity and the project of Enlightenment, Western literature has been established as one among other laboratories and observatory arrangements, or as a kind of 'playground' for testing hypothetical knowledge and simulating alternative knowledge and epistemic plurality (see Klausnitzer 2008: 6). In this sense, literature serves as a medium for a symbolic *behavior in rehearsal*, yielding the human capacity for imagination and thus allowing for a potential expansion of empirical existence (ibid.: 6-7). By crossing the boundaries of reality and empiricism in the willing suspension of disbelief, literary texts can yield novel forms of life, experiences, affects, and concepts which would otherwise be absent from culture, but importantly interact with other discourses and meanings in our cultural ecology.

What is important about the idea of literature as thought experiment, besides the deliberate challenging of empirical facts and the aspect of the reader's exemption from the necessity or pressure to act, is of course its temporal delimitation: unlike most real-life situations in which decisions have a lasting, direct consequence and personal involvement cannot easily be cancelled, the aesthetic experience of literary texts is confined by a relatively clear beginning and end point. The reader is willing to engage with a literary text *as* thought experiment because she knows that this experience is terminated and, moreover, can be withdrawn at any given point. This clear temporal delimitation is thus constitutive for the function of literature as thought experiment.

In her essay "The Laboratory of the Mind," Catherine Elgin transfers the central ideas from James Robert Brown's (1991) homonymous work on the role of thought experiments in science to the field of literature.[9] Elgin takes as her point of departure the question of why we believe that the encounter with literary texts

9 For the notion of literature as laboratory, see also Swirski: "Literature is not a crutch but an intellectual and emotional laboratory as we time-travel to the future one day at a time. It contains the narrative and cognitive machinery for examining issues that challenged thinkers of yesterday, and will continue to challenge thinkers of tomorrow. Because [...] we are not just information processors but storytelling homeostats who experience the world much in the same fashion, and for much the same reasons, as in the days of *Gilgamesh*." (2007: 11)

makes us think that we are "cognitively better off for having read the work" (Elgin 2007: 43). Elgin emphatically supports the cognitive value of literature, which can be located in its ability to constitute thought experiments, conceptualized as an "imaginative exercise that asks: what would happen if certain conditions obtained" (ibid.: 48):

> Like an experiment, a work of fiction selects and isolates, manipulating circumstances so that particular properties, patterns, and connections, as well as disparities and irregularities are brought to the fore. It may localize and isolate factors that underlie or are interwoven into everyday life, but that are apt to pass unnoticed because other, more prominent concerns typically overshadow them. (ibid.: 49)

However, literary texts are not like the rather simple, reductive thought experiments from other disciplines. More complex than thought experiments with their usually strictly limited set of parameters, but at the same time much less complex than life, literary texts can create for us the possibility of thinking and living through certain situations which will either never occur to us 'in reality' or in which we may find ourselves, at least in a similar way, at some point in our lives. Elgin thus implicitly answers the question of why we should not rather study real life instead: In comparison with the abundance of interrelations and influencing factors in real life, literary works constitute "tightly controlled thought experiments" (Elgin 2007: 49) that allow for the isolation of some factors and circumstances. Another answer to the question "But why not life itself?" comes from Martha Nussbaum, who argues that "we have never lived enough. Our experience is, without fiction, too confined and too parochial. Literature extends it, making us reflect and feel about what might otherwise be too distant for feeling." (Nussbaum 1990: 47) The isolation of particular factors along with the capacity to widen our cognitive and affective horizon by imagining new or 'distant' circumstances is what characterizes the potential of literary fiction to serves as thought experiment.

However, thought experiments – whether in science, philosophy, or literature – are anything but epistemologically unproblematic or uncontested. If one looks at the origins, use, and functions of thought experiments in science, it becomes clear that they pose a certain epistemological problem or puzzle, at least in a scientific context (see Davies 2007). Roughly, the main arguments are about whether or not thought experiments are suited to provide any new information or knowledge about the world, and whether or not they can be "reduced without epistemic loss to inferences of any standard kind (deductive, inductive, or abductive)" (Davies 2007: 157). What seems most important about thought experiments, however, is their heuristic potential, which allows for the actualization of previously intuitive or tacit knowledge that can then be carried over to real-life situations:

> Ernst Mach, who is widely acknowledged as the progenitor of this approach, argued that we have 'instinctive knowledge', derived from experience but never articulated and perhaps even incapable of being articulated or made explicit, and that this knowledge is activated when we imagine ourselves in a hypothetical experimental situation. (ibid.: 159)

This strikes me as a very useful explanation of what so often happens during the act of reading a work of literary fiction: Exposing readers to certain situations under certain conditions, literary texts activate their readers' previous knowledge by asking them to simultaneously adopt the perspective of one or several characters and to position themselves (morally, emotionally, etc.) toward the events and characters, thus imagining their own reaction in a similar situation (again, the notion of the 'doubling structure' of literary fiction is crucial here). A literary text – understood as a particular kind of thought experiment – requires that readers build their own mental models. Narrative fictions become instruments of the mind (see Herman 2013: 227), but they are always interwoven with the readers' understanding of, and embodied situatedness in, the world. In "constructing and manipulating the model, the receiver mobilizes a number of other cognitive resources: her everyday understandings of the world, based on practical experience, practical know-how, an 'embodied familiarity' with the world" (Davies 2007: 159).

But how can we be sure that the knowledge thus activated in the reception of a literary text is really based in some inter-subjective reality, and is not simply a result of the deceptive power of literature decried by Plato in his decision to evict the poets from the polis? Is a feeling of 'rightness' gained in the reading process not rather proof of the author's ability to effectively (and affectively) manipulate the reader than of the correctness of the reader's intuitions (see ibid.: 161)? How, in other words, can we rule out the possibility and danger that readers become the victims of some ideologically and cognitively questionable ideas about reality or, for that matter, life? The answer, perhaps, is simply that we should refrain from any generalizing knowledge-claims and "grant that all we can get from such engagements [with fictional narratives] are *possible* cognitive benefits that stand in need of independent testing" (ibid.: 162).[10] As philosophers and historians of sci-

10 "[T]he claim, again, is not that, in the case of the relevant kinds of cognitive resources, a reader's sense of having learned from fiction itself justifies her belief that she has so

ence have taught us, there are not timeless truths in science either, but rather theories that are replaced by other, better theories as soon as new experiments and empirical findings suggest so.

The abandonment of a general theory of knowledge and universal truth, however, does not take away from literature's experimental, explorative function. Wolfgang Iser's (2000) concept of "exploratory fictions" is very helpful here: Taking as his starting point the anthropological considerations of Clifford Geertz and Eric Gans, Iser outlines a 'literary anthropology' and discusses what he regards as one of the main functions of literature within culture, namely its representation of something otherwise absent. By representing the absent,[11] literature is able to "mobiliz[e] the imaginary" (2000: 165) and thus to produce something that is not available or "unfathomable" (ibid.: 171) in other spheres of human life. Iser's differentiation between 'explanatory' and 'exploratory' fictions strikes me as crucial: In contrast to fiction/fictionality in an anthropological context, where it primarily works as an instrument for explaining reality, fictionality in a literary context has a significantly different function: "fictionality in literature functions basically as a means of exploration" (ibid.: 170). What this means is that literary fictions do not *directly* refer to an extratextual reality which they merely illuminate or explain. Instead, by its very definition literary fiction puts such 'reality' in brackets, suspending or disrupting its "extratextual fields of reference" (ibid.). This is exactly what turns fictional literature into an exploratory rather than explanatory medium: "Literary fictions decompose existing organizations outside the text, and recompose them in order to overstep given boundaries. Explanatory fictions have an implicit teleology, which the 'as if' of the exploratory fiction deliberately suspends" (ibid.: 171).

This distinction between explanatory and exploratory fictions points to the anthropologic and cultural functions of literature: by mobilizing the imaginary, rep-

learned. The claim is only that, when the sense of having learned from a fiction is *in fact* grounded in the right kind of unarticulated knowledge, the reader can indeed be said to have learned what she believes herself to have learned." (Davies 2007: 162-3.)

11 Iser is well aware of the problematic paradox a phrase like 'representing the absent' entails. He tries to solve this paradox by proposing that fiction creates a "clothing of sorts" (2000: 165); the act of representation in fiction "creates an absence by means of deferral" and "simultaneously gives a fictional clothing to that absence by making the center into the appearance of the inaccessible." (ibid.)

resenting the otherwise 'unfathomable', and de- and recomposing reality, literature generates gaps of meaning and therefore a plurality of interpretation.[12] Hence, Iser's model helps us to come to terms with the complex interrelationships between life and literature/fiction as well as with the question of literary life knowledge. Fictional literature does not merely represent life in the sense of mirroring an extra-textual reality and thereby serving to explain such reality. Instead, literature suspends reality in an 'as if' status and thus allows us to explore reality. 'Life' in literature is not simply a copy or image of 'life' in reality. Rather, literature "present[s] what is absent, it makes the workings of human culture transparent" (ibid.: 167), and thereby produces its very own and specific (life) knowledge, creating something "that is irrevocably absent in the life that humans lead" (ibid.: 167).

I have now delineated the central role of aesthetic experience, the doubling structure inherent in the concept of fiction as well as the notion of literature as thought experiment and the explorative function of literary fiction, which all help to cast light on how narrative literary texts potentially endows the reader with 'knowledge of life'. What these approaches and conceptual frameworks have in common is that they shift the overall perspective from a literary theory of meaning ("What does a text mean?") to a functional approach that foregrounds the ways in which literary texts participate in the socio-cultural construction of (life) knowledge ("What does a text do?"). It is through this shift that literary studies gains significance and relevance as a form of life science (or as discipline that provides ample opportunities for transdisciplinary work *with* the life sciences, see Zapf 2016: 125-68). What does a literary text *do* with regard to our understanding of our own life, the lives of others and living together? As Nicholas Gaskill, drawing on the works of John Dewey and Charles S. Peirce, argues,

> Dewey and Peirce provide a way of looking at art as a direct phase of experience – or category of sign production – that is nonetheless continuous with, and dynamically related to, other modes of life. They emphasize that meaning resides in process and in the dynamic relations of elements in a situation and thus call us to abandon aesthetic inquiries based on, or directed towards, autonomous 'texts' or 'readers' or 'language' and instead engage the relations and modes of experience literature makes available. (Gaskill 2008: 168)

12 See also Fluck: "Denn der Zuschuß des Imaginären macht aus Wirklichkeit Möglichkeit, um aus imaginierter Möglichkeit neue Wirklichkeit entstehen zu lassen." (1997: 21)

Literature does not linger in a separate realm of the aesthetic. From a pragmatist point of view, it is through experience that the meaning – or knowledge – of literary texts is tightly interwoven with our other 'modes of life'. For Gaskill, a literary pragmatism thus needs to center on the complex ways in which "event, reader, text, and context enter into a dynamic constellation within which virtual reconstructions of relations are created and pushed forth into future experience" (Gaskill 2008: 165; also see Basseler 2009). The special potential of literature to *do* this, i.e. to create new possibilities, knowledge, and "new models of living" (Gaskill 2008: 170) within aesthetic experience, resides in literature's capability to speak to both our emotional and cognitive senses: "Literary language carries the fullness of sense but in a medium more resonant with the ways in which we carry out our intelligent lives." (ibid.: 171)[13]

Aesthetic experience is thus by no means restricted to mere 'pleasure', but provides the key to an understanding of how literature can be conceptualized as a source or medium of (life) knowledge. In a literary experience, the boundaries between the text, context, and reader become permeable and thus a whole new experience is created. In this way, new relations and possibilities emerge:[14]

> In an experience of literary signs, a reader's transaction with these affects and percepts modifies the relations she recognizes and pursues; the qualitative constellations made palpable in the aesthetic experience change the reader's modes of relating to both self and environment. These modes are multiple and involve our ways of feeling, thinking, and associating in the world. (ibid.: 172)

Rather than simply presenting ideas or 'thought experiments', then, literary texts create new possibilities of thinking, feeling, and acting. They have the potential to produce a knowledge which cannot only be transferred but is always already interrelated with other spheres of our lives:

---

13 Gaskill grounds his argument on Peirce's tripartite concept of Firstness, Secondness, and Thirdness: "In brief, Firstness is the category of quality, Secondness of actual existents, and Thirdness of laws or mediating relations." (Gaskill 2008: 168) Whereas Firstness thus refers to qualities and 'virtual possibilities', Secondness could be understood here as the actual instantiation of these possibilities in concrete objects, and Thirdness as the representation or mediation thereof.

14 "Literature does not help us to 'identify' with others; it helps us to experience nonpreexisting relations and to form new habits of relating that alter the possible configurations of self and community that inform social practice." (Gaskill 2008: 174)

> Literature [...] *creates possibilities* that might be carried into new situations. Its distinctive sign-structure enables it to reconfigure 'habits of feeling' and social relations, and its effects reverberate through the individual vital body to the social process of community reconstruction. (ibid.: 174, emphases added, M.B.)

To sum up, the aesthetic experience that literary texts induce seems to be a key to the understanding of how literary texts can generate or impart knowledge, and not an impediment to literature's cognitive value, even though this latter idea arguably runs counter to the mainstream in literary aesthetics, which neatly separates the cognitive from the aesthetic. In the act of reading, the narrative of the literary text is doubled, as readers produce a second narrative that is invested with their own knowledge, hopes, fears, etc. Read 'as if for life', literary texts can have a lasting impact on our system of beliefs and our life knowledge, influencing the ways in which we regard our lives and the lives of others as well as providing answers to the question of how to live. Several critics have therefore suggested that literature serves to fulfill similar functions as thought experiments do in philosophy and science, working as an "intellectual and emotional laboratory" (Swirski 2007: 11) of the mind. Drawing on this notion, the chapters in the next part will now further analyze the ways in which the formal specificities as well as the reading experience of the short story endow the genre as a medium in which life knowledge is reflected and produced in an experience of literary signs and forms.

Part Two:
The Genericity of Literary Life Knowledge in the Short Story

4. The Short Story as an Organon of Life Knowledge:

An Epistemological Approach to the Genre

> Genres have no essence: they have historically changing use values.
> (Frow 2010: 134)

So far, I have only talked about 'the knowledge of literature', making virtually no distinctions as to the specificities in form and content of such knowledge that may come into view when one looks at the different kinds or genres of literature. As a matter of fact, the tendency to neglect the generic disposition of literary knowledge can be regarded as a result of the analytic approach that still dominates the scholarly debate about the knowledge of literature. What philosophers of literature are usually interested in, as the previous chapters have shown, tend to be very broad, abstract questions: What constitutes a text as a work of literary art and what is the significance of its cognitive content or import in this respect? What is the relationship between knowledge, truth, and fiction? How can a transfer take place between the fictional world of a literary text and the 'real world', i.e. how can literary knowledge be translated into 'real-life' knowledge (and is there a need to do so in the first place)?

While these are no doubt all relevant questions, they tend to draw the attention away from the fact that such signifiers as 'literature' or 'fictional literary work' are themselves great abstractions. "Literature," as Terry Eagleton reminds us, "does not exist" (2008 [1983]: 9). Therefore, in order to come to terms with literature's relation to (life) knowledge it seems indispensable to consider the particularities – both formal and thematic – of the different kinds, or genres, that constitute 'fictional literature'. Particularly with regard to 'life knowledge', the generic dimension of a literary text already has a great bearing on the ways in which such knowledge is configured, transmitted, and perspectivized (see Nussbaum 1990:

5). "Everything describable as knowledge is shaped and structured in some fashion." (Walsh 1969: 137) Knowledge, whether literary, scientific, or other, is never pure or innocent. It always depends on the media and formats of its representation. These are in turn marked by very specific symbolic principles, rules of communication, dispositives, and ideologies. Since knowledge by definition must be communicable, there simply is no knowledge that can be detached from its forms and genres of representation. In this very basic sense, epistemic content (i.e. knowledge) is always inextricably intertwined with the structural and ideational specificities of its respective formal representation. In this regard, genres arguably fulfill an important role in structuring what we might refer to as the 'life knowledge' of literature. Whether a sense of life manifests itself in a short story or a novel, or is expressed in a poem, arguably makes a great difference: Life knowledge can be represented *as* a short story, novel, or poem (or as a soap opera, for that matter). Literary (life) knowledge is thus always and inescapably generic; any discussion about 'the knowledge of literature' that does not acknowledge this generic dimension seems limited in a very essential way.

Although 'genre' has for a long time constituted one of the major categories of literary theory, relatively little scholarly work exists that explicitly tackles the question of how genres constitute formats of knowledge, i.e. how the practical and theoretical implications of literary genres have an influence on certain historical orders of knowledge (see Bies/Gamper/Kleeberg 2013b: 7; see also Klausnitzer 2008: 25-48). The emergence of new forms and objects of knowledge, as Joseph Vogl (1999) has argued in his poetological approach to knowledge, can only be fully understood in conjunction with its concrete representation and production (or 'staging'). To conceive of genres as formats of literary (life) knowledge thus means to go beyond the content and discursivity of a work and take into account the formal constitution and stabilization of such knowledge. Genres, from this vantage, become the *sine qua non* of knowledge:

> In reality, knowledge and genre are inescapably intertwined, if only because all forms of knowing, whether poetic or political, exquisitely lyrical or numbingly matter-of-fact – rely on an array of formal resources, stylistic conventions, and conceptual schemata [...] In this sense, form and genre are not an impediment to knowledge, but the only conceivable means of attaining it. (Felski 2008: 83-4.)

Based on the premise that literary (life) knowledge can only be adequately defined as the interrelation between content and form, this chapter addresses the short story genre as a format of knowledge. Like all genres, the short story has developed certain formal principles, conventions, historical use values, and ways of representation.[1] These principles, forms, and conventions, as I will argue, are interwoven with certain cultural notions of (human) life as well as with epistemic notions of how life can be understood. I will discuss several recursive positions from the field of short story theory which attribute to the short story a certain epistemic quality, especially with regard to its potential to capture or express a certain sense of life the 'larger' genres, and especially the novel, tend to overlook.

Some of the epistemic qualities of the short story form have been so central in the early theorizing of the genre that they arguably still influence our very conception of it. Frank O'Connor, in his seminal study *The Lonely Voice*, held that the short story entails an "intense awareness of human loneliness" (1963: 19), shaped by the genre's condensed form of representation: "Because [the short story writer's] frame of reference can never be the totality of a human life, he must be forever selecting the point at which he can approach it" (ibid.: 21). O'Connor's approach to the short story is both ideological and formal. His genre definition rests upon a certain epistemic quality of the short story, i.e. its capacity to reveal a reality of human life that for O'Connor is transgenerational and transnational (see ibid.: 18-45), and which he couples with the genre's formal characteristics.

In the theorizing of the short story throughout the 20th century, there have been numerous attempts to define the qualities of the genre along similar lines, and to "identify the short story form with particular modes of cognition or attitudes to life" (Scofield 2006: 4). One of the inherent problems with such approaches, as Scofield points out, is that "it is usually easy to come up with instances that contradict or at least trouble the principles laid down" (ibid.: 4). As all essentializing, normative theories, such definitions of the short story seem too limited to adequately capture the variety of sub-genres and forms of the short story that have emerged over the last centuries. The remarkable persistence of these attempts, however, at least seems to point toward a particular "use value" (Frow 2010: 134) of the short story. As a literary form that is closely entwined with modern sensibility and forms of life, its representation of life as fragmented, selective, and ephemeral has become almost metonymic for a modernist aesthetics and epistemology. As G.K. Chesterton once remarked, "[t]he moderns […] describe life in short stories because they are possessed with the sentiment that life is an uncommonly short story, and perhaps not a true one" (qtd. in March-Russell 2009: 25).

In a number of what I have elsewhere called "epistemological approaches" (see Basseler 2011a), the short story has been associated with certain kinds or modes of knowledge and human experience. Epistemological approaches start

1 Cf. Gymnich/Neumann/Nünning (2007) and Horn (1998) for an overview, and Gymnich/Neumann (2007) for a fruitful reconceptualization of genre theory.

from the assumption that many short stories, especially since modernism, deal with brief but decisive, critical moments in the lives of their characters, and that these moments have a revelatory quality for either a character or the reader. Often, in these brief situations some previously obscure meaning is revealed to the reader/character, building up toward a "climatic moment of brilliant transforming clarification" (Baxter 1997: 55). James Joyce, in *Stephen Hero*, famously described this as epiphany: "a sudden spiritual manifestation, whether in the vulgarity of speech or of gesture or in a memorable phase of the mind itself," triggered by a "trivial incident". In such incidents, the short story performs its epistemological work: "Then all at once I see it and I know at once what it is: epiphany." (Joyce 1974 [1944]: 99) While 'epiphany' is probably the most established term for this generic feature, similar ideas find their expression in a variety of other critical and poetological writings about the short story. Among the concepts which introduce such a notion of a fleeting and often hurtful or disillusioning insight into the secrets of the human condition are Aldous Huxley's 'diaphany', and Virginia Woolf's 'moment of being'. At least by the 1960s, this notion of the short story as the primary form to depict climactic moments of sudden insight had been reinforced by theoreticians of the form. T.O. Beachcroft's *The Modest Art* (1968), for instance, claimed that "[t]he particular domain of the short story is unique. It is a *flash of insight* that leads to a story; [...] It is a *vision* of people." (Beachcroft 1968: 260, emphasis added, M.B.) Like Joyce's epiphany ("then all at once I see it"), Beachcroft thus draws on optical metaphors ("flash of insight") and the visual effect of a "glimpse through" to define the key feature of the short story genre in terms of its epistemic quality. Exactly twenty years later, John Bayley maintains that it is the short story in which the epistemology of epiphanic moments finds its most accomplished literary expression:

> 'There are in our existence spots of time' – moments which are essential to moral meaning and the moral well-being of the individual, but which can be exploited in a different spirit by the artist. The significant moment is at once art's demonstration of its own completeness, and of the mystery of being which lies outside art. [...] The short story effect, if we can agree to call it that, the epiphany, or 'spot of time', may be met with everywhere, and in almost any genre – poems, novels, *nouvelles* – though the short story itself, of course, affords it complete and conscious existence. (Bayley 1988: 9)

The short story is defined as a meaning-making tool, a form of thought experiment in which art proves its ability to shed light on the "mystery of being". Despite the creativity in the production of terms ("spots of time", "moments of being", etc.), the central idea remains the same: The short story evolves toward a quasi-religious moment of revelation in which some mystery, truth, or meaning of life is exposed to the character and/or the reader in a visual or quasi-visual manner: "A moment of radiant vision brings forth the sensation if not the content of meaning." (Baxter 1997: 55)[2] Formally speaking, epiphanies require some alienation or de-familiarization of the ordinary: in order to "achieve such epiphanous and unique ordinariness, we are required [...] to 'make the ordinary strange.'" (Bruner 2004: 696) In the literary epiphanies of writers like Joyce, Sherwood Anderson, and John Cheever, the "crust of conventional schemata" is broken through in order "to call up new forms of consciousness, other ways of seeing" (Felski 2008: 79).

While epiphany may not be an 'essential' feature of the short story form (there exists, of course, a plethora of stories which lack such moments of sudden insight), the logic of unveiling nevertheless constitutes one of its main "use values" (Frow). As Charles Baxter remarks, the "logic of unveiling has become a dominant mode in Anglo-American writing, certainly in fiction, particularly short stories [...]. Some of the most beautiful stories ever written, at least in the last 150 years, follow this pattern." (1997: 58-60)[3] Epiphanies may not be built into the very logic or 'essence' of the short story, yet they are arguably more frequently found in this genre than in any other literary form. From a literary-historical perspective, one might argue that the modernist short story's penchant for epiphanies corresponds with the "discovery" of point of view, highlighting the "link between observation, epistemology, power, narrative, perspective and aesthetics-at-large" (Klepper 2011: 5).

Along the lines of the defamiliarizing effect of epiphanies, more recent short story theory has further developed these links between epistemology and aesthetics in the short story. Charles May (1984), Thomas Leitch (1989), and most recently David Trotter (2010) have all claimed that the short story has a special potential to defamiliarize, debunk, and "dis-enable" (cf. the title of Trotter's essay)

---

2 See Tigges (1999) on aspects of the literary epiphany.

3 His essay tellingly entitled "Against Epiphanies," Baxter complains about the ways in which epiphany has become a stale or even rotten convention in American short fiction. "The mass-marketing of literary epiphanies and climactic insights," Baxter writes, "produces in editors and readers an expectation that stories must end with an insight. This insight-ending, as a result, has become something of a weird norm in contemporary writing [...] That old insight train just comes chugging into the station, time after time" (1997: 62-7). He then even provides some quasi-statistical, empirical evidence for this: "In most anthologies of short stories published since the 1940s, insight endings or epiphanic endings account for approximately 50 to 85 percent of all the climactic moments." (ibid.: 67)

what is considered as knowledge in society. In his essay "The Nature of Knowledge in Short Fiction," May expresses his notion of an essential, epistemological and ontological difference between the short story and the novel: "The short story is short precisely because of the kind of experience or reality embodied in it. And the kind of experience we find in the short story reflects a mode of knowing which differs *essentially* from the mode of knowing in the novel." (May 1984: 328, emphasis added, M.B.) May further unfolds this thesis, claiming that whereas the novel is connected to a form of experience that is "conceptually created and considered" (ibid.), the short story typically deals with *an* experience that is "directly and emotionally created and encountered" (ibid.).[4] He concurs with the prevalent theories of the novel held at that time (especially those propounded by Lionel Trilling and Ian Watt), which regarded the novel as concerned with the social reality, and in contrast conceives of the short story as an 'anti-social' form, which is ostensibly closer to dreams and the unconscious. Where the novel reaffirms the everyday world, the short story 'defamiliarizes' it (May 1984: 329).[5]

In order to support this thesis, May adopts the phenomenological notion of reality and Husserlian life-world as presented by Alfred Schütz and Thomas Luckmann in *Strukturen der Lebenswelt* and associates the short story "with characters in their essential aloneness," rather than in intersubjective encounters with others (as in the novel): "The short story breaks up the familiar life-world of the everyday, defamiliarizes our assumption that reality is simply the conceptual construct we take it to be, and throws into doubt that our propositional and categorical mode of perceiving can be applied to human beings as well as objects." (May 1984: 333) This, May contends, also explains why 'we' (he probably refers to readers in a Western cultural context) prefer the novel over the short story, since it does not disrupt or unsettle 'our' general sense of the "security of the everyday life-world" (ibid.). Moreover, he attempts to reconcile the short story's alleged inclination toward the supernatural, spiritual or dreamlike with its relation to 'reality' – simply by expanding the notion of reality itself, so that it includes what William James has named 'sub-universes of reality':

4 Here, May is clearly inspired by Dewey's differentiation between the general, non-aesthetic experiences that occur continually, and 'an' experience that is typically realized in art.

5 May refers to a whole variety of sources in which the defamiliarizing quality of art and particularly literature is emphasized, from Shelley's "Defense of Poetry" through the Russian formalists and Morse Peckham's study *Man's Rage for Chaos*.

> The reality the short story presents us with is the reality of those sub-universes of the supernatural and the fable which exist in the so-called 'real' world of sense perception and conceptual construction. It presents moments in which we become aware of anxiety, loneliness, dread, concern, and thus find the safe, secure and systematic life we usually lead disrupted and momentarily destroyed. The short story is the most adequate form to confront us with reality as we perceive it in our most profound moments. (ibid.: 337-8)

The short story's epistemology thus aims at the very foundations of our knowledge of life. As Thomas Leitch has argued, short stories are not so much characterized by a movement from nescience to knowledge, but in fact 'debunk' formerly uncontested certainties and beliefs: "[I]t is quite possible to challenge the character's, and the audience's, assumptions about the world without substituting any more-authoritative knowledge, so that such stories constitute not a form of knowledge but a challenge to knowledge, that is, a way of debunking assumptions which are not really true." (Leitch 1989: 133) The short story constitutes "essentially a means of unknowing rather than a means to knowledge" (ibid.). The emergence of the short story form in the United States is therefore connected with a deep epistemological skepticism, particularly with regard to the concept of a public identity, i.e. the notion that "a self acts in such a knowable, deliberate way as to assert a stable, discrete identity" (ibid.). Stories as different in form, style, and content as Poe's "The Tell-Tale Heart", Melville's "Bartleby, the Scrivener", Anderson's "The Man Who Became a Woman", and O'Connor's "Good Country People" all share this "antithetical structure" (ibid.: 140) that aims at the destabilization of affirmed notions of identity and subjectivity. The "debunking rhythm", i.e. an epistemological structure proceeding from stable assumptions and authoritative knowledge to their dissolution, pervades American short fiction, and especially the sub-genre of initiation stories (see ibid.: 134). In this regard, the short story may be said to dismantle rather than produce cultural life knowledge, functioning as a counter-discourse (sensu Zapf) in which dominant models and forms of life as well as truth claims and hegemonic life narratives of a unified public self are being contested.

Another example of approaches that associate the short story with a radical epistemological skepticism is David Trotter's recent essay on "Dis-Enablement: Subject and Method in the Modernist Short Story." Trotter (2010: 6) holds that whereas the novel is fundamentally an affirmative genre meant to enable the bourgeois subject to maintain a stable identity with regard to morality, nationality, ethnicity, sexuality etc., the short story 'dis-affirms' such categories, "render[ing] meaning incompatible with existence." Fundamentally a genre of crisis, the short story's main cultural function is dis-affirmation. If novels present crises in order to overcome them and to arrive at a certain knowledge, "the crisis of a short story does not necessarily produce affirmative knowledge" (ibid.: 8). Similar to May and Leitch's texts, Trotter suggests an epistemological approach to the short story that associates the genre with a certain critical positionality toward culturally dominant forms of knowledge. Drawing on earlier notions of epiphany, all three of them credit the short story with a certain critical potential that 'debunks', 'disenables', or 'defamiliarizes' socially sanctioned perceptions of life as well as systems of knowledge. Short stories, in all three accounts, aim at our epistemic certainties, confronting the reader with moments that cannot be easily understood and thus undermine the very foundations of our knowledge.

May's, Leitch's, and Trotter's theoretical accounts of the short story are instructive in that they acknowledge that literary genres are not merely sets of certain artistic techniques, but also formats of knowledge in which formal, stylistic, and conceptual schemata contribute to the ways in which meaning is produced (or deconstructed, for that matter) and communicated in the interaction between author, text, and reader. Of course, to assign the short story with such expressive and epistemological qualities always risks to essentialize the form. As John Frow remarks with regard to the novel, "it's most powerful theorists, those who have achieved the most intense illumination of the expressive capacities of the genre, have all bought their insights at the price of an essentialisation of those capacities" (Frow 2010: 134).[6] The same holds true for the short story. In fact, there is probably no other literary form or genre that is better suited to corroborate the recently expressed notion that 'genre' and 'theory' are mutually exclusive terms. As various critics, including Ralph Cohen and Hayden White (2003) have argued, the very concept of genre is 'resistant to theory'.

Although it does not make much sense to define the epistemic nature of the short story in abstract theoretical and transhistorical terms, one can however find literary-historical evidence for a specific connection between the form and a desire to represent a 'deeper', sub-surface knowledge of human life. From a genre- historical point of view, it is unnecessary to make generalizing formalist claims about a genre in order to describe the cultural work it does. Genres can never be described as holistic entities: "The reason a genre cannot be present in its entirety is that it undergoes change with each new genre member so that there is no 'entirety.'" (Cohen 2003: vii) At the same time, short story theories and collective conceptions of the 'nature' of the short story have of course had an inestimable influence on its cultural life: Just like individual authors respond "to communal

6 The theorists Frow refers to include Georg Lukács, Mikhail Bakhtin, and Ian Watt.

rules and expectations," these rules and expectations are in turn shaped and transformed by the individual contributions (see Levy 1993: 4). Each short story responds to the existing expectations and conventions that govern literary communication, whether it is by affirmation, expansion or subversion. Genres, understood as products of certain social and historical processes rather than ontological entities, constitute a horizon of expectation (cf. Frow 2010: 69) for both authors and readers. Genres arguably do possess certain "historically specific and variable *expressive qualities*: they offer frameworks for constructing meaning and value" (ibid.: 72).

Bakhtin and Medvedev have described genre as the "organic unity of theme with what lies beyond it" (1994: 178), pointing to the reciprocity of genre and social reality, of particular means of representation and their rootedness in life. Very much in a Bakhtinian sense, then, genres can be regarded as specific modes of experience, or as forms of "manifesting or expressing a world view" or "carriers of world view" (Morson 2003: 411). Genres may be understood as frameworks or formats which offer "certain expressive qualities over others in a particular set of circumstances" (Frow 2010: 72). In their particular historical and cultural contexts, genres possess certain "truth effects" (ibid.), which are generated by their specific "discursive qualities" (ibid.). These discursive qualities refer to the processes and structures of authorial production on the one hand, and the reception on the other. Generic strategies refer to the textual or medial characteristics, including the *formal features*, *thematic structures*, certain *topoi* as well as a certain "structure of address" (ibid.: 73). Following this idea of the very specific discursive qualities of genres, the short story (like any other genre) may be said to produce or project certain "effects of truth and authority" (ibid.), i.e. a generically specific 'world'. What is more, the relationship between generic representation and extra-textual knowledge is one of reciprocity: "Over time, readers are shaped by what they read, even as they cannot help but impose on texts what they already know. Here again we can apprise the relevance of genre not as a rigid set of formal rules, but as flexible criteria that we impute or ascribe to texts." (Felski 2008: 87)

In this chapter, I have drawn on several scholarly positions to delineate an epistemological approach to the short story in order to supplement and substantiate the more general theoretical framework ("the knowledge of literature") outlined in the previous chapters. The persistence of approaches according to which the short story is characterized by its special relation to meaning and knowing – expressed in a variety of terms and conceptual frameworks – suggests that the American short story has emerged and developed as a genre in which the very foundations of culturally prevailing life knowledge are being critically reflected, expanded, and in some cases undermined. The abundance of epiphanic moments, the tendency to defamiliarize reality and create an awareness of the limits of what we can possibly know and understand about life, arguably constitutes one of the most crucial generic features of the short story. In contrast to formalist attempts at defining the genre, however, such an epistemological structure should be conceptualized as a particular 'use value' of the short story, rather than a universal or essential quality. The 'life knowledge' that the short story explores or presents thus should not be understood as a knowledge that precedes its literary or generic representation in the sense that it is simply 'depicted' or 'captured' in the short story form. Rather, it must be conceptualized as a decidedly generic knowledge, i.e. a knowledge that only exists in this specific form. The life knowledge that the short story presents, mediates, and generates is inextricably connected to its generic representation as well as the discursive qualities of the short story. The next chapter will therefore further explore the ways in which the discursive qualities of the short story as a medium of life knowledge play out in the interaction between author, text, and reader.

5. Life Knowledge as Projection:

The Cognitive Work of Short Stories

In chapter 3, I have argued that the aesthetic experience of literary texts is not only conducive to, but even constitutive of the knowledge they impart. By providing us with multifarious possibilities to imaginatively 'live through' certain situations or make experiences that would otherwise not be accessible to us, literary works offer a unique source of knowledge. This idea is in keeping with the pragmatist notion of art as experience (Dewey) and a decidedly pragmatic view of literature that regards literary texts not as autonomous aesthetic entities but puts them at work in the world, and in the lives of their readers.

The question remains, however, how short stories, by means of their particular generic setup, enable the transfer of meaning or knowledge between the text and the reader. What characterizes the reading experience of the short story? What equips the short story with a special potential to perform cognitive work as an 'organon of life knowledge'? How does the short story's brevity effect the ways in which readers interact with stories and endow them with meaning? If brevity, as Paul Zumthor reminded us, "is never random but *constitutes a structuring model*" (2016: 74, emphasis in the original), then how does brevity as structuring model contribute to the 'truth effects' of the genre?

Combining reader response theories with narratological categories, Renate Brosch has addressed similar questions in her study *Short Story: Textsorte und Leseerfahrung*. Brosch importantly expands the focus of short story criticism to include not only the questions of what a story means, or what the formal constituents of short stories are, but also and very importantly the functions of short stories with regard to the emotional and cognitive processes the genre evokes in the reader (see Brosch 2007: 14-5). As the subtitle of her book suggests, Brosch approaches the short story from a double perspective that considers the ways in which the textual features, generic conventions and narrative techniques (*in medias res* beginnings, open endings, limited personnel, and transitional settings etc.) shape the reception process and reading experience. Brosch's basic assumption is that short stories produce a very particular reading experience, which differs especially from the reading experience of longer narrative forms like the novel. The relative brevity of the short story genre, its tendency toward compression, omission, and linguistic sparingness all contribute to this effect which determines not only how short stories are processed during the perusal, but also how they coax the reader into transgressing the textual boundaries and produce meaning beyond the confines of the story itself.

If compared to novels, short stories do not allow for the same degree of immersion on the part of the reader because of the rather short time needed for their consumption. Nevertheless, short stories do require a very high amount of active reader participation in the construction of meaning. Whereas readers of a novel tend to immerse more or less fully in the given textual world, the short story forces the reader to oscillate between the textual world and the extratextual frame references that are needed for the interpretation:

> Die Besonderheit des Lesens von Kurzgeschichten liegt in der Kürze. Zwar stehen sie im Zusammenhang mit unseren natürlichen narrativen Fähigkeiten und ihren weitreichenden Einflüssen auf Bewusstseinsvorgänge, doch können sie weniger als narrative Langformen durch detailreiche Ausgestaltung einer fiktionalen Welt den Leser vereinnahmen und zu vertieftem Lesen verleiten. Die Leseerfahrung der Kurzgeschichte ist daher zwischen der automatisierten Desambiguierung von syntaktischen Einheiten in der Alltagskommunikation und dem bewussten Verfolgen von bedeutungskonstitutiven mentalen Prozessen, die einen literarischen Text begleiten, angesiedelt. Sie erlaubt weder die völlige Immersion illusionistischer Lektüre noch die unproblematische Informationsextraktion der Gesprächskommunikation. Die Lesestrategien bewegen sich zwischen Eindeutigkeitsstreben und Mehrdeutigkeitsvergnügen. (Brosch 2007: 15-16)

As a general tendency, short stories arguably require from the reader a greater amount of attention and hermeneutic effort ("Deutungsanstrengung," ibid.: 57) than novels. Whereas it is possible to skip several pages in the course of a novel of several hundred pages without dramatically affecting the general reading experience, a short story needs to be read with the same amount of attention throughout. Short stories in general, and modernist and postmodernist stories in particular, tend to employ a comparatively high degree of gaps of indeterminacy, requiring the reader to fill these gaps. As a result, meaning in the short story often resides in different (textual and contextual) layers of meaning, in contrast to the more gradual, successive unfolding of meaning in the novel (see ibid.: 58). According to Brosch, then, this quality of the genre leads to the profound and lasting effect of many short stories, i.e. the phenomenon that readers often remember short stories better and more fully than longer narratives. The particular reading experience of short stories is closely intertwined with their narrative economy, demanding constant attention and a relatively high interpretative investment on the part of the reader.

Hence what distinguishes the specific reading experience of short stories is that they tend to evoke a kind of "projective reading". This concept basically refers to a distinctive receptional stance that readers of short stories take when they are forced to constantly transgress the material boundaries of the respective story, investing the reading with a wide net of extratextual frame references. As a consequence, 'meaning' does not merely reside *in* the text itself, but in its many potential references and 'projections' onto other domains. Of course, reading is always necessarily 'projective' to a certain degree, as various reader response theories have convincingly argued: Without referring the textual elements to some other, extratextual schemata, mental models, and frames of reference, an understanding of any literary text, and not only short stories, would not be possible in the first place. These frames of reference include other literary texts, historical events, basic social and psychological assumptions, and also the very system of language. Hence, a reading completely without projection would be impossible. However, Brosch argues that the short story as a genre stimulates this kind of projective reading in a particular way:

> Wir werden vom Text angehalten oder angeregt, das Dargestellte projektiv zu lesen, und wir reagieren auf den kurzen Erzähltext, indem wir dazu neigen, ihn zu erweitern. Unsere Bereitschaft zu solchem projektiven Lesen ist ungleich größer als bei Romanen. Kurzgeschichten stellen aufgrund der von ihnen erzeugten kognitiven Dissonanz ein Projektions- und Transgressionsangebot für den Leser bereit. (ibid.: 200)

As a result of this potential for transgression and projection that the short story as a genre offers the reader, the reading of short stories is therefore marked by a "cognitive sustainability" (ibid.: 97, transl. M.B.). Because of this reading experience, short stories possess a particular cognitive significance: They are able to convey certain insights and cognitive impulses that go far beyond the mere semantic understanding of the content. As Monika Fludernik (1996) has argued, every reading act constitutes a process of adaptation and naturalization, i.e. the meaning of a text is constructed by the reader and integrated into his or her world knowledge and system of beliefs. In this way, readers are able to even make sense of seemingly incomprehensible, inconsistent texts and create their own meaningful narratives during the reading process. And whereas this holds true for all (narrative) texts, Brosch claims that the reading experience of short stories rests upon this principle to a particularly high extent: "Kurzgeschichten nutzen diese natürliche Disposition von Lesern schamlos aus." (Brosch 2007: 94)

But short stories do not only invite the reader to invest the text with extratextual meaning in an act of projective reading, they also frequently produce cognitive dissonances and thus build up what Brosch calls "pressure of dissonance" (see ibid., transl. M.B.). Cognitive dissonances occur whenever certain events, settings, motives or other elements of a story's plot or discourse do not correspond with our existing knowledge, or are difficult to interpret within our value and belief system. Reading a story like George Saunders's "The Semplica Girl Diaries" (2013) makes it difficult for the reader to adequately respond and to 'naturalize' the plot. Presenting the world of a highly idiosyncratic first-person narrator, where girls from third-world countries are trafficked as ornaments and then hung upon strings in people's front-yards as a symbol of prosperity, Saunders's story forces the reader to reconcile these cognitive dissonances, to test the story's implications for their own models of reality.

For the reading experience of short stories, this has two important consequences: on the one hand, the reader can control these pressures and contradictions by referring to their system of beliefs in the process of adaptation or naturalization. On the other hand, however, the cognitive dissonance may be so strong that the reader feels the pressure to change their beliefs, and thus their interpretation of the given text (see Brosch 2007: 96). Consequently, this pressure of dissonance forces the reader to match or adjust his or her own assumptions and reality models with the ideas and models presented by the text. In the case of "The Semplica Girl Diaries", this process might lead the reader to ponder on the difference between the obviously grotesque, inhuman situation depicted in the story and other, similarly inhuman circumstances that the globalization of labor in late Capitalism has produced. Projective reading thus means that the reading process potentially has a 'transformative emotional effect' (ibid.: 103) and transcends the textual frame. For Brosch, this particular reading experience of short stories is directly linked to the brevity of the genre – and hence to the textual features that this brevity engenders.

This idea of 'projection' that characterizes the reception of short stories may be both supported and further differentiated by Mark Turner's more comprehensive cognition framework developed in *The Literary Mind*. In contrast to Brosch, who ascribes 'projective reading' to the generic disposition of short stories, Turner regards projection as a fundamental category that applies to, and in fact characterizes, narrative in general, and not only short stories. What is even more, Turner conceptualizes narrative projection as a cognitive principle that governs the way we make sense of the world: From a cognitivist perspective Turner aims to explain why our very thinking is generally ruled by narrative structures and principles and how the concept of 'story' therefore does not merely refer to the cultural products we call stories (short stories, novels, anecdotes, etc.) but to "a basic principle of the mind" (Turner 1996: v).

More precisely, Turner uses the three categories 'story', 'projection', and 'parable' in order to demonstrate the narrative structure of our cognition. Whereas 'story' simply refers to the basic cognitive activity of "narrative imagination" (ibid.: 4) per se, 'projection' means the capability to project one story onto another in order to create coherence and meaning. The concept of 'parable' derives from the literary genre of the same name, yet it serves to denominate the more fundamental process or "mental instrument" (ibid.: 7) of using stories and projecting them onto other stories: "The essence of parable is its intricate combining of two forms of knowledge – story and projection." (ibid.: 5)

Hence, in Turner's conceptual framework, story, projection, and parable do not merely describe certain cultural or linguistic products, but fundamental cognitive principles that are at work when we make sense of our everyday lives. Although we tend to think of such mental processes as literary, we use them all the time and mostly unconsciously when we "imagine realities and construct meanings" (ibid.: 11). From this vantage, stories are not merely aesthetic or cultural products, but "indispensable to human cognition generally" (ibid.: 5): it is in this sense that the human mind is a literary mind. What is more, projection is inextricably connected with all kinds of stories, whether in the sense of an everyday mental process or a literary artifact. According to Turner, because of our human capability of, and propensity towards, narrative imagining we cannot help but project meaning, using the principle of 'parable' to make sense of stories by means of other stories.

Turner's cognitivist theory fundamentally challenges the (evolutionary) view that human language preceded and thus produced the storytelling capacity of humankind. The widely-held notion that language developed first, and later allowed for the more complex symbolic forms of storytelling is obsolete for him. On the contrary, he claims that stories, understood as the basic principle of the mind, brought about language (i.e. the use of grammatical structures) in the first place, and not *vice versa*: "Grammar results from the projection of story structure." (ibid.: 141) Turner thus reverses the traditional view that literary narrative is the refined result of more basic linguistic skills: "It works the other way round. With story, projection, and their powerful combination in parable, we have a cognitive basis from which language can originate." (ibid.: 168)

Due to the broad scope and fundamental claim of his argument, which is first and foremost interested in narrative as a basic cognitive principle, Turner is rather abstemious when it comes to providing explanations for how readers of literary works project these literary narratives onto their own lives. His focus is primarily on how the principles of narrative are always at work in our experiencing and interpreting the world. Interestingly enough, however, Turner, in one of the few passages that do offer some concrete examples as to how literary narratives may have an impact on our lives, draws on the short story form:

> Often a short story will contain no overt mark that it stands for anything but what it purports to represent, and yet we will interpret it as projecting to a much larger abstract narrative, one that applies to our own specific lives, however far our lives are removed from the detail of the story. Such an emblematic story, however unyieldingly specific in its reference, can seem pregnant with general meaning. (Turner 1996: 7)

What this means is as simple as it is compelling. Short stories are not about our lives. Short stories are not even about life in general. They are always only about specific, imagined characters, events, and plots. Generally, very few of these stories have any direct correlation with the lives of their readers. More often than not, they are detached and fundamentally different from the historical, social, and cultural circumstances of their readers' lives. Nevertheless, when cast against the readers' own life narratives, short stories can become expressive of a 'general meaning', enlightening one's understanding or knowledge of life by means of projection. As they invite self-implication in literary reading (see Kuiken et al. 2004), the formal characteristics of the short story importantly contribute to their capacity to transcend the borders of the text and trigger projective reading. The shorter, the more compressed a narrative becomes, the more it tends toward such implication of general, trans-individual, and exemplary issues (see Nischik 1993: 214; see also Basseler 2018).

From a cognitive point of view, therefore, theories of projection seem to provide a useful framework to describe and explain the ways in which short stories are particularly well equipped to impart general meaning and life knowledge, even though this knowledge is not 'contained in' the text in any direct, propositional sense. The short story's life knowledge, whether practical or theoretical, is not so much a propositional knowledge, but a relational knowledge. It is only in the act of reading that this cognitive significance can be activated, so to speak. And of course, short stories are not the only or even necessarily the foremost genre in which this process occurs: A novel can be read projectively, as could a poem or a play. However, it seems that the narrative form of the short story, its brevity and tendency for polysemy and indeterminacy, abets such a reading. Hence, if stories build the very foundation of our knowledge since our cognitive faculty basically functions on the principle of narrative projection (as Turner claims), and if the short story genre relies on this principle to a greater degree than most other genres (as Brosch claims), then it makes sense to conceive of the short story as a medium or organon of life knowledge: Providing us with very particular themes, plots, and characters – the lives of others as it were – *and* with the possibility to project these plots to the 'much larger abstract stories' of our own lives, short stories add to our very knowledge of and about life.

Of course, the principle of projection alone does not sufficiently explain why and how short stories might serve as a medium of life knowledge. In order to come to terms with this question it is also necessary to look at the formal peculiarities and the typical subjects and topoi of short stories. It is to these that I will now turn.

6. Life-Changing Experiences and Turning Points:

The Crisis-Ridden Life Knowledge of the Short Story

Theorists of the short story tend not to agree on too many things. One aspect, however, which has almost become a commonplace in critical writing about the short story is the notion that the genre lends itself particularly well to the depiction of crises and turning points.[1] In the *Cambridge Introduction to the American Short Story*, Martin Scofield (2006: 238) observes that the "short story is perhaps the exemplary form for the perception of crisis, crux, turning point; and as such it has proved ideal for recording decisive moments, intimately private but often with broad social resonances". According to Scofield, a moment of crisis is constitutive for the genre: "Like the lyric poem, but always with the emphasis on narrative and event, it focuses on the most intense and *life-changing experiences*." (ibid., emphasis added, M.B.) As a favored thematic domain, short stories often zero in on situations which, embedded in the larger framework of the protagonists' lives, bring about a fundamental change the characters' and/or readers' perception of life.[2] Charles May (2004: 22) even maintains that the "short story insists that the self must be challenged by crisis and confrontation" (ibid.), whereas the novel usually tends to resolve crises and integrate them into the "ordinary flow of everyday experience" (ibid.: 24). And Kasia Boddy emphasizes the direct interrelation between the short story's formal and thematic characteristics along the same lines: "Given its brevity, its formal constitution in and as crisis, the short story

1 Cf. Robert Vogt's (2012) insightful essay on other literary (sub-)genres that rely heavily on turning points, namely alternate history, science fiction, and 'multiverse narratives.'

2 Frank O'Connor famously launched this notion in his seminal study *The Lonely Voice* (1963). In this book, O'Connor argues that the short story is all about crisis and in this sense turns on itself (see Boddy 2010: 100).

gravitates towards certain kinds of subject matter; in particular, towards the representation of moments of condensed significance, moments in time which allow or enforce a stepping out of routine, out of time." (2010: 101) From this vantage, the short story is more radical than the novel in terms of the presentation of crises and their epistemological resonances. On the level of subject matter, then, the short story has often been associated with plots of crisis and turning points, focusing not so much on the causality of events and the life course, but on "the moment which marks a radical change in the life of an individual, a group or [...] a whole nation" (Scofield 2006: 10).

What is most intriguing about such notions of the short story as a genre of 'crisis, crux, and turning points', however, are perhaps the epistemological assumptions that are implicated in these notions. To quote Scofield once again, "the short story can *bring home to a reader* the experience of a moral crisis which has had a profound effect on a life and its beliefs" (2006: 210, emphasis added, M.B.). Whereas the novel is a "cognitive form concerned to map the causal processes underlying events, the short story, by contrast, can yield us some single bizarre occurrence of epiphany of terror whose impact would merely be blunted by lengthy realist elaboration" (May 2004: 16). Note the shift in the argument here: whereas the first sense of the short story as a genre of crisis refers to the level of the story/plot, this second sense is more concerned with what Renate Brosch (2007) has called the particular reading experience of the short story:

> Short stories sind bekannt als Texte, die bevorzugt grenzgängerische Themen darstellen, Menschen in *Übergangssituationen, Krisen und Umbrüchen*. Doch sie machen solche Grenzgänge nicht nur zum Thema, vielmehr werden Grenzgänge vom Text angeregt und vom Leser vollzogen; die Grenzen, die andeutend, darstellend oder imaginativ überschritten werden, finden sich auf den verschiedenen [...] Ebenen. (Brosch 2007: 23, emphasis added, M.B.)

Short stories can thus deal with crises and turning points on the story level, reflect them on the discourse level, and trigger processes of imaginative transgression on the part of the reader. As a kind of border-crossing genre, short stories tend to focus on the moment of crisis and turning point itself, rather than its resolution. Providing the reader with the experience of a transitional phase, crisis and/or turning point – short stories have the potential to retroact on the reader's understanding of life and its underlying values and norms. Hence, the central idea is basically an Aristotelian one, namely that a representation of crisis can cause a quasi-cathartic effect on the part of the reader.

As a closer look therefore reveals, critics do not always refer to the same phenomenon when they ascribe to the short story an inclination towards crises and turning points. Given the related yet slightly different meanings of this notion, it makes sense to differentiate between the various levels on which these critical moments potentially manifest themselves. In the following, therefore, I will discriminate between 1) moments of crisis represented on the story level; 2) a narrator's explicit reflection on crises and turning points on the discourse level; and 3) turning points and moments of crisis or cognitive dissonance in the reader's reception, i.e. the notion that the short story is particularly well-equipped to create a reading experience that has the potential to challenge or change the reader's sense of life (by means of projective reading). Of course, these different levels on which crises and turning points manifest themselves often overlap and interrelate. Without any crisis moment or turning point on either the story or discourse level, a reader will hardly be led to an imaginative transgression of the kind described by Brosch in the above quotation. Nevertheless, it strikes me as useful to separate them on an analytical level in order to qualify the relatively vague assumption of the short story as a genre of crises and turning points.

Before turning to these issues, however, it seems necessary to briefly elaborate on the very terms 'crisis' and 'turning point', which – despite the common habit to use them as rather obvious and self-explanatory concepts – are less natural givens than cultural constructs. As a matter of fact, the very idea that crises and turning points 'occur' in peoples' lives, and that they have a significant impact on the further life course, is already part of the genre's life knowledge: rather than a neutral reflection of a preceding, *a priori* 'reality', crisis and turning point are part of the specific 'world-making' which the short story performs. The very idea that turning points and crises are important moments in the narrative comprehension of life, the making of meaning, and the construction of identity is part of the genre's larger narrative framework that shapes cultural knowledge of life. By staging crises and turning points, I argue, and by creating an aesthetic experience in which these 'life-changing events' can be imaginatively 'lived through' by the reader, short stories contribute to our very understanding of life, offering models of explanation and meaning-making.

A central problem with the notion of the short story as a genre of crisis and turning point is that so far nobody has really bothered to clarify what 'crisis' or 'turning point' actually mean in a narrative. In one of the few narratological attempts to define 'turning points', Ansgar Nünning has persuasively argued that "[t]he definition of the key concept of 'crisis', the meaning of which seems self-evident at first glance, is already problematic: Intuitively, everybody knows what a crisis is, and what an event is" (Nünning 2009: 234). Crisis, as Nünning reminds us, is first and foremost a metaphor. Despite the ubiquitous use of this metaphor in the media as well as everyday life, there has been virtually no serious academic research into crisis metaphors and narratives so far. Defined by the *Oxford English Dictionary* as a "point in the progress of a disease when an important development or change takes place which is decisive of recovery or death; the turning-point of a disease for better or worse," the literal meaning of crisis obviously derives from the field of medicine. In its figurative use, however, crisis can refer to all kinds of situations "in which a decisive change for better or worse is imminent". Thus, we speak of economic and financial crises, political crises, crises in sports, as well as personal crises, e.g. in a relationship or marriage, and emotional crises of identity, as in 'midlife crisis' (see chapter 9). Inherent to the notion of crises is a diagnosis of the significance of certain events, or series of events. What connects all these different kinds of crises on a structural level is the moment of indecision and openness: the outcome of the critical situation is still in limbo: "Crises are a special kind of event, or perhaps rather non-event, since they – according to their etymology – precisely mark the critical point at which a decision about the further progress of the incident is made amongst a number of possibilities." (Nünning 2009: 239)

Drawing on Wolf Schmid's narratological definition of 'event' and 'eventfulness', Nünning suggests several criteria and characteristics of a (narrative) crisis, three of which seem particularly useful in the context of this study: 1) a crisis is always a "moment of surprise or the extraordinary" (ibid.: 240) that stands out from the everyday flux of incidents and challenges normality; 2) there has to be a certain consequentiality of this moment, which is perceived by the protagonists; 3) crises are always discursively created and are thus constructs rather than givens, "made by the people and media 'reporting' on them" (ibid.). The following explication of 'crisis' thus can serve as a very helpful step towards the description of the 'crisis-ridden life knowledge' of the short story:

> Based on the differentiation between occurrences and events, crises can be conceptualized as the results of narrative transformations by means of which an occurrence first of all becomes an event, then becomes a story and finally becomes a certain kind of story or a specific plot pattern, namely a crisis narrative. From the point of view of literary and cultural studies, crises can only become tangible, and are only observable, in their textual or medial manifestations, i.e. in the discursive presentation as crisis narratives in a concrete text or another media product. (ibid.: 242)

Crises are thus essentially a phenomenon of storytelling, the result of narrative transformation by which occurrences first become events and then stories. To analyze the short story as a genre of crisis, then, one first of all needs to analyze the narrative patterns by which the transformation from occurrence to crisis is shaped. In contrast to crisis narratives in the media, however, short stories as crisis narratives typically deal with invented, or imagined, events (though one might think of numerous examples in which short stories draw on 'real' events, such as Eudora Welty's exquisite "Where is the Voice Coming From", written in direct response to the assassination of Civil-Rights leader Medgar Evans in 1963). As 'crisis narratives', short stories provide a generic model of how people transform their experiences in the form of stories, constituting a particular 'mode of emplotment' for crises.

Like crisis, the term 'turning point' is – for the most part – used metaphorically to denote "peculiarly essential junctures" (Abbott 1997: 99). As another quick glance at the *OED* reveals, more often than not – at least in everyday speech – 'turning point' is used as a synonym for 'crisis': "a point at which a decisive change of any kind takes place; a critical point, crisis."[3] As we have also seen above, turning point and crisis are defined interdependently. The source domain of the turning-point metaphor, however, is a categorically different one: Whereas crisis derives from the source domain of medicine, turning point is a spatio-temporal metaphor which implies a certain movement – or travelling – through space and time. With regard to human beings' perception and interpretation of their lives, the 'turning point' metaphor is therefore closely connected to another conceptual metaphor, namely that of 'life as a journey'.

Drawing on Lakoff and Turner's (1989) famous definition of the 'life as a journey' metaphor, Nünning and Sicks (2012: 14) offer a valuable list of the characteristic features of the metaphor of turning points. These features include a) a subject that can be envisaged as a traveler; b) the movement along a particular path; c) the reaching of a crossroads connected with a choice among several other 'paths;' d) a heightened degree of self-awareness as well as a conscious reflection about the options on the traveler's side; e) an understanding of the problems, conflicts, and importance involved in the decision; f) a decision on which of the options and paths to choose and take; g) a "change of direction resulting from whatever decision is made;" h) a (relatively) high degree of eventfulness as well as i)

3 Somewhat enigmatically, Marshall Brown comments that "[t]he turning point is both a moment of balance and a moment of unbalance, of decision and of indecision, of determination [...] and of indetermination" (1997: 10). In this quote, the term 'turning point' is arguably completely interchangeable with the term 'crisis.'

a "sense of the importance of the decision and the changes and effects that it entails" (ibid.). Turning point is understood metaphorically as the moment of juncture in the course of the journey of life. As conceptual metaphors crises and turning points, though often conflated in their actual usage in the media and everyday language, thus imply quite different notions of a larger cultural concept. While the notion of crisis is temporal (describing the moment between illness and recovery or death), turning point is a spatial metaphor that projects this moment onto the realm of traveling.

As the products of narrative transformation, crises and turning points never exist 'out there' but are always already the product of a diagnosis and interpretation: "Just like other events, crises are also the result of selection, abstraction, and distinction." (Nünning 2009: 239) By selecting a certain situation and presenting it *as* a (life) crisis, thus, the short story already engages in the production of a kind of life knowledge which only becomes visible in critical situations. Hence, the very idea of 'life-changing experiences', which seems to underlie the short story form to a certain degree, already affirms a cultural pattern of explanation: namely that change and progress always require a critical moment of uncertainty, indetermination, and indecision. Moreover, both the turning point and the crisis metaphor make use of narrative patterns, either projecting a temporal or a spatial model onto human experience.

Jerome Bruner's work on the subject of narrative turning points may help to throw further light on the psychological and psycho-social functions of turning points as narrative phenomena. According to Bruner, turning points "represent a way in which people free themselves in their self-consciousness from their history, their banal destiny, their conventionality" (Bruner 1991: 74). From a psychological point of view, turning points serve to function as a means to change one's direction in life. Bruner differentiates three core features of turning points: First, turning points are usually linked to some external events or happenings, but are "finally attributed to a happening 'inside' – a new belief, new courage, moral disgust, 'having had enough'" (ibid.: 50). Second, turning points depend on an act of remembering since they are based on "a wave of episodic memory retrieval, rich in detail and color" (ibid.). Turning points are a means of retrospective meaning-making. Third, turning points typically trigger off "a new and intense line of activity" (ibid.). Turning points primarily serve to produce order and meaning in life stories and to connect those individual stories to the larger social and cultural contexts. While Bruner, in his definition of turning points and their functions, primarily had autobiographic and biographic narratives in mind, his definition arguably does apply to fiction as well: it is in and through fiction that the patterns, motifs, metaphors, and plots that humans are created by which 'our lives become stories', to borrow Paul John Eakin's (1999) powerful phrase.

It seems crucial that a turning point is always a spatio-temporal construct that refers to the human experience of time, or more precisely *lived* time, but imposes on this a spatial concept (travel). Turning points can be considered as a narrative function in order to structure and give shape to people's experience of an otherwise abstract time. This might actually differentiate turning points from crises: whereas turning points can only be marked and attributed retrospectively ("I didn't realize it back then, but this was a turning point in my life"), crises can be experienced *at the time*, as an instant diagnosis of a crucial, unstable or threatening experience in the life of an individual or a collective.

Based on these considerations, the functions of turning points as a narrative phenomenon come into a clearer focus. Ansgar Nünning (2012) has outlined these functions as follows: First, turning points serve to enhance the tellability (see Ryan 2005) of a story, i.e. they generate interest and excitement. Second, turning points offer "a means of creating coherence and causality" (Nünning 2012: 47). Third, turning points "impose form upon an amorphous reality" (ibid.: 48), i.e. they structure a complex reality by means of selection and abstraction. Fourth, they fulfill heuristic functions, allowing people to describe and account for change in their lives. Fifth, turning points serve to "temporalise someone's experience" (ibid.: 49). Sixth, the "construction of turning points is one of the most important sense-making, and self-making, strategies that narrators have at their disposal" (ibid.: 50).

These preliminary definitions of the conceptual metaphors, narrative plots, and primary functions of crises and turning points allow us to come to terms with what the title of this chapter calls the 'crisis-ridden life knowledge of the short story'. As a literary genre that seems to dwell on such moments of life-changing quality, the short story engages with the question of how people select, structure, and make sense of certain incidents in their lives. The knowledge that results from this process is inherently metaphoric, since, as we have seen, crisis and turning point are themselves first and foremost conceptual 'metaphors we live by', to borrow Lakoff and Johnson's famous phrase. As such, they fulfill important functions with regard to the way in which people conceive of their lives. In the words of Lakoff and Turner:

> Part of the power of such a metaphor is its ability to create structure in our understanding of life. Life, after all, need not be viewed as a journey. It need not be viewed as having a path, or destinations, or impediments to travel, or vehicles. That structuring of our knowledge of life comes from the structure of our knowledge about journeys. (1989: 62)

Quite frequently, short stories – explicitly or implicitly – draw on the conceptual metaphors of crisis and turning points in order to convey a sense of life. In so doing, they give a narrative shape to the idea of life-changing experiences that are embedded in, but at the same time stand out from the experience of everyday life. At the end of such moments of crisis there is often a recognition of great cognitive importance: the realization of the futility and emptiness of one's life, an insight into some 'deeper' truth or wisdom, the recognition of missed opportunities or 'the road not taken', etc. Among the many stories that centrally employ spatio-temporal patterns and metaphors of crisis and turning point to convey such notions are, for example, Nathaniel Hawthorne's "Young Goodman Brown", Stephen Crane's "The Open Boat", Eudora Welty's "A Still Moment", "A Worn Path", and "Death of a Traveling Salesman", Flannery O'Connor's "A Good Man is Hard to Find", Sherwood Anderson's "I Want to Know Why", and Edith Wharton's "A Journey". In all of these stories, the metaphors and narratives of crisis and turning point have a certain epistemological force or surplus when it comes to understand life and to consider one's life as meaningful.

As a variation of this pattern, short stories can of course also deny the possibility or desire for coherence by emphasizing the meaninglessness and the lack of real 'turning points'. Sometimes, as in the postmodern stories of John Barth or Donald Barthelme for example, the notion of the existence of turning points is even outright rejected, deconstructed and exposed as a culturally dominant yet ultimately arbitrary fiction based on narrative conventions and expectations. Ronald Sukenick, in *The Death of the Novel* (1969), described the postmodern condition as one in which reality, time, and personality do not exist. In this climate of radical epistemological skepticism – when *everything* is perceived as crisis and reality becomes a series of discontinuous moments – it is obvious that ideas like 'turning point' lose their meaning. Particularly the notion of a causal organization of life, one of the salient features of the turning-point metaphor and narrative, become obsolete: in the postmodern funhouse of life, there are no longer turning points or life paths but only labyrinths and distorting mirrors.

As the short story form capitalizes on, and gives shape to, the psychological and anthropological constant of crises and turning points, it often stages them as non-temporal or even a-temporal. What we find in many short stories is a character's experience of momentary "step out of time" (Boddy 2010: 101). As Kasia Boddy remarks, in modern short stories such "interruptions and dislocations [...usually] take place in the temporary hiatus of a railway station, a doctor's waiting room, a hotel lobby, a bar in the early morning – settings that, like the short story itself, suggest both impermanence and enclosure" (ibid.). Short stories frequently devise such chronotopes of crisis and turning point, spatio-temporal constructions which enable us to make meaning and narratively transform occurrences into events, events into stories.

Interestingly enough, at least in their metaphorical sense, crises inevitably constitute situations in which something like secure, ready-made 'knowledge' is not available. In crises, knowledge erodes. If a person – or a literary character for that matter – finds himself in a crisis, this usually implies a lack of theoretical, and, maybe even more importantly, practical knowledge. In moments of crisis, either the theoretical or the practical life knowledge (or both) of a person are challenged, or else there would be no crisis in the first place. People in crises usually do not know what actions and strategies would be advisable or right. Hence, the short story's preference for crises and turning points correlates with this epistemic structure: what is at stake in many short stories is the very possibility of knowledge of life.

Sometimes, as Thomas Leitch (1989) has argued, the erosion and 'debunking' of cognitive certainties in short stories do not lead to the creation of new, authoritative knowledge: "it is quite possible to challenge the character's, and the audience's, assumptions about the world without substituting any more-authoritative knowledge, so that such stories constitute not a form of knowledge but a challenge to knowledge, that is, a way of debunking assumptions which are not really true" (Leitch 1989: 133). In this sense, the relation of the short story to something like life knowledge could be described by what Paul Fry has called 'ostension:' "Ostension [...] is that indicative gesture toward reality which precedes and underlies the construction of meaning [...] it is the deferral of knowledge by the disclosure, as a possibility, that existence can be meaning-*free*." (qtd. from Wood 2005: 7) By focusing on the depiction of the crisis or turning point itself rather than its resolution in the larger framework of a life story, short stories often move the epistemological uncertainty center stage, and thereby reflect on the problematic relationship of life and knowledge, emphasizing the "paradoxes and aporias of knowledge for living" (Ette 2010a: 984-85).

The idea that crises and turning points can either yield an understanding of life or point to the impossibility to know or even fully understand life is constitutive for several, if not most, of the subgenres I will discuss in the third part of this study. The story of initiation, for instance, is fundamentally based on the idea that at least in some stages of life, lessons must be learned the hard way, and that is by going through crises. The initiate is always confronted with an 'unknown world' whose secrets he or she needs to find out in order to become a part of that world, as for example in Sherwood Anderson's "I Want to Know Why," Robert Penn Warren's "Blackberry Winter" or Junot Díaz's "Ysrael." In other genres, such as the 'story of midlife crisis' or the 'story of unlived life', this idea is equally constitutive, as the examples of John Cheever's "The Country Husband" (see chapter 9) or Henry James's "The Beast in the Jungle" (chapter 10) will show.

Whereas crisis and turning points thus already point to the temporality of conceptions and knowledge of human life, the short story's special relation towards time needs to be further unpacked. Therefore, the next chapter will address how the short story genre handles time (lifetime, lived time, life as temporal project) in its compressed narrative structures, but it will also consider the ways in which the form itself – as a particularly time-sensitive genre – relates to larger socio-cultural contexts, thus telling us something about a culture's very conceptions of human (life-)time.

7. The American Short Story and the Temporalization of Life in Modernity:

Washington Irving's "Rip Van Winkle" and F. Scott Fitzgerald's "The Curious Case of Benjamin Button"

> The short story wants to stop time. [...] In its brief span, a short story frequently spurns us by denying our wish to get to know its characters the way we do when we read a novel. We don't identify with the people in a short story as we do with the central figures of a novel. Instead, we peer at them from a distance, through a finely crafted glass. Often, they are frozen in an attitude, a moment, a gesture. The short story tends to give us portraits of the unfinished life, or the life already over: hard vignettes of regret and loss. [...] In every case, though, the short story makes brevity work for it.
>
> (Mikics 2013: 185)

Particularly in a modern context, 'time' has become a crucial category and an increasingly important dimension of life, both from an individual and a collective perspective. That human life unfolds in a temporal sequence may be a universal fact, a biologically predetermined condition that holds true for traditional as well as modern societies: People are born, they grow up, and finally grow old (and eventually die) in all cultures and historical epochs, at least until today. As a consequence, "people throughout the world necessarily have to deal with time as an element of their lives as self-conscious humans" (Silber 2009: 107). Yet the patterns of sequencing, i.e. the ways in which life is structured on a temporal level, are not only culturally and historically highly variable but have also tremendously gained in significance in modernity.[1] Whereas in traditional societies place was the main category for maintaining a stable identity and social security, the processes of mobilization in modernity required a different form of social and individual stability (see Kohli 1986: 190). As sociologist Martin Kohli argues, the development toward modernity is therefore essentially the process of a 'temporalization of life' (ibid.: 184).

Obviously, 'modernity' or 'modernism' are temporal constructs themselves, since they are used in order to delimitate eras from one another as well as to integrate them in a larger historical framework. What is more, the socio-historical epoch as well as the corresponding aesthetic movement they denominate are also marked by very specific notions of temporality and concepts of time. Very famously, for instance, Virginia Woolf's differentiation between the conventional 'clock time' indifferent to human beings and a subjective, non-chronological 'mind time' exemplifies how in modernism culturally established notions of time are questioned and complemented with, or even replaced by, others. The central idea underlying the temporal concepts of Woolf and other modernist writers like Faulkner or Hemingway is that time not only has an 'objective' dimension, which can be measured in equal lengths, but that it also depends on the experience of individuals and therefore can be highly diverse in its perception.[2] For example, an hour may always consist of 60 minutes or 3,600 seconds, but its perceived length can vary significantly in the experience of individuals. Also, the subjective perception of time is not bound to the strict linearity of clock time (or, for that matter, calendar time) and, by contrast, can be essentially anachronous or cyclical, for instance in many of Faulkner's novels and short stories, where the present is always inextricably interwoven with the past. What these now commonplace ideas serve to demonstrate is the temporal dimension of human life, or more precisely, the cultural and historical variability of life-time-models, which are often influenced or even shaped by literary texts and genres.

Within literary and cultural studies, cultural concepts, models, and perceptions of time have moved center stage in recent years. Time, as Aleida Assmann (2006: 121) maintains, hardly appears to us as clear and unambiguous as the date on a

---

1 See Georges Poulet's classic *Studies in Human Time* (1956), especially the introduction, for an informative account of the changing conceptions of time from the Middle Ages through Renaissance and late modernity.

2 Of course, the scientific and philosophical discussions of time around 1900 – Einstein's theory of relativity or Bergson's theory of duration, to name only two of the most prominent examples – had a tremendous impact on modernist writer's conceptions of time. See, for instance, Douglass (1986).

calendar or the arms of a clock. Instead, it permanently influences and manifests itself in multiple forms and practices of human experience and action, remembering, and meaning-making. Assmann (ibid.) therefore highlights the importance of time concepts for the project of cultural studies, emphasizing that time is usually less clear than what a clock or calendar may suggest, manifesting instead in a variety of experiences, practices, interpretations and memories. Space and time are therefore not exclusively physical phenomena or given categories that structure human perception, but rather cultural constructs themselves (ibid.). To find out about the temporality of human life from a cultural-studies perspective involves an analysis of the ways in which time shapes human action, perception, interpretation and remembrance. This goes far beyond the traditional concepts of time in literary studies, e.g. the analysis of narrative time in structural narratology (very influentially, for example, in the works of Gérard Genette). The question of how ideas and categories of human time are cultural constructs rather than givens involves notions about the contingency and ambivalence of time, the idea of 'lifetime' as a major structuring principle of human life and experience, the relationship between generations, the acceleration (or deceleration) of time, as well as the staging of temporal concepts in literature and other cultural artifacts, for example the notion of an intensified perception of brief, single moments in modernist literature (see ibid: 121-48).

With regard to theoretical and practical life knowledge, one may ask how living always presupposes an (often rather implicit) knowledge of and about the temporality of life, how such knowledge is culturally and historically specific, and how this knowledge is both reflected in and shaped by literature and other media. In this chapter, I will attempt to examine a) this temporal dimension of life in the wider literary and cultural historical context of this study (c.1850-2000s) and b) the ways in which literature, and particularly the short story, can contribute to a life knowledge that involves individual as well as collectively shared concepts and patterns of (life-)time; and c) look at some exemplary short stories in order to illustrate these ideas. If "[m]odernity is about the acceleration of time" (Conrad 1999: 9) and if the short story is essentially a modern genre (see Allen 1981: 3; Hunter 2007: 2; March-Russell 2009), then the question as to how the temporal structure of the short story correlates with the general shift of temporal experience in modernity takes center stage. In fact, the very name as well as the reading experience of the genre seem to support this idea: in contrast to lengthy, time-consuming novels, *short* stories appear to be "somehow 'up to speed' with the realities of modern life" (Hunter 2007: 3). Short stories are *short stories* because of the importance of time in the modern context out of which they emerged.[3] In order to validate and specify this general thesis of the short story's affinity with modern life-time-models, however, it is necessary to briefly explore what exactly characterizes the temporal structures of modernity. As a next step, I will discuss how these findings may be interpreted with regard to the short story, taking into account genre-theoretical considerations on time and temporality in the short story.

First of all, however, let me briefly comment on the related yet not entirely synonymous terms 'modernity' and 'modernism'. Modernity as a socio-historical concept usually designates the rather large historical period from c.1500 to the present, subdivided into early modernity (1500-1789), classical modernity (the 'long' 19th century), and late modernity (the 20th century), whereas modernism refers to the comparatively short and specific literary-historical era (c.1920-1960). When I speak about 'modern' life and society in the following, I sometimes move back and forth between these different concepts of 'modernity' and 'modernism' in the social sciences and literary studies. This has mainly two reasons: 1) the literary understanding of modernism/the modern can be regarded as a culmination of the socio-historical processes described by the social sciences' conception of 'modernity;' and 2) the 'emergence' of the American short story in the early to mid-19th century falls into a key period in this process of modernization in the United States: It is in the early decades of the 19th century that America begins to change from a rural, agrarian nation to a modern, industrialized nation with a steadfast belief in technological progress. From this vantage, i.e. applying a wider understanding of 'modern' America that includes the transitional phase of the early 19th century, the short story as a genre can be considered as a 'modern' genre

3 The historical and cultural variability of understandings and especially the social evaluation of 'shortness' in connection with narrative forms can be observed, for example, in Mark Twain's famous story of "The Celebrated Jumping Frog of Calaveras County" (1865). Other than the title may suggest, Twain's story is decidedly eventless and not very much 'to the point' – hence the annoyance that this story usually causes, especially with students. Much to the annoyance of the genteel frame narrator, the intradiegetic narrator, Simon Wheeler, indulges in long-winded narrative that never culminates in a final climax or punchline. As Holger Kersten (2011: 132) has persuasively argued, however, Wheeler's peripatetic storytelling is quite appropriate in the story's setting of the Western frontier: "in an environment in which nothing much happens, *where time is not an article in short supply*, and where questions of usefulness are not an issue, a long, spun-out story may well have been a boon rather than a boring, 'long and tedious', 'useless', 'monotonous narrative.'" (emphasis added, M.B.)

whose formal beginnings coincide with other milestones in the project of an American modernity, for example the construction of the Erie Canal, the first steamboats on the Hudson River, Andrew Jackson's presidency, and the invention of the telegraph.

Many studies on modernity and the processes of modernization agree that a fundamental change of the conception and perception of time is one of its salient features. In a sense, the very idea of modernism is based on temporal notions: as the British sociologist Anthony Giddens points out, a 'modern' society "unlike any preceding societies, lives in the future, rather than the past" (1998: 94). This future orientation of modern societies also explains why time has become an ever more important issue in modernity, since the future (at least in a Western context) always suggests a 'not yet' that can only be achieved by 'speeding up'. The 'beauty of speed', as Filippo Tommaso Marinetti famously puts it in his manifesto of futurism, has become the emblem of (late) modernity with its many 'speedy', time-saving inventions like the automobile, the telephone, or the jet plane.

In his brilliant study *Social Acceleration*, Hartmut Rosa (2013) develops a sociological theory of acceleration as the most characteristic collective time structure in modernity. He intriguingly argues that social acceleration affects or involves at least three different areas: (1) technical/technological acceleration; (2) acceleration of the pace of life;[4] (3) acceleration of social and cultural change ratio. These dimensions or forces of acceleration can be differentiated and separated for analytical purposes, yet they are interdependently connected in a circle of acceleration (Rosa 2013: 151-59), creating a self-sustaining process of acceleration in modernity. Technical and technological acceleration (the invention of 'time savers' such as the railway, automobile, telephone, or internet) triggers social change; the acceleration of life tempo is a direct result of the acceleration of social change; the need for technical acceleration increases with the acceleration of life tempo and thus the scarcity of time resources.

Hence, according to recent works from the fields of sociology and anthropology, the category 'time' pervades our lives on at least three different levels (see

4 The often-stated (yet seldom specified) acceleration of the 'pace of life' in modernity involves both the speed of actions (such as walking, eating, reading etc.) as well as a general perception or experience of time. It can therefore be described as a temporal compression of activities and techniques (multi-tasking, speed-dating etc.), technical innovations (railroad etc.) and new modes of perception as well as patterns of behavior ("compression of compression of episodes of action and experience in the face of time pressure," Rosa 2013: 156). Thus sped-up, accelerated social change becomes "a potent driver of the acceleration of the pace of life" (ibid.).

ibid.: 8-9). First, there is our *everyday time*, i.e. the temporal structure of our day-to-day lives, which is marked by a highly repetitive and cyclical character (e.g. sleeping and eating, work, leisure activities, and other recurring activities and routines). Second, individuals also develop a more comprehensive perspective of the temporality of their lives as a whole, and this dimension can be referred to as *life-time* or *biographical time* (here, the question of how one wants to spend one's life is central). Third, the temporal aspect of someone's life is also necessarily embedded in an overarching *societal* and *historical* time. These three dimensions with their respective temporal patterns, rhythms, sequences, tempos, practices, synchronization requirements as well as perspectives (e.g. the notions of past, present, and future, and their relevance for one's own actions) constitute 'our time' (see ibid.: 8.) Since these three time levels usually differ to a significant degree with regard to their patterns, rhythms etc., it requires narrative patterns and structures to (re)connect them:[5]

> The interconnection of the three levels of time in the perspective of actors always follows narrative patterns. Everyday time, biographical time, and historical time are related to each other, and mutually criticized and justified, in cultural and individual narratives. The meaning and relative weight of the past, present, and future and thus also the relevance and relative weight of tradition and change are determined simultaneously in narrative schemata (*Entwürfe*). (ibid.: 11)

What is even more interesting than the mere observation of the acceleration in the realms of technology, everyday life, and social change, is therefore the question of how this affects our concepts and patterns of identity, or in other words: how notions of (biographical) life are shaped by temporal structures. Moreover, the function of narratives in adjusting to and making sense of the temporal patterns and processes of acceleration is already highlighted: narratives provide an instrument by which everyday time, biographical time and historical time are integrated or related to each other. Jerome Bruner (2004: 692) therefore remarks:

5 For example, Martin Kohli (1986: 192) has illustrated how in retrospect individuals interrelate the chronology of their own biography with the overarching historical narrative in order to verify and contextualize it: "Es ist für das Individuum selbstverständlich, daß es den Ablauf seiner Lebenszeit ständig in die historische Jahreserzählung übersetzt und daran überprüft; die beiden Chronologien werden in eins gesetzt."

> We seem to have no other way of describing 'lived time' save in the form of a narrative. Which is not to say that there are no other temporal forms that can be imposed on the experience of time, but none of them succeeds in capturing the sense of *lived* time: not calendrical time forms, not serial or cyclical orders, not any of these.

The temporality of life and narration are thus inextricably intertwined, tremendously affecting people's identity concepts and shaping our sense of lived time. The continual acceleration of life throughout modernity led to a fundamental shift of identity patterns and concepts, and consequently life itself was regarded more and more as a temporal and thus narrative project. For the classical modern subject, individualization means a turning away from the atemporal, fixed identity concepts of premodern societies. In America, Benjamin Franklin's *Autobiography* (1791) marks this shift: Franklin relates his life story as a project of 'self-making' acted out over different periods or stages of his life. As a typically and essentially modern process, individualization thus correlates with a temporalization of life: identity becomes a self-reflexive project ('self-making') that unfolds in (life)time.[6] Accordingly, classical modernity (i.e. roughly the period of the 'long' 19th century 1789-1900) is characterized by the institutionalization of the course of life (*Lebenslauf*) as a well-organized and predictable biographical pattern (see Kohli 1985: 358; Cole 2006: 3-5). Hence, classical modernity can be conceptualized as the age of temporal identity patterns – Martin Kohli (1985) refers to this as life-course regime ("Lebenslaufregime").[7] Following these temporal structures and

6 These ideas correlate with Ulrich Beck's assumption of an individualization of biographies in the wake of modernity, e.g. in his influential study *Risikogesellschaft: Auf dem Weg in eine andere Moderne* (1986). According to Beck, individualization means the formation of new life forms and circumstances in which the individual has to produce, stage, and patch up his or her own biography (see also Abels 2008: 142).

7 See also Weymann (2008: 199, emphasis in the original), who describes the impact of modern life-course politics on the patterns of socialization: "*Lebenslaufpolitik schafft oder verändert Institutionen des Lebenslaufregimes einer Gesellschaft und damit Muster der Erwachsensozialisation.*" The main characteristic of life-course politics is the liberation of the individual from the authority of religion, tradition, aristocracy, family etc.: "Anstelle traditionaler Gemeinschaften strukturieren hochspezialisierte Institutionen das Leben in modernen Gesellschaften von der Wiege bis zur Bahre."

patterns, which provided schemata for orientation and identity formation, biographies – and in fact lives – became more and more normalized ('normal biography').[8]

What sociologists call 'normal biography' is therefore an invention of modernity and a direct upshot of the acceleration of life in this period. Typically arranged around the working life, normative life events (marriage, employment, parenthood, etc.) are connected with particular phases of life. The result may be described as an 'external sequentialization' of life (see Kohli 1986). And it is of course no coincidence that this development corresponds with the rise of the novel and especially the *Bildungsroman*, the literary genre that prototypically employs the temporal patterns of the life-course regime in order to create narrative coherence and a stable identity for the protagonists.

Rosa also describes this shift towards temporal identity concepts as a direct consequence of the acceleration processes outlined above and differentiates three major historical stages: (1) In a Taylorian sense, pre-modern, traditional societies, understood identity as substantial identity *a priori* (Rosa 2013: 227), well-grounded in stable social structures and order. The acceleration of social change was relatively low; major changes occurred in intergenerational intervals, i.e. every 80-100 years (or three generations). Hence, personal biographies were primarily predetermined by the status of the parents and were therefore more or less given. (2) With the increasing social acceleration in modernity, identity was more and more understood as an individual project, based on the liquidation of traditional social structures and role models. Like Martin Kohli, Rosa (2013: 226-31) describes this process as a 'temporalization of life'. Nevertheless, identity is still considered as a fairly stable category, because the social change ratio is 'generational' and therefore provides enough reliable structures in which a stable identity can be developed; here, Rosa speaks of a "*stable a posteriori identity*" (2013: 229). (3) In late modernity (or what correlates with the literary-historical construct of modernism/postmodernism), finally, the social change ratio exceeds the pattern of generational exchange. As a result, the notion of a stable identity can no longer be maintained (see ibid.). The main difference between classical modernity and late

8 In the sociology of life course (*Soziologie des Lebenslaufs*), which is interested in the temporal dimension of human life, the construct of 'normal biography' basically refers to the normalization or standardization of biographies in modernity; a 'normal biography' determines the appropriate chronology of certain life phases and events such as employment, marriage, parenthood, etc. See also Heinz/Krüger (2001: 33): "The resulting concepts for mapping the modern life course are temporalization, chronologization and biographization of life events."

modernity resides in the ways in which time and temporalization are either understood as a continuous project of organizing life along temporal patterns (classical modernity), or as a situative project that leads to the detemporalization and fluidity of identity (late modernity):

> *what is the difference between the classical modern and late modern forms of the liquefaction and dynamization of identity?* My thesis [...] is that the difference lies in the fact that the predominance of *individualization* in the transformation of relationships to self and world in classical modernity leads to a *temporalization of life*, i.e., to a perspective on one's own life as a project to be given shape in time, while the same process of dynamization in the late modern phase of its development effects a "detemporalized," *situational* definition of identity. (Rosa 2013: 226)

The further increase in possibilities and contingencies as well as the decreasing stability of social structures leads to an individualization of biographies, and the concept of the 'normal biography' can no longer provide useful schemas for orientation:

> one can no longer read off who someone is from a traditionally defined cultural and social model of order that lasts for many generations (as in premodernity), nor can one determine it for an entire individual lifespan (as in classical modernity). Instead, it depends on the particular *point in time* within an individual's life. Identity thus becomes *transitory*; it alters at an *intragenerational* rate of change. (Rosa 2013: 232-33, emphasis in the original)

This identity concept can be called 'situational' because it is no longer necessarily embedded in a causally structured linear-chronological framework. Situational identity emphasizes the specific moment rather than its integration into the lifespan and can be regarded as a consequence of the acceleration of social change. It leads to an individualization of biographies due to the increase of possibilities and contingencies with regard to personal biography, but it also renders problematic the notion of a stable identity that lasts – or is developed – over an entire lifetime.

* * *

The question now is whether and how these modern notions of (life-)time may find their correspondent and reflection in short stories. 'Reflection' here does not merely mean 'mirroring' in a traditionally mimetic sense but involves the exchange processes that come into sight with Paul Ricœur's (1983-85) hermeneutic, three-partite model of mimesis. Prefiguration (or mimesis I) describes how our understanding – of literary texts, other artifacts, as well as reality – is symbolically mediated. Time, from this perspective, also becomes a prefigured concept, as our conception of time is always already shaped by symbolic representations. In the process of configuration (or mimesis II), it is particularly through narratives that fictional and historical representations actively shape our models of time. Through refiguration (or mimesis III), finally, these 'configured' models and notions of time become meaningful as readers adopt them as ordering models and patterns for structuring and understanding life as a temporal project. Literature does not merely reflect but in fact interpret, influence, and determine our very notion of reality, thus "rework[ing] the work of culture" (Felski 2008: 85). In this sense, the representation of the temporal dimensions of life in (short) fiction serves to generate new perspectives and life knowledge. As Rita Felski holds with reference to Ricœur: "Over time, readers are shaped by what they read, even as they cannot help but impose on texts what they already know. Here again we can apprise the relevance of genre not as a rigid set of formal rules, but as flexible criteria that we impute or ascribe to texts." (Felski 2008: 87) The way in which short stories configure models and knowledge of human life-time may be therefore understood as one central aspect in the short story's semantics and knowledge of life.

Against the backdrop of the sociological and cultural-historical diagnoses of the temporal structures in modernity outlined above, it is tempting to conclude that the short story directly corresponds with the altered perceptions and concepts of time and identity in the (late) modern era. If the novel, rising to prominence in classical modernity, favors the model of a 'temporalization of life' and a 'stable identity *a posteriori*', the short story seems to correlate with, or anticipate, the notion of a situational identity as the result of a 'temporalization of time'. Where the novel suggests and invents temporal patterns according to which life becomes a temporal project and in which identity is formed over the course of a human life (the model of the *Bildungsroman*), the short story tends to reject such long-term perspectives, focusing instead on the momentary and fluidity of identity. This becomes most obvious, of course, in the genre's preference for moments of heightened awareness and sudden revelation, which has become a generic trademark in the 20th century, as I have argued in the previous chapter. Many modern short stories in America and beyond insist that time can only be perceived as presence, that identity is therefore fragmented, and that it manifests itself in fleeting and often apparently insignificant and trivial moments. Hence, the 'life knowledge' of the short story seems more in keeping with a high modern or late modern concept of a transitory, temporal identity.

Generally speaking, time seems to be the most fundamental element of all narratives, even more fundamental than characters, setting or action. According to Paul Ricœur, "temporality and narrativity are closely related" (2002: 35), and their structural interrelationship is one of reciprocity: narratives follow a temporal pattern and our understanding of temporality is based on narrative principles. Stories are always about the passage of time and so "the sequence of any fiction is, by its nature, the path of time evaporating" (Silber 2009: 111). In his famous essay on chronotopes, Mikhail Bakhtin (2000: 22) argues along similar lines that the spatio-temporal structure is the very center of each work of fiction: "It can be said without qualification that to them [the chronotopes, M.B.] belongs the meaning that shapes narrative." Narrative and time are closely interwoven; in and through narratives time becomes intelligible as stories impose a concrete form upon the abstract phenomenon of time. The ways in which different storytelling genres handle time and thus project meaning onto (life) narratives become crucial for understanding the generic construction of life knowledge.

In short story theory and criticism, the analysis of the genre's peculiar temporality has received relatively little serious critical attention.[9] What is more or less uncontested, however, is the assumption that due to the obvious restrictions in length, time and timing are of particular importance in short stories, as they are generally marked by a fairly high degree of complexity and functionality with regard to all textual or narrative constituents such as space, characters, time etc. As Günter Ahrends (2005: 41) maintains, this leads to the result that short stories usually tend to dispense with the description of long time spans (see also Pratt 1994) in favor of brief, representative moments. This also has a bearing on the typical plot structure of short stories, which usually focus on the depiction of singular events, episodes, scenes, and situations of revelatory character (Ahrends 2005: 41).

This notion of the episodic quality or 'momentariness' of the short story is arguably still the most persistent and commonplace claim about the specific temporality of the genre.[10] It is guided by the understanding that in a short story, a

9 An exception is the collection *Time and the Short Story* (Chialant/Lops 2012). The essays in this volume, diverse and insightful as they are, do not, however, add up to any coherent theory of the genre's particular relation to time.

10 In one of the most recent monographs on the American short story, Kasia Boddy (2010: 101, emphasis added, M.B.) writes: "Given its brevity, its formal constitution in and as crisis, the short story gravitates towards certain kinds of subject matter; in particular, towards the representation of moments of condensed significance, moments in time which allow or enforce a stepping out of routine, *out of time*."

certain episode in a character's life is highlighted, leading to a sudden insight (epiphany) or a 'shock of recognition'. Thus, whereas novels typically depict a 'change through time', short stories highlight brief moments or representative 'snapshots' of life to which the reader must imagine the larger (temporal) context (see Pickering 1989). Referring to J. Hillis Miller's claim that time is the main dimension of the novel, Jean Pickering maintains: "This narration of the *life in time* is [...] closely connected to the principle of causality." (1989: 49, emphasis added, M.B.) By contrast, in the short story such strong causal notions of time are abandoned: instead of a linearity of events, short stories typically deal with 'isolated incidents' and 'episodic movements' – one might even say that the narration of *life in time* is replaced by a narration of life *outside of time*. For Pickering, 'evolution' describes the progression of time in novels, whereas the short story's particular relation to time can be described as 'revelation', a short flash of insight that reveals or represents a whole life.[11] In a similar vein, Paul March-Russell (2009) argues alongside Georg Lukács that "chronological time cannot be fully rendered [in the short story, M.B.], but is also more fully a product of the disenchanted modern age" (ibid.: 121). "Without the presence of chronological time," he continues, "the heroes of short stories cannot age and develop in relation to historical change but are *suspended at a single point in their lives*" (ibid., emphasis added, M.B.).

However, this view of the momentariness of the short story must be critiqued as a typical upshot of the reductionism of formalist genre conceptions that dominated short story theory up until the 1980s (see Basseler 2011a). As, for instance, Renate Brosch has convincingly demonstrated, there are numerous examples which contradict this view, and even in those stories that deal with such decisive moments, there is often a larger chronological framework in which they are embedded and without which the whole idea of a 'moment of truth' would be meaningless in the first place. At the same time, other genres also stage such 'moments of being', so that it appears as a modern phenomenon rather than a short story

11 According to Pickering, the short story thus "tends to deal with the unchanging elements of character and emphasises the stability of the essential self" (1989: 48); this conclusion, of course, stands in stark contrast to the idea of the situational identity that has replaced the notion of a stable identity in the process of modernization: "The moment of revelation that stands at the heart of the short story, that moment of insight that comes before language, constitutes a discrete moment of certainty in a nebulous universe." (ibid.: 53)

phenomenon.[12] "Die erwähnte These von der Momenthaftigkeit der short story ist also offensichtlich unzureichend." (Brosch 2007: 174)[13]

Nevertheless, qua its temporal particularities the short story has a special potential to reflect upon the temporality (and temporalization) of life, i.e. the many time patterns, structures, models, etc. which underlie our lives. In real life, these patterns and structures usually remain unnoticed. Fiction does not only imagine for us "a stopping point from which life can be seen as intelligible" (Silber 2009: 8) because it has at its disposal the privilege of the storyteller's hindsight.[14] It can also create an awareness of our life as a 'temporal project', including e.g. the many processes of (de-)synchronization of everyday-time, lifetime, and historical or social time, or the acceleration and deceleration of life in certain situations. But more than that, narrative literary genres provide us with the very temporal structures and patterns by which we organize and make sense of our lives.

There are two major opposing principles by which a story can be structured temporally: it can either depict a very short time span by means of a relative time congruence, i.e. a concurrence of the narrated time and narrative time (or more precisely: story time and discourse time), or it can cover a long time span by means of condensing or compression. What does this mean with regard to the 'life knowledge' of the genre?

First, short stories can present a relatively short time span and thus single out and highlight a brief decisive moment or a succession of moments, thus focusing on formative moments or phases in which identity is challenged, (re-)formed or

12 See Assmann (2006: 138): "Wirklichkeit wurde von vielen Autoren um 1900 nicht mehr wie in der realistischen Literatur des 19. Jahrhunderts als das schlechthin Offenbare, sondern umgekehrt als das schlechthin Verborgene verstanden, das sich in unerwarteten Augenblicken selbst offenbart."

13 With reference to Jean Pickering (1989), Brosch (2007: 176) argues that the thesis of the short story's momentariness probably arises from a (false) transferral of a receptional aspect on the textual level: "Wenn uns eine Kurzgeschichte imaginativ packt, kann die Zeit des Leseerlebnisses völlig aus dem Gedächtnis verschwinden, von einer mächtigen Erinnerung an den Erzählinhalt verdrängt. Diese Diskrepanz mag zu den Bestimmungen von der 'Momenthaftigkeit' der short story geführt haben, die auf einer Übertragung eines Rezeptionsmerkmals auf die Textform beruhen."

14 Here, Joan Silber refers to the chronological paradox pointed out by Kierkegaard, namely that "life can only be understood backward but has to be lived forward" (2009: 8).

decomposed.[15] Hence the notion of 'moment of truth' stories or epiphanic stories: "Moment of truth stories focus on a single point of crisis in the life of a central character, a crisis which provokes some basic realization that will change the character's life forever." (Pratt 1994: 99) For Pratt, however, this leads to the conclusion that the moment of truth "stands as a model for the short story the way the life stands as a model for the novel" (ibid.).[16] This is somewhat misleading, because it suggests that the 'moment of truth' is not part of the character's life. Although many short stories (especially high modernist ones) do in fact favor the staging of an isolated incident/event in a moment that is disjointed from, or at least contrasted with, the lifetime of the protagonists (e.g. Anderson's "I Want to Know Why", Welty's "A Memory" and "Why I Live at the P.O.," Faulkner's "Barn Burning" etc.), the opposition between 'life' and 'moment of truth' seems a little forced. Nevertheless, the relationship between the short story and the high/late modernist conception of a situative identity can be maintained, as Nadine Gordimer famously suggested:

> Each of us has a thousand lives and a novel gives a character only one. *For the sake of the form.* The novelist may juggle about with chronology and throw narrative overboard; all the time his characters have the reader by the hand, there is a consistency of relationship throughout the experience that cannot and does not convey the quality of human life, where contact is more like the flash of fire-flies, in and out, now here, now there, in darkness. Short story writers see by the light of the flash; theirs is the art of the only thing one can be sure of – the present moment. Ideally, they have learned to do without explanation of what went before, and what happens beyond this point. (Nadine Gordimer 1968; qtd. from Hunter 2007: 2)

The temporality of the form is crucial. Like Pratt, Gordimer stresses the short story's preference for the momentary over consistency, revelation over explanation. The quality of human life is presented not in one coherent narrative, but in a 'flash of fire-flies' that substitutes chronology with fragments.

15 See Bates (qtd. in Pickering 1989: 149): "The method by which the short story is told is not by the carefully engineered plot but by the implication of certain isolated incidents, by the capture and arrangement of casual episodic movements."

16 Avoiding the essentialism she criticizes earlier, Pratt is quick to add that "[t]he novel form is not 'by its very nature' too big for the moment of truth structure; nor is the short story inherently too small to tell a whole life. It is neither a logical nor an empirical necessity, but rather a fact of literary history" (1994: 100).

Second, short stories can compress a whole lifetime in a few pages, thereby providing a very different potential to reflect on the temporalization of life and identity by means of condensation. When long time spans and entire life courses are summarized and thus 'sped up', the processes which govern the temporal development of identity, as well as the narrative patterns that underlie them, are aesthetically foreshortened and thus become more visible. Emulating the temporal life model of the novel yet radically curtailing it, such 'condensed' or 'miniature' novels often demonstrate how certain singular events, decisions or coincidences can have a bearing on the lives of individuals and groups in very long terms. In William James's "The Beast in the Jungle," for instance, it is only through this long-term perspective that John Marcher's hesitation to marry May Bartram can be depicted as the central decision, or rather non-decision, which keeps him from actually living his life; in "The Curious Case of Benjamin Button," the structure of a condensed novel allows Fitzgerald to reverse the human life-course and thus render visible the absurdities and contingencies of such temporal regime; Katherine Anne Porter's "The Journey" even unfolds the complete family history of a genteel slave-owning family in the antebellum South, using the 'condensed novel' form to contrast the life courses of Sophia Jane and her former slave Nannie (Alvarez 2010: 269-70).

What both types – the 'moment of truth story' and the 'condensed novel' – have in common is that they aesthetically foreground the temporal dimension of human life. This can be regarded as one of the short story's aesthetic-epistemological principles, which even holds true for such stories in which there is virtually no stable chronological order at all or in which the chronology of human life-course models is questioned – for example the experimental postmodern stories in John Barth's *Lost in the Funhouse* –, and which can therefore be described as 'timeless narration' ("zeitloses Erzählen," Brosch 2007: 172) Again, this emphasis on the temporality of life seems to underlie narratives in general, as Joan Silber points out:

> So by now it seems to me that narrative – because it shows events unfolding – always has time itself as an element of its subject matter. This can be seen more clearly as we turn to stories that do this quite directly, stories whose characters announce themselves as engaged in a particular struggle with time. There's the plot of remembering […], the plot of revised time […], the plot of forgetting […], and the plot of unused time. (Silber 2009: 83)

Short stories, through their relative brevity, frequently employ such struggle with time that is, as Frank O'Connor famously remarked, a struggle with the novelist's time: "it is an attempt to reach some point of vantage from which past and future are equally visible. The crisis of the short story is the short story and not as in a novel the mere logical inescapable result of what preceded it." (Frank O'Connor, qtd. in Boddy 2010: 100) In conjunction with the short story's preference for crisis and turning point, its peculiar temporal quality is part and parcel of the genre's function as an organon of life knowledge. To further demonstrate this, in the following I will discuss two very prominent examples of the American short story, Washington Irving's masterpiece "Rip Van Winkle" and F. Scott Fitzgerald's "The Curious Case of Benjamin Button," in order to demonstrate how short stories often dwell on, and thus produce a particular knowledge about, the temporal dimension of life.

* * *

Washington Irving's early masterpiece "Rip Van Winkle" (1819) is a case in point for the ways in which the short story works on cultural time models qua its own temporal peculiarities. A formative piece in the early development of the short story, it is a sterling example of the genre's potential to reflect and aesthetically condense culturally and socially prevalent notions of (life)time – and perhaps even to anticipate upheavals in a society's conception of time. Essentially, "Rip Van Winkle" is a story about the acceleration of the speed of life in an increasingly modern America. As such, it also constitutes a model for the genre's predilection for the presentation of temporally condensed crises and turning points. The story not only dramatizes the temporalization of life in so far as it depicts a quick-aging protagonist who, after his foray into the mountains, is *temporally* alienated from society. As the cultural historian Thomas Cole (2006: 75) persuasively argues in his study on the changing perception of old age in America, Irving's piece also "foreshadows both the marginality *and* the sentimental devotion that American society would soon associate with old men," as the fate of poor Rip forestalls "the obsolescence of the old man in a secular society where women become rulers of the home, productivity becomes the primary criterion of man's worth, and patriarchy becomes a maudlin compensation for powerlessness." Thus embedded in emerging cultural notions of life as a temporal project in which traditional social structures and institutions become increasingly porous, "Rip Van Winkle" lends itself to an analysis that foregrounds the ways in which the short story genre becomes a genre through which cultural meanings and knowledge of life are aesthetically shaped and negotiated.

In the remote "little village of great antiquity" ("Rip," 18) near the Catskill Mountains where Rip lives, time is not a scarce good:

Here they used to sit in the shade through a long lazy summer's day, talking listlessly over village gossip, or telling endless sleepy stories about nothing. But it would have been worth any statesman's money to have heard the profound discussions that sometimes took place, when by chance and old newspaper fell into their hands from some passing traveller. ("Rip," 21)

Irving's story, usually considered as one of the foundational texts of the (American) short story genre, invites its readers to a world in which time abounds. The villagers indulge in their time-consuming activities that seem to have no particular goal or even benefit ("telling endless sleepy stories about nothing"). Their days are long and eventless, and so are the stories they tell each other. As the 'old newspaper' symbolizes, information arrives and societal change comes only very slowly, if at all. It seems that the entire village consists solely of "sages, philosophers, and other idle personages" ("Rip," 21) who have time on their hands. Interestingly enough, even in this realm of tranquility and temporal indifference, Rip is described as a particularly hassle-free character who 'takes the world easy'. "If left to himself," the narrator expounds, "he would have whistled life away in perfect contentment" ("Rip," 20). There is arguably no other character in literature who is as oblivious to time as Rip Van Winkle.

When Rip leaves the village one fine day together with his congenial dog Wolf in order to find temporary relief from his termagant wife, he can be assured that nothing will change during his absence. However, when he returns after his long sleep caused by the mysterious liquor that the ghostly Hendrick Hudson and his men had offered him, he finds, quite to his surprise, that literally the whole world has changed: "everything was strange." During Rip's absence, time has taken its toll. In an iterary representation of time in which the objects and space relate the passing of time, the narrator describes how Rip's house has "gone to decay – the roof fallen in, the windows shattered, and the doors off the hinges." ("Rip," 27) Finally, Rip realizes that 20 years have passed since he walked away into the Catskills. In the meantime, the whole world – like the door of his house – seems unhinged. Peter Freese (1999b: 153) summarizes the profound changes that await Rip at his return:

His wife is dead, his little son has grown into 'a precise counterpart of himself', and the old inn, 'designated by a rubicund portrait of His Majesty George the Third', where Rip used to gossip with his cronies, is now 'The Union Hotel, by Jonathan Doolittle', and it shows, instead of the King, a portrait of 'GENERAL WASHINGTON.'

What lies between Rip's foray into the woods and his return to his village is the American revolutionary war: the old "British colony has turned into the American republic, and the peaceful old village [...] has become 'larger and more populous'" (ibid.: 154). Rip's twenty-year long sleep serves as a narrative device to bring into sharp contrast "the two competing ways of life" (ibid.) of the old British colony and the New American Republic and thus emphasizes the socio-critical level of the story. What awaits poor Rip after his return is the hustle and bustle of the Jacksonian era, marked by a competitive democracy and a passion for material wealth (see Cole 2006: 77).

In the long history of its reception, "Rip Van Winkle" has brought about a whole plethora of interpretations; for example, it has been read as a timeless (!) myth, as a "private fantasy of escape from marital strife and marital responsibilities" (Cunliffe et al., qtd. in Freese 1999b: 156), and as a tale of the socio-cultural changes after the American Revolutionary War (see, e.g., Freese 1999b; Scofield 2006: 12). What has so far been neglected in the critical discussions of the story, however, is the fact that "Rip Van Winkle" is basically a story about the acceleration of life that involves the three time levels of daily time, biographical time, and epochal or historical time. Rip's inability to cope with the new social reality in his native village, I would argue, is basically a result or effect of a desynchronization of these levels: Whereas his own individual perception of time remain the same after his 'night' in the mountains, the social paradigm of time has changed dramatically. Where life once used to be a tranquil flow of events and daily affairs in which there was plenty of time for otiosity, the 'times have changed' in the old village.

This effect of desynchronization is also the source of Rip's identity crisis: Being the tardy character that he is, from that moment on when he returns from the mountains he is completely unable to adapt to the new life tempo in his village and until his death remains a tragic figure 'lost in time', even if the new generation reverences him as "one of the patriarchs of the village, and a chronicle of the old times" ("Rip," 31). Quite literally, Rip has become history:

> Rip's heart died away at hearing of these sad changes in his home and friends, and finding himself thus alone in the world. Every answer puzzled him too, by treating of such *enormous lapses of time*, and of matters he could not understand. ("Rip," 29, emphasis added, M.B.)

Centered around the ellipsis of Rip's sleep in the Catskill mountains, the specific temporal structure of the story allows it to emphasize the acceleration of social change and its consequences for the individual. The story uses a narrative 'trick', or what Joan Silber (2009) calls "fabulous time," to stage the contrast between a pre-modern society and a modern one. The cause of all these changes – the Revolutionary War – is erased in the "enormous lapses of time." Among other things such as the general way of life or the political climate, the social changes that accompanied the revolution manifest themselves on a temporal level: for poor old Rip, life seems to go too fast, leaving him 'alone in the world' and unable to comprehend what is happening around him.

Hence, time is not only an important structural element of the story, but becomes its main subject. Collectively shared concepts and perceptions of time determine our life models and concepts of identity. In "Rip Van Winkle," the shift from the colonial period to the Early Republic is depicted as a transgression from one societal time order to another, with far-reaching consequences for the individual. Although the story diverges from, and even dismantles, 'realistic' or conventional time, it nevertheless sheds light on the historical changeability of the patterns, rhythms, and tempos of (life)time. Moreover, Rip's identity crisis as a result of the acceleration of social change seems to echo the thesis of the process of modernization as a temporalization of life. Whereas in the old village time was not an issue, it now determines the people's behavior: "The very character of the people seemed changed. There was a busy, bustling, disputatious tone about it, instead of the accustomed phlegm and drowsy tranquility." ("Rip," 27)

* * *

The "dominant fiction of chronological aging," as Mary Russo put it, "plots our lives in continually increasing numbers" (1999: 25). Literary texts have a particular potential to reflect upon culturally preconceived and normalized models of life and life phases. But they also contribute to, as well as complicate, these cultural plots by producing real-world models, providing the narrative schemata a culture uses to tell stories of childhood, adolescence, adulthood, etc. Sometimes, however, such extra-literary life-course models are also subverted and caricatured. This often has an effect of alienation: By imagining other than the 'real' or realistic models and phases of life, literary texts are able to expose the constructedness, cultural specificity, and contingency of these models and thus undermine or put into question culturally available schemata as well as the underlying norms and values.

Because of its acute temporality, the short story form is particularly apt to break with realistic models of human lifetime. Whereas Irving deploys an ellipsis to intersperse Rip's biography with a 20-year-long sleep to accentuate the acceleration of life in modern America, F. Scott Fitzgerald's "The Curious Case of

Benjamin Button," published in his collection *Tales of the Jazz Age* (1922),[17] uses a different strategy to achieve a similarly alienating effect. The story exposes what can be considered a Western and arguably even decidedly American life-course model by imagining an alternative and highly contrastive one. One of Fitzgerald's "fantastic tales" (Buell 1982), the story creates a tension between a realist mode and the older form of romance, a tension that some theorists of the short story have characterized as typical of the genre (cf. May 2002). Similar to Melville's "Bartleby," in Fitzgerald's story a highly aesthetic character – Benjamin Button – enters the world of 'everyday reality'. For example, there are numerous references to the Civil War and the Spanish-American War, Baltimore's high society in the late 19th century, or the American educational system, which firmly ground the story in a socio-historical reality. As Charles May (2002: 38) argues with regard to "Bartleby," this narrative technique involves a blending of the traditions of romance and realism and forces the reader to take the protagonist as a symbolic and an 'as-if-real' character at the same time.

According to Fitzgerald, "The Curious Case of Benjamin Button" was written as a response to Mark Twain's quip that "it was a pity that the best part of life came at the beginning and the worst part at the end" (Fitzgerald 2010: viii). The working principle of Fitzgerald's story is basically that of inversion: When Benjamin Button enters life in a Baltimore hospital in 1860, he has the physique and mental state of a septuagenarian, much to the annoyance and terror of the doctors and nurses who fear for the hospital's reputation. His parents, the Roger Buttons from an honorable family of enviable social and financial position, are equally appalled at the first sight of their aged infant:

> Wrapped in a voluminous white blanket, and partly crammed into one of the cribs, there sat an old man apparently about seventy years of age. His sparse hair was almost white, and from his chin dripped a long smoke-colored beard, which waved absurdly back and forth, fanned by the breeze coming in at the window. ("Benjamin Button," 179)

Rather reluctantly, the Buttons take their 'baby' home and eventually come to accept their fate, even though Roger Button does everything to conceal the physical and psychological age of his son ("But Mr. Button persisted in his unwavering purpose. Benjamin was a baby, and a baby he should remain." "Benjamin Button," 184).

---

17 Interestingly, the story has not received nearly as much critical attention as the Hollywood movie that is based on it, David Fincher's *The Curious Case of Benjamin Button* (2008), starring Brad Pitt and Cate Blanchett.

As Benjamin 'grows up', it becomes more and more obvious to everyone that he is turning younger – physically and mentally – instead of older: at age twenty, he has the looks of a fifty-year-old; at thirty-five he is at the height of his life, a successful business man with a wife and son, but the people in Baltimore already recognize that he "seems to grow younger every year" ("Benjamin Button," 195). Thus rejuvenating, he finally becomes a playmate for his own grandson, and in the end his world consists only of his crib, his nanny, and the faint smell of milk. In the story's closing scene, the seventy-year-old Benjamin Button has become a baby, barely able to perceive anything around him: "Then it was all dark, and his white crib and the dim faces that moved above him, and the warm sweet aroma of the milk, faded out altogether from his mind." In the end, as Henry Alexander (2009: 7) remarks, it is as if for Benjamin "there had never been any life at all" – his whole existence just fades into nothingness. Hence, what makes Benjamin Button's case so curious is first and foremost the paradoxical fact that he is old while he's young, and young when he's old.

The story's eponymous character is doubtless a literary 'freak of nature', but just like other literary freaks, such as Gregor Samsa or Bartleby, he is also more than just that: Benjam Button serves as an agent for demonstrating certain norms and collective notions of 'life' in a given culture. Fitzgerald takes what in a Western cultural, i.e. Judeo-Christian context is traditionally considered as a *lifetime* – seventy years[18] – and imagines what might happen if life started at the other end, if only for one person: in a world of perfect chronology, Benjamin is the only one living 'against the clock'.

However, a closer look reveals that the temporal structure of the story is slightly more complex than that. Henry Alexander (2009: 2) has differentiated between three lines or threads of time/age in Benjamin's life, namely a chronological one, a physical one, and a psychological one. Chronologically speaking, Benjamin lives his life just like everybody else, turning older each year from his birth in 1860 to his death in 1930. By contrast, his physical age moves in the direct opposite direction, i.e. he grows younger and younger. The most complicated temporal thread is his psychological age, which hardly seems to undergo much change, except for his final years when he gradually loses his ability to speak and finally his consciousness. On a psychological level, there is neither a considerable process of maturation nor of regress. The story's grotesque and ironic effects are of course produced by the circumstance that these temporal threads – chronological, physiological, and psychological age – are "seldom congruent:" "The theme comes out

18 See Psalms 90 ("God's Eternity and Man's Transitoriness"): "The days of our years *are* threescore years and ten;/ and if by reason of strength they *be* fourscore years."

in cases where we are surprised or shocked by the discrepancies between age and appearance or by changes in appearance or by psychological shifts which strike one as dissonant with one's own or another age." (Alexander 2009: 2) Only in Benjamin's middle years do the threads seem to converge, and it is certainly no coincidence that these are his happiest years: he marries his wife Hildegard, his son Roscoe is born, he successfully runs his own business and returns from war as a decorated veteran.

However fantastic and unbelievable this story of the curious case of Benjamin Button might be, it nevertheless succeeds in its exposure of what can be regarded as a typical American life (cycle) or 'normal biography' at the turn of the 20th century. As a matter of fact, it is precisely the fantastic reversal of Benjamin's life story that creates this effect. In the story, Benjamin is the only person moving (or rather living) in the wrong direction – "only one man in a perfectly normal world" (Fitzgerald 2010: viii-ix) –, which turns him into an outsider, a complete alien: When other children in his age attend kindergarten and learn how to paste green paper on orange paper, Benjamin is more interested in cigars and the *Encyclopedia Britannica*. When it is time to go to college, Benjamin is rejected from Yale because the registrar does not believe that he is only eighteen. Similarly, he is expelled from the army in 1914, because he has the looks of a little boy. Thus deconstructing cultural models of lifetime and life phases, the story manages to draw attention to the ways in which these models are culturally made.

More specifically, the unnatural birth of Benjamin Button signals the transition from a traditional – and thus spatially organized – to a modern – and thus temporally organized – society. As the story's beginning suggests, firm social structures are still in place at the time of Benjamin's birth: "The Roger Buttons held an enviable position, both social and financial, in ante-bellum Baltimore." ("Benjamin Button," 176) The personal biography of baby Benjamin, at least so it seems, is predetermined by the status of his parents. What follows, however, is a story of temporalization in which the upheavals and transformations of an increasingly modern society are foregrounded. Interestingly enough, despite the anomalies of his aging process Benjamin's life still resembles to a certain degree a typical upper-middle-class American biography in the age of modernity: "If the chronological inversion of Benjamin's life is ignored, the pattern of events seems normal, for he attends college, finds work, gets married, becomes brigadier general." (Kuehl 1991: 29) In this regard, his biography reads like that of many other Americans at the turn of the 20th century. Benjamin's identity is thus based on what sociologists call the institutionalization of life course models: his life is not a succession of random events, but follows a highly conventionalized and pre-structured pattern, the 'normal biography'.

At the same time, however, by contrasting Benjamin's chronological, physical, and psychological age by means of imagining a 'fabulous time' (Joan Silber), Fitzgerald's story exposes the arbitrariness and absurdities of the concept of a socially sanctioned normal biography as the foundation of an individual's identity. As Martin Kohli (1985: 14) points out, the organization of life courses in modern Western societies usually follows the chronological age and disregards the psychological or physical age (Kohli speaks of the 'functional age') of an individual. Chronological age regularizes the life course and makes it predictable: children go to kindergarten when they are three, school starts at age six, people marry in their twenties, etc. Thomas Cole therefore writes: "In an increasingly rationalized, urban, industrial society, chronological age came to function as a uniform criterion for sequencing the multiple roles and responsibilities that individuals assumed over a lifetime." (2006: 3) For the most part of Benjamin Button's life, the discrepancies between his chronological and physical/psychological age render the concept of normal biography preposterous for him. What is more, the social pressure of the modern life-course regime deprive Benjamin of coherent models for his identity, as he is forced to pass through the normal biographical stages, even if this leads to obviously grotesque results.[19] Thus, Benjamin is "apparently unable to grasp or to hold a grasp of what is happening to him, of how the disparity between his physical and chronological ages affects his life" (Alexander 2009: 3). "Benjamin Button" thus illustrates what happens if a person cannot revert to such models, and how this lack creates an extreme disorientation in life (see ibid.).[20]

The story's many social and historical references further serve to contextualize Benjamin's individual fate in the acceleration processes of modernity and thus illustrate how an individual's lifetime is always embedded in an overarching historical or epochal time. Benjamin is born in the antebellum South in the year before the outbreak of the Civil War and thus at a nodal point in American history. In the 'old order' of the South, the wealthy Buttons are a part of the ruling class. After the war, however, the social structures change tremendously, not only in the

19 For instance, as a 'toddler' he is discovered smoking a Havana with a "guilty expression on his face," and in kindergarten he dozes off in the middle of play; at Yale he is evicted because the registrar scents a spoof.

20 Despite his fate, Alice Hall Petry (1989: 79) calls Benjamin Button the "happiest character in the Fitzgerald canon," because at the time of his death he "simply cannot remember the few unhappy events of his life." An innocent baby with absolutely no memories at all, he is saved from the disillusionment that befalls many people at the end of their lives.

South but in the United States in general, creating existential crises (financial, social, political, generational etc.) for families like the Buttons. Quite literally, then, Benjamin is a child of modernism – his own rejuvenation also mirrors the rejuvenation and reformation of the American nation during the late 19th and early 20th century.

In sum, Fitzgerald's story can be read as a critical assessment of the erosion of certainties in modernism as a result of the acceleration of life tempo and social change. In this condensed story of Benjamin Button's extraordinary biography, time is the main subject; the story is essentially about the human experience of life in time and the many conflicts and desynchronization processes between everyday time, lifetime, and epochal time.[21] By turning it around, the story thematizes and satirizes the way in which chronological age is used to regulate the life course. Fitzgerald's story could thus be regarded as a thought experiment on the question of 'what would happen if life began at the other end?' Here, the short story form seems to be the perfect vehicle or medium for such experimental thinking: In the condensed temporal frame of a short story, Benjamin's life can be depicted in a fast forward mode that serves to highlight the absurdities of his inverted existence. His life merely appears as a succession of conventional, socially normalized and sanctioned life phases which are characterized by their typical events and activities, most of which seem oddly out of place in Benjamin's particular, 'curious' case. For instance, in his childhood he attends kindergarten and is forced by his father to engage in the playful activities of other children, even though Benjamin is more interested in cigars and encyclopedias. When it is time to go to college, he is rejected by the registrar at Yale who first mistakes Benjamin for his father and then angrily throws him out of his office. By reversing the life phases from the cradle to the grave, the story highlights and caricatures them, making the reader aware of the typical behaviors and events of each phase. In this way, it critically engages with the temporalization of patterns of identity and (normalized) life models and demonstrates how "[o]ur awareness of chronological age is part of a more basic historical development – the emergence of individual lifetime as a structural feature of modern society" (Cole 2006: 3).

21 Additionally, one might argue that the story satirizes the assumption held by medieval theologians that a rare child (*puer senex*) could transcend its chronological age and reach the wisdom and virtue of a more advanced spiritual age, whereas an older person "might display the virtues of *infantia spiritualis*, the simplicity and purity of a small child" (Cole 2006: 7-8).

Part III:
Stages of Life – Staging Life in the Short Story

Part III: Stages of Life – Staging Life in the Short Story

It is one of the commonplaces of short story theory that the genre deals with brief moments or phases in the life of a character, presenting to the reader a 'slice of life' instead of the 'whole thing'. In an essay that compares the typical subjects and methods of short stories and novels, David Trotter notes: "Most nineteenth-century novels implicitly or explicitly divide the human life-span into a long rise stretching to the age of 60, measured in social and moral terms, and a short (physical) decline." (Trotter 2010: 5) In a short story, by contrast, such a wide narrative arc would be the exception rather than the rule, even though nothing in the form of the short story automatically renders it impossible (as we have seen in Fitzgerald's inversion of this pattern). Typically, however, short stories tend to emphasize the momentary over the "expansive, substantial, complex [and] broad perspectives" (Malcolm 2011: 100) of the novel: "The short story offers a model of the human life-course which privileges the single moment, rather than the longer term." (ibid.)[1] Based on this – genre-theoretically problematic but literary-historically plausible – thesis that short stories tend to depict 'fragments' or phases of life, whereas novels usually depict a whole lifetime (or even a succession of lifetimes, as in the family saga), the discussion of short stories in the third part of this study is arranged around the concept of life stages or phases. The first section will deal with stories about childhood, youth, and adolescence; the second section with adulthood; and the third section with (old) age.

Admittedly, this arrangement is a somewhat artificial construct, since it is not always possible to make clear-cut decisions as to the compartmentalization of the

1 See also Allen who claims that "we recognize a short story as such because we feel that we are reading something that is the fruit of a single moment of time, of a single incident, a single perception" (1981: 7).

individual stories within the different stages or phases of life. Often enough, stories deal with intergenerational aspects and conflicts, depicting characters in different life phases and their social interactions and relationships. Eudora Welty's "A Visit of Charity," for instance, could be placed in at least two camps, as it is a story about the encounter of two characters from vastly different generations: the young campfire girl Marian meets old Addie, who lives in a home for the elderly. It is therefore both a story of youth/adolescence *and* of old age, depending on whose character's perspective one takes into consideration. Although it has been read as a story of initiation and thus an example of a story of youth, it would also fit into the category of 'stories of aging'. Also, as the example of Fitzgerald's "The Curious Case of Benjamin Button" has shown, short stories can cover the full life course of their protagonists by means of rather extreme summary narration: the full life cycle, unfolding over 70 years, can be depicted in no more than 30 pages (or possibly even less). What is more, some of the discussed stories actually fall into more than one category, since they deal with adult characters *remembering* crucial scenes from their childhood or youth. Hence, the life-phase oriented categories applied to structure the text discussions in this study should be regarded as *possible* heuristic constructs, not as a definitive typology.

The idea (and ideal) of different stages of life, which are distinct from each other and together form a typical life cycle or life course, is of course not a universal anthropological constant, an *a priori* fact of human nature, even if "the process of birth, growth, maturity, decay and death appear as parts of the cycle of organic life" (Cole 2006: xxxii). As cultural historians, anthropologists, and sociologists have argued over the last decades, the Western life-course model – although it may appear as a completely 'natural' and self-evident reality – is to a great extent a discursive product, i.e. the result of social interaction and structural-historical processes. The notion of the 'discovery' or even 'invention' of childhood (see Heywood 2001; Cunningham 2006), for example, has become a commonplace in the social sciences and in cultural studies. From this vantage, childhood is not regarded as a biological fact but as the upshot of societal transformation processes and cultural representations of children in art, literature, and other discourses, especially since the Renaissance. Similarly, adolescence and old age can be seen as socio-cultural phenomena and as results of the processes of modernization and particularly the functional differentiation in modern Western societies. As David Bakan argued, "the invention of adolescence in America was largely in response to the social changes that accompanied America's development in the latter half of the nineteenth and the early twentieth century" (1971: 980). Adolescence is thus not merely and individual, biopsychological phenomenon, but a psycho-social phenomenon that is inextricably tied to larger social developments and cultural notions. Thomas R. Cole follows a similar line of thought when he maintains that during the process of modernization in both Europe and America (old) age was stripped of its formerly positive connotations and the "ancient and medieval understandings of aging as a mysterious part of the eternal order of things". As a consequence, it was "removed from its ambiguous place in life's spiritual journey, rationalized, and redefined as a scientific problem" (2006: xx).

In general, the concept of life stages and the very notion of 'age' is closely connected to modern progress and the institutionalization of the life-course model I have outlined in the previous chapter. In traditional societies, age did not play any important role: "Since numerical age had virtually no social significance, few people knew exactly how old they were." (Cole 2006: 5) Only with the temporalization, chronologization, and biographization of life in modernity did the concept of 'age' gain social relevance. Thus, the idea of different life stages is not only an essentially *temporal* construct that structures life according to certain patterns, each of which are marked by their own specific meanings, life events, lifestyles, experiences, and forms of life. It also reflects modern societies' tendency to compartmentalize and fragment life, creating social images of, and roles for, people in certain life phases. Human beings obviously have the need to make sense of what Thomas Cole calls "the mystery of human temporality" (ibid.: xxxi).

According to a dominant position in the social sciences, different ages or stages of life should not merely be understood as results of a biological process (which undoubtedly forms the basis of the life-course model),[2] but also as an individual *and* collective experience. Cultural knowledge of the stages of life is inextricably intertwined with the personal 'living through' of these stages: "We come to know the ages of life by living a personal journey from vulnerable, dependent childhood to apparently independent adulthood and on to vulnerability and dependence again in old age. Moving from stage to stage, we come to know ourselves." (Cole 2006: xxxiv) At the same time, this personal experience of the stages of life, along with the diverse meanings, values, norms, attitudes, and virtues attached to them, is significantly shaped by the culturally available images, symbols, rituals, and narratives. These cultural forms serve to provide a kind of knowledge for orientation, helping people to cope with the challenges that each of the life stages holds in store, but they also sanction and control collective notions of a 'normal' or 'ideal' life.

2 See Richter (2011) for a brief discussion of the biology of aging.

In the third part of this study, my aim is to analyze the North American short story's cultural work as an organon of life knowledge, and especially its active role in the formation of modern configurations of life stages. As Sabine Coelsch-Foisner notes, the "cult of childhood, the focus on initiation or, conversely, ageing, life extension, and immortality are indicative of what has been valued about life and how life-course models have been shaped according to these ideals" (2011: X). Far from being neutral containers, these concepts and stages are laden with complex and often contested meanings. Literature, and the various literary genres have arguably played a significant role in disseminating values and knowledge of the human life course and its various constituents. Literature has the privilege to aesthetically shape the human life-course, to endow it with metaphors, plots, and allegories. As powerful meaning-making tools, literary genres always privilege certain perspectives on the life-course model, as I have briefly argued above. The task is therefore to further examine how the literary form of the short story has contributed to such notions, values, and configurations of life stages: How does literature, and how do short stories, reflect on culturally prefigured forms of life and life-course models? What is the short story's role in producing and disseminating certain notions of life phases and an 'ideal' life? In other words, how does the short story contribute to a poetics of life and the human life course? Where do the literary representations of life phases divert from the culturally dominant notions? Where do they foreshadow or anticipate culturally latent developments?

8. Epistemological Uncertainty and Knowledge of Maturation in Stories of Initiation:

Sherwood Anderson's "I Want to Know Why", Eudora Welty's "A Visit of Charity" and "A Memory", and Junot Díaz's "Ysrael"

In a famous essay dating from 1958, Ihab Hassan observed a 'cult of adolescence' in modern American literature. Hassan claimed that no one could fail "to notice the sheer physical presence of the adolescent in our world" and "to recognize in the sad and angry youths who populate American fiction a striking literary manifestation rife with extra-literary import" (1958: 312). This extra-literary import, as sociologists have argued, resides in the general valorization of youth and youthfulness as the paradigm of a modern lifestyle (see e.g. Abels et al. 2008: 8). America, at least in the early decades of the 20th century, is the land of adolescence. As some critics have even asserted, this favoritism of youth and adolescence over the other ages of life, especially old age, is grounded in the American mentality, representing the United States' peculiar relationship with history. Peter Freese comments on this matter:

> America [...] has always connected the individual developmental phase of adolescence with the collective chance of beginning anew in the virgin land of a continent free of the fetters of history, and has thus linked the promise of individual youth with [...] 'the American Dream.' (Freese 1999c: 178-79)

Thus casting an individual phase of human development onto the collective, historical situation of the nation, adolescence comes to represent something of an American national character: Youth is more than a mere age of life, it is a state of mind and a precondition of the American Dream. Historically speaking, the American preference for youth and adolescence has been interpreted as a reaction to the demographic and economic changes after the Civil War (see Bergmann 2003: 40-41). In fact, the very 'discovery' or 'invention' of adolescence falls into this period, as the American psychologist Stanley Hall coined the term in his influential study *Adolescence* in 1904. Adolescence is hence a construct of the late 19th to early 20th century (see Bergmann 2003: 39; see also Freese 1999c), adding another culturally specific life phase to the modern project of a 'temporalization of life'.

But what are youth and adolescence, then, if we regard them as a response to the dawn of modernism and the changing life-world of the 20th century? For sociologists, youth is connected with a certain longing for unity and 'soulfulness' in a fragmented world ("Sehnsucht nach einem 'beseelten Ganzen' in einer fragmentierten Welt," Abels 2008: 84). As a stage of life, youth and adolescence are associated with the development of identity, the implementation of a meaning of/in life, the idea of a life plan, and a growing into the separate areas of life such as relationships, sexuality, work, family, etc. Adolescence has accordingly been described as a transitional phase between the more stable, long-term phases of childhood and adulthood, rather than an independent life phase in itself. As such, adolescence corresponds to and can even be said to be a direct upshot or invention of the modern society as a society of differentiation, and of the ensuing division of labor: "It is only with the differentiation of the society, the division of labor and the respective specialized qualifications, that the phenomenon of youth emerges." (Abels 2008: 112, transl. M.B.) The German-American psychoanalyst Erik H. Erikson, an important pioneer in life-course studies, has famously described adolescence as a psychosocial moratorium, a kind of shelter in which the individual can develop his or her own personality and find answers to the most existential questions ('Who am I? How do I fit in? What is my purpose in life?' etc.). From this vantage, the invention and, somewhat later, the prolongation of the life phase 'youth/adolescence' can be regarded as a result of the structural change of life patterns described in the previous chapter.

Literature, as Hassan's early observations already suggest, has played an inestimable part in the construction of images and perceptions of adolescence and youth, and has thus contributed to this new 'cult'. Particularly the short story had a prominent role in this development, disseminating a wide range of representations of youthful protagonists and their struggle with society, from Hawthorne's Robin to Hemingway's Nick Adams to Salinger's Babe Gladwaller and Holden Caulfield. Mary Louise Pratt (1994: 106) even maintains that short stories often portray childhood experience, whereas novels rarely deal with this phase of life, except for the genres of the picaresque novel and *Bildungsroman*. One might therefore assume that the short story provides a privileged outlet for staging the conflictive phase of adolescence, with its focus on crisis and turning point as well as the tendency to single out brief moments of life. Along the same lines, Kasia Boddy argues that adolescence is the life phase most congenial to the short story, since adolescence is

> all turning point. Adolescence is a point of vantage equally on childhood and on adult life, on innocence and on experience. The short story, a form constituted by and as crisis, well suits adolescence, a state of mind and body constituted by and as crisis. (2010: 102)

The following questions derive from these observations: What is the short story's role in the sociological and psychological 'invention' of adolescence as a distinct age of life? With its focus on crisis and turning point and the transition from childhood to adulthood, how does especially the emergence and proliferation of the story of initiation interrelate with the growing epistemological uncertainty that characterizes the modern age? Most importantly, what kind of life knowledge is addressed and produced by stories of initiation? What are the pragmatic repercussions of stories of initiation on the question of how to live? And how has the genre developed throughout the 20th century, with the changing conceptions and shifting temporal delimitations of the life stage youth/adolescence? In the following, I will address these questions by looking at a number of short stories dealing with adolescence and initiation, the examples ranging from classics like Anderson's "I Want to Know Why" to Junot Díaz's recent story "Ysrael" that transfers the initiation theme into a 21st century American multicultural society. As I will argue, the genre of the story of initiation continues to be one of the most powerful literary genres by which a cultural notions of adolescence – as part of a cultural life knowledge – are being negotiated and disseminated.

* * *

With the focus on adolescence, initiation became a major theme in American literature at least since the mid-19th century (see Bergmann 2003: 11). Famously introduced into literary criticism by Ray B. West and somewhat later and more systematically by Mordecai Marcus (1960), the 'story of initiation' represents the American preference for youthful protagonists who struggle with their integration into society. Stories of initiation are the primary genre for the literary treatment of the theme of how the child becomes a man or woman (see Bergmann 2003). Unlike the *Bildungsroman*, for instance, which depicts the process of socialization over a longer period of time and thus emphasizes the successful or, in the case of the negative *Bildungsroman*, failed social (re-)integration of the individual, the initiation story usually focuses on "the decisive turning point or climax of such a process" (Freese 1999c: 179).[1]

Given the fact that the story of initiation is a well-established subgenre of the short story and that there are numerous studies devoted to its definition and classification, it is needless to discuss its formal, structural, and thematic characteristics in detail here.[2] The focus of this chapter is rather to examine to what extent the genre is imbued with a certain life knowledge. As the above quotation from Boddy already suggests, the genre's perspective on human life is dominated by notions of crisis and turning point. In stories of initiation, the protagonists enter situations in which their former lives and identities are profoundly shaken, forcing them to respond to this crisis and often constituting a decisive change in the course of their lives. Peter Freese, in what can still be considered the most concise definition of the generic features of the story of initiation to date, stresses this contrastive tension between knowing and unknowing, reality and appearance, as well as innocence and experience:

> The youthful protagonist of a story of initiation gains his experience during a *journey* which consists of the three phases of *exit*, *transition* and *(re-)entrance* and leads the traveler from *innocence* to *experience*. In the course of this real or metaphorical journey the initiate experiences manifold *confrontations* with a world hitherto unknown to him, and is exposed to the temptations of a *tempter* but can, on the other hand, find advice and help from a fatherly *mentor*. His experiences culminate in a *recognition* or an *insight* which changes his life and

1 I am not so much concerned here with the differentiation between 'tentative', 'uncompleted', or 'decisive' initiations. For a discussion and persuasive critique of these different 'types' of initiation see Bergmann (2003: 46).

2 Peter Freese's (1999c [1981]) important work on the story of initiation, though already some thirty years old, arguably still provides the most comprehensive definition as well as insightful discussions of several exemplary texts of the genre. Ina Bergmann's study *And Then the Child Becomes a Woman* (2003) is an important addition to Freese's works as it discusses the female version of the genre, which was long neglected and marginalized in the discourse on stories of initiation. Taken together, Freese and Bergmann provide an excellent overview of the cultural construction of the concepts of adolescence and initiation, their adaptation in literary studies, as well as a number of illuminating interpretations of exemplary stories of initiation. Also see the concise discussion of stories of female initiation in Bergmann (2011).

which often refers to the disillusioning discovery of the disparity between *appearance* and *reality*. (Freese 1999c: 184, emphasis in the original)

The acquisition of life knowledge, staged at the story level as the protagonist's journey from innocence to experience, is part and parcel of the story of initiation. In his early definition, Mordecai Marcus already acknowledged this epistemological dimension when he pointed out that the initiate experiences "a significant change of knowledge about the world or himself" (1960: 222). Later definitions also center on the idea of knowledge and recognition (see Lubbers 1977; Freese 1999c). This focus on the change of knowledge can already be observed in Hawthorne's "My Kinsman, Major Molineux" (1832), which, as Freese convincingly shows, introduced "the very constituents which from now on will dominate the American story of initiation in constant variation" (1999c: 181). As a general rule, the acquisition of knowledge in stories of initiation comes at a high price, as "the initiate's gaining of insight and maturity has to be paid for by his losing of his innocence and spontaneity" (ibid.: 184).

Given the supposed self-evidence of the term or concept of 'initiation' in the discussions of the early 20th century, it is remarkable that it is precisely this notion that many short stories put into question. Henry James's "The Tree of Knowledge" (1900), for instance, already problematizes the notion of initiation, questioning "that it occurs, and (if it occurs) that its occurrence can be located in time, can itself be 'known'" (Ohi 2008: 118). James's epistemological skepticism toward initiation as a knowable and tellable event in a person's life is further radicalized in the postmodern anti-stories, most notably in John Barth's "Lost in the Funhouse" (1968), which renders not only the concepts of adolescence and initiation, but also the genre conventions of the initiation story and the very notion of storytelling as a means of identity formation and self-knowledge problematic. Barth's postmodernist, anti-illusionary mockery of the initiation story culminates in the scene where Ambrose, the awkward protagonist, admiringly watches a sailor and his girl, his admiration for the sailor contrasting sharply with his own innocence and clumsiness:

Ambrose understood not only that they were all so relieved to be rid of his burdensome company that they didn't even notice his absence, but that he himself shared their relief. Stepping from the treacherous passage at last into the mirror-maze, he saw once again, *more clearly than ever*, how readily he deceived himself into supposing he was a person. He even foresaw, wincing at *this dreadful self-knowledge*, that he would repeat the deception, at even-rarer intervals, all his wretched life, so fearful were the alternatives. Fame, madness,

> suicide; perhaps all three. It's not believable that so young a boy could articulate that reflection, and in fiction the merely true must always yield to the plausible. ("Lost in the Funhouse", 93-4, emphasis added, M.B.)

Note how Barth's narrator deploys the thematic and formal conventions of the story of initiation, only to immediately ridicule and subvert them. The adolescent's recognition ("more clearly than ever", "this dreadful self-knowledge"), presented through Ambrose's inner perspective by means of focalization, gives way to the meta-narrative commentary that exposes the foregoing paragraph as a stale literary convention: "Is anything more tiresome, in fiction, than the problems of sensitive adolescents?" (Barth 1988: 91-2) Many stories of initiation, especially since postmodernism, thus not only present the *rite de passage* as an anthropological constant, but consciously reflect on its epistemological underpinnings, narrative conventions, and cultural specificities.

From the perspective of literary studies as a form of life science, stories of initiation are an epistemological genre *par excellence*, since they are primarily concerned with the protagonist's process of 'wising up' to the realities of life and the many problems and challenges connected with this idea. Depicting youthful protagonists in borderline situations in which their prior world-view becomes questionable, they exemplify the short story's general tendency towards crisis and turning point: Stories of initiation foreground epistemological uncertainty as something that frequently befalls adolescents as a result of the new, incomprehensible situation they find themselves in, and in which their knowledge of the world seems to erode. As a genre, they are therefore explicitly concerned with questions of life knowledge or how to live, even though for the protagonist such knowledge is marked by its very absence or suspension: in these stories, the dynamic and inherently problematic interrelation between literature, life, and knowledge takes center stage. By focusing on moments of suspension rather than resolution, the genre also problematizes the unbridgeable discrepancy between knowledge and life in situations of transition and crisis.

Furthermore, it seems helpful to differentiate again between the intra-textual and the extra-textual dimensions of life knowledge in order to fully understand the ways in which the story of initiation responds to socio-historically specific models of life and the cultural practices of living. On an intra-textual level, i.e. on the level of the story/plot, stories of initiation explicitly stage the cognitive and emotional processes that characterize the transition from childhood to adulthood, from innocence to experience. However, they do of course not merely reflect, but in fact model this process by applying to it a certain form, which usually involves some sort of travel, confrontations with other individuals, and a shock of recognition.

Quite frequently, stories of initiation explicitly stage encounters between characters from different ages of life in order to foreground the idea that what separates the initiate from these other, grown-up characters is a distinctive life knowledge. The transition from youth to adulthood is not so much marked by biological processes but by the acquisition of cultural knowledge. For the initiates, the recognition of the inadequacy of their previous knowledge and perception of life is often rather disillusioning and unsettling, forcing them to adapt their own system of beliefs.

On an extra-textual level, stories of initiation also produce and disseminate cultural life knowledge insofar as they stage adolescence as a distinct age of life and thus take part in the modern process of the temporalization of life and biography, as outlined in the previous chapters. The main question is therefore how the knowledge in the story translates into real-life knowledge. Stories of initiation deal with anthropological constants, but they also engage in the cultural negotiation of such concepts as youth or adolescence and therefore contribute to, and sometimes critically examine or put into question, culturally prevalent notions of life stages/ages. Moreover, many proponents of this genre juxtapose different ages, confronting the initiate with crucial life events such as birth and death (see Bergmann 2003: 33-4). They also create a figurative knowledge by championing the figure of the American Adam, i.e. the young protagonist or 'man-boy' as the favorite American literary hero (see ibid.). One may thus ask what this valorization or 'cult' of adolescence in modern American literature, and especially the story of initiation, means for the literary production of life knowledge? And to what extend can initiation be regarded as a theme that leads to 'American self-understanding' (Freese)? In the following, I would like to address these questions by looking at three very different stories of initiation, Sherwood Anderson's "I Want to Know Why," Eudora Welty's "A Visit of Charity," and Junot Díaz's "Ysrael."

* * *

Published in the collection *The Triumph of the Egg* (1921) and one of Anderson's most-anthologized pieces, "I Want to Know Why" relates the protagonist's first experience of the ugliness of adult life and adult sexuality.[3] Concerning its central theme, characters, and structure, the story is one of the foremost examples of the initiation story in America, and one of Mordecai Marcus's sources for his early

3 The first parts of this section draw on an earlier discussion of Anderson's story (Basseler 2011b).

definition of the genre. The nameless 16-year-old protagonist and first-person narrator goes on an adventurous trip that takes him far from his rural Kentucky home to the glittering world of horse-racing. He and a few friends break away from home in order to bet on horses in Saratoga where they spend six days. At the races, the narrator encounters his childhood idol, the famous trainer Jerry Tillford and his stallion Sunstreak. Exchanging glances with Tillford before the race the narrator believes he senses a deep, secret bond between him and Tillford: "I looked up, and then that man and I looked into each other's eyes. Something happened to me. I guess I loved the man as much as I did the horse because he knew what I knew." ("I Want to Know Why", 394) After Sunstreak wins the race and "busted the world's record for a mile" (ibid.) his admiration for Tillford grows into outright adoration, which has a transformative power: "It was the first time I ever felt for a man like that." (ibid.: 395) However, when the narrator steals away from his friends in the evening after the race to "be near Jerry Tillford" (ibid.), he furtively watches Tillford and some other men passing their time with "bad women" (ibid.), whom the I-narrator describes as "ugly mean-looking, not nice to look at or be near" (ibid.). Terrified by the recognition that Tillford glances at one of those "bad women" in the same way he had glanced at Sunstreak only a few hours ago, the narrator all of a sudden begins "to hate that man" (ibid.: 396). The story then closes with the narrator's desperate recognition that nothing ever will be the same after this experience: "At the tracks the air don't taste as good or smell as good. It's because a man like Jerry Tillford, who knows what he does, could see a horse like Sunstreak run, and kiss a woman like that the same day. [...] What did he do it for? I want to know why." (ibid.)

The story shows all of the features associated with the story of initiation: The protagonist belongs to the transitional phase between childhood and adulthood; his geographical journey from Kentucky to Saratoga resembles or symbolizes his rite of passage from the realm of his sheltered youth to the world of adults; in the course of the story, the initiate is confronted with several other people – most importantly, of course, Jerry Tillford – and these encounters "culminate in a sudden insight or illumination which most often effects a lasting change in the initiate's life and might be best termed, in Melville's words, a 'shock of recognition'" (Freese 1999c: 182-3); and the young protagonist passes through all three typical phases of initiation stories as outlined by Freese (ibid.), namely exit, transition, and (re-)entrance. The last and most crucial phase, the phase of (re-)entrance, is not yet completed in the story, thus leaving the protagonist in a liminal state. What he saw that evening when he watched Jerry Tillford at the "rummy looking farmhouse" ("I Want to Know Why", 395) leaves the first-person narrator deeply confused, distraught and stuck between his old life as a child and his new, disenchanted life in the harsh world of adults. Almost a year after the events, he is still emotionally involved in his experiences, as his meta-narrative comments reveals: "That's what I'm writing this story about. I'm puzzled. I'm getting to be a man and want to think straight and be O.K., and there's something I saw at the race meeting at the eastern track I can't figure out." (ibid.: 391)

The narrative perspective of the adolescent protagonist serves to fulfill important functions within this short story, especially with regard to the dimension of knowledge and recognition associated with initiation stories. Presented from the point of view of a teenager, the story displays his somewhat naïve and inexperienced perspective and mindset. This results in the effect that the discrepancy between the limited perspective and knowledge of the protagonist and the more knowledgeable perspective of the adult reader creates dramatic irony. The reader is not presented with any superordinate, knowledgeable perspective of a third-person narrator, but must draw his or her own conclusions from what the narrator – often implicitly – reveals about his experiences. Whereas life knowledge – and the temporary suspension thereof – is thus staged as the central content or theme of Anderson's story, the narrative perspective serves to foreground the epistemological process at the discourse level as well.

Part of this is that the story self-reflexively accentuates the act of narration itself. Telling the story – however inchoate it might seem to the narrator-protagonist himself – becomes an important means for the narrator to come to terms with his experiences, even if this process is still incomplete. His digressive reports of the events at the tracks are repeatedly interrupted by metanarrative comments that reveal his need for comprehension: "It got me upset. I think about it at night. Here it is." (ibid.: 393). The act of narration is intertwined with the narrator's psychological and moral crisis and his longing for understanding. The use of a first-person narrator thus serves to aesthetically stage the loss of certainty and knowledge that this story – and the story of initiation at large – addresses. Focusing on a crucial phase in the psychological development of the protagonist, "I Want to Know Why" mimics the nature of human understanding and making sense of the world, and emphasizes the role of language and storytelling in this endeavor by staging the discrepancy and even contradiction between life and knowledge, between living and understanding one's life.

In the way that it thematizes and presents the tension between life and knowledge on the story and discourse levels, "I Want to Know Why" illustrates how the genre of the initiation story, and the short story in general, are literary and cultural forms of life knowledge in which epistemological, social, cultural, and aesthetic dimensions complexly overlap. The epistemological crisis of the teenage protagonist, his wanting to know why, provides the major conflict and the narrative fuel on which the story operates. Far from being a singular story, however, this motif is embedded in the larger social context of a modern American society in which adolescence emerges as a social phenomenon in response to changing life worlds and time regimes. As a story of initiation, "I Want to Know Why" contributes to the cultural framing of this social phenomenon, providing a narrative framework and aesthetic structure that shapes cultural notions of adolescence and initiation, of childhood and adulthood.

Initiation is a dominant theme in the modern American short story, and many writers have either replicated or complicated and expanded the model that Anderson's story presents. Eudora Welty's "A Visit of Charity" from her collection *A Curtain of Green* (1941) is a case in point for how the initiation theme is further developed in the American short story of the first half of the 20th century. In its pronounced literariness – especially the rich, suggestive mythological and intertextual references as well as the extensive use of symbols and metaphors, the high degree of aesthetic compression, its focus on a single, significant moment in time (or 'slice of life'), and its deployment of the theme of initiation – Welty's story is heavily indebted to what is probably the most foundational text of the modern short story in America, Anderson's *Winesburg, Ohio* (1919). No wonder, then, that Welty's stories served as a preferred example for the New Critics' method of close reading, most prominently perhaps in Brooks and Warren's influential textbook *Understanding Fiction*: they almost cry out for a close reading that analyzes its formal aspects and highlights the peculiarity of the cognition or knowledge it provides.[4]

In contrast to many other modern stories of initiation that favor a first-person narrator in order to underscore the epistemological uncertainty that the crisis has caused (e.g. in "I Want to Know Why" or Robert Penn Warren's "Blackberry Winter"), "A Visit" is told from the perspective of a heterodiegetic narrator, establishing a notable distance between the protagonist and the reader. The story begins in the morning of a "very cold, bright day" ("A Visit," 113) and creates a strong visual image of a young girl standing in front of a retirement home:

> Holding a potted plant before her, a girl of fourteen jumped off the bus in front of the Old Ladies' home, on the outskirts of town. She wore a red coat, and her straight yellow hair was hanging down loose from the pointed white cap all the little girls were wearing that year. She stopped for a moment beside one of the prickly dark shrubs with which the city

4 See Lombardy (2005) for an informative discussion of the New Critics' (particularly Allen Tate's) understanding of literature as a distinct form of knowledge.

> had beautified the Home, and then proceeded slowly toward the building, which was of whitewashed brick and reflected the winter sunlight like a block of ice. As she walked vaguely up the steps she shifted the small pot from hand to hand; then she had to set it down and remove her mittens before she could open the heavy door. ("A Visit," 113)

The girl's name is Marian, and she is a "Campfire Girl" on one of her obligatory 'visits of charity' that earn her points in her score. Her arrival at the old ladies' home signals the moment of transgression for her; she is, quite literally, standing at the threshold of an experience that will lastingly change her perception of life. In her informative interpretation of Welty's story, Ina Bergmann (2003: 273-82) provides a very detailed and well-researched analysis of the textual elements that render it a story of female initiation. Here are the most important ones.

In terms of the story's spatial structure, the location of the retirement home "on the outskirts of town" hints at the seclusion in which initiations usually take place. The home is described as looking "like a block of ice," symbolizing the lack of emotionality and humanness. Moreover, the element of travel, referred to in the above passage by the mentioning of the bus, is also constitutive of the genre's emphasis on the stages of exit, transition, and re-entrance. When at the end of the story Marian jumps on the bus again, this frames her initiation and signals the end of her journey and the return into society: "she jumps aboard the bus to make good her escape from the stages of aging that she has been forced for a moment to confront." (Cline 1999: 171) Hence, the story's spatial frames, i.e. the "shifting scenes of action" (Ryan 2009), serve to underscore the protagonist's initiation process: whereas the bus symbolizes Marian's leaving and returning to society, the remote setting of the retirement home is the location where here transformation from child to woman can take place.

The characters that the young girl meets on her journey, especially the two old women she pays a visit to, play an important part in the story as they initiate her into her role as a woman (see Bergmann 2003: 274). However, it is significant that the elderly ladies are not described in human terms, but are portrayed as (almost object-like) animals. Whereas one of the old ladies is repeatedly described as a sheep ("an old lady of some kind cleared her throat like a sheep bleating," "A Visit", 113; "She had a bunchy white forehead and red eyes like a sheep," "said the old woman like a sheep," ibid.), the other one resembles a bird with hands like claws ("A Visit," 114). Other than the reader might expect, the old women are not particularly pleased about Marian's visit but instead quarrel all the time, spitefully insulting each other and complaining about their lives. As Ralph Cline nicely sums up, the two are "unpleasant in the extreme and in all aspects of their interrelations. They bicker about every topic of conversation breached [...] until one is reduced to weeping like an infant and the other to begging like a toddler for pennies and nickels." (1999: 171) Welty's story thereby seems to suggest that such acts of organized charity dehumanize rather than humanize, turning all participants into caricatures (see Bradham, qtd. in Bergmann 2003: 276).

Like many other of Welty's stories, "A Visit" is marked by a wide net of mythological and other intertextual references which expand and deepen its cultural meanings. For example, Marian's journey can be read as a modern actualization of the myth of Persephone's descent to the underworld, or even more obviously, as a 20th-century version of the fairy tale of Little Red Riding Hood, who also undertakes a visit of charity to her grandmother. Also, there is the reference to the Biblical story of the fall of mankind, sealed by the bite into the forbidden fruit. When at the end of the story Marian "took a big bite out of the apple" ("A Visit," 118), Welty clearly frames Marian's initiation process in this religio-cultural context, which also centers on the moment of acquiring dangerous, even forbidden knowledge. Thus, the purpose of all of these mythological and intertextual references is to underscore and condense the theme of initiation, placing it in a long tradition of similar stories and further charging it with cultural meaning. The numerous symbolic and metaphorical elements in the story serve to fulfill a similar function, since they also add conventionalized, cultural meaning to it. The "potted plant" with the heart-shaped leaves that Marian brings as a gift for the old women, for example, symbolizes the lack of emotionality and the heartlessness of the girl. Moreover, it links up to the story's mythical elements, particularly the *Aeneas* story, and represents life and death at the same time (see Bergmann 2003: 279).

It is significant that Welty juxtaposes the different ages of life – youth, maturity, and old age – in Marian's visit to the retirement home, thereby aesthetically condensing and foregrounding the temporal dimension of life. As Cline notes, Marian arrives at the home as a young girl, where she first encounters a "middle-aged, virtually genderless nurse" and then symbolically passes from middle age to old age when she enters the old ladies' room, thus proceeding "through the 'Ages of Woman'" (1999: 171). This results in an entirely new perspective:

> Marian gains a new perspective, and from it a fuller understanding of herself, the old ladies, and charity. When she steps to the bed of old Addie, the person nearest death, Marian has reached the nadir of her new world. There she is privileged to comprehend much more than the short years of her life have ever revealed. [...] Marian, as a protagonist, undergoes the experience of gaining a new awareness. (Bradham, qtd. from Bergmann 2003: 277)

During the short time of her visit, Marian makes an experience that confronts her with the abrupt finality of life and initiates her into a new reality, the reality of lived human time. What makes Welty's story interesting in the context of the study at hand, thus, is primarily its peculiar treatment of the initiation theme, which is quite special in at least two regards. First, "A Visit of Charity" is a story of female initiation and thus expands the male-centered definitions that have dominated the discussion of the story of initiation genre ever since West's and Marcus's contributions (see Bergmann 2003). Second, Welty's story depicts the intergenerational encounter between a young girl and two elderly ladies and in this way stages notions of life phases and the understanding of the meaning of age in a modern American context. As in all initiation stories, life knowledge is the major theme of the story, as the young initiate gains a new perspective. At the same time, however, by presenting the protagonist's initiation at the conflictive intersection between gender and age, and by aestheticizing the process of temporalization of life in the American society, "A Visit" also is an example of the short story genre's tendency to debunk hegemonic knowledge and power structures governing sociocultural notions of life.

This complex of female initiation and societal norms, gender roles and expectations, as well as life knowledge is further explored by Welty in a number of her short stories. In "A Memory", also published in *A Curtain of Green*, a nameless narrator remembers a scene from her childhood when she lay on the beach of a small lake near her home. As so many of Welty's stories, this one begins with a strong visual image that serves to introduce the general mood of the story. The narrator, snugly ensconced in the warm sand, describes the scenery in almost photographic accuracy, catching details in the far distance as much as objects close by:

> The sun beat down – it was almost noon. The water shone like steel, motionless except for the feathery curl behind a distant swimmer. From my position I was looking at a rectangle brightly lit, actually glaring at me, with sun, sand, water, a little pavilion, a few solitary people in fixed attitudes, and around it all a border of dark rounded oak trees, like the engraved thunderclouds surrounding illustrations in the Bible. Ever since I had begun taking painting lessons, I had made small frames with my fingers, to look out at everything. ("A Memory," 75)

While this description evokes the impression of a photograph or a very detailed landscape painting, it also rather implicitly reveals some information about the narrator (for instance her religious upbringing, hinted at by the reference to the Bible illustrations). Even at her young age, she appears to be a very responsive, heedful person who carefully observes everything in her surrounding, drawing her conclusions from these observations. Similar to the adolescent narrator in Anderson's "I Want to Know Why", she is upset and even "terrified" by the things she sees, and like him she is still resistant to the cruelties of the adult world, which fill her with "a vision of abandonment and wildness which tore my heart with a kind of sorrow" ("A Memory," 75).

Unlike Anderson's protagonist, however, she is much more wised up already: Whereas her parents still deem her to be an innocent child, who sees "nothing in the world which was not strictly coaxed into a place", she knows that they "would have been badly concerned if they had guessed how frequently the weak and inferior and strangely turned examples of what was to come showed themselves to me" (ibid.). Thus, her gift of close observation already thrusts upon her the secrets of life which are usually beyond the perception of children, and to find them out has become "a *need*" (ibid.) or even an obsession for the narrator during the summer: "It did not matter to me what I looked at; from any observation I would conclude that a secret of life had been nearly revealed to me – for I was obsessed with notions about concealment, and from the smallest gesture of a stranger I would wrest what was to me a communication or a presentiment." (ibid.: 76)

Her emotional responsiveness is even heightened by her being in love for the first time: one day in school she has, more accidentally than intentionally, touched the hand of a boy, a fleeting and almost imperceptible moment of (mutual?) affection. Although she knows or rather feels that she has "identified love at once" (ibid.), she is not yet able to process this emotion: "The truth is that never since has any passion I have felt remained so hopelessly unexpressed within me or appeared so grotesquely altered in the outward world." (ibid.) What Welty captures so powerfully here is the feeling of first love with all its "overwhelming beauty" (ibid.) and fragility, as well as the alertness that accompanies it. The whole life of the nameless protagonist is shaken by this tiny gesture – the touching of a boy's hand –, leaving her with uneasy feelings. Soon, however, the narrator's youthful innocence is taken away when the boy she is in love with bleeds from his nose during a Latin class: Seeing the "red – vermillion – blood" (76), the narrator is shell-shocked and faints over her desk. On a symbolical level, of course, the blood signifies the narrator's loss of innocence and the recognition of sexuality. Once she gets a glimpse of the joys and emotional heights of (spiritual) love, she also has to face the sorrows of love which are also real, manifesting themselves on the physical level of the body.

Interestingly enough, like Welty's "Old Mr. Marblehall," "A Memory" explores the notion of a doubled life (see chapter 9). For the narrator, her interstitial position between dreamer (of her own life) and observer (of the lives of others) almost amounts to the feeling of living a "dual life" (ibid.: 76). Life in the short moments captured in these stories is not the dull, everyday life submerged by routine and inattentiveness, but a life that is perceived in its entire richness, pleasures, and sorrows. Here, Welty is very close to the intensified 'moments of being' of Virginia Woolf, whose writing she admired. The central moment in the story, however, is when all of a sudden, a family arrives at the beach and settles close to where the narrator lies. The family is described by the narrator as a "group of loud, squirming, ill-assorted people who seemed thrown together only by the most confused accident" (ibid.: 77), consisting of a man, his wife, their daughter and two sons. The narrator is instantaneously vexed by their presence and behavior, trying to withdraw to her dream of "touching the wrist of the boy I loved on the stair" (ibid.: 79) and even wishing "that they were all dead" (ibid.: 78).

It is not quite clear what it is exactly that upsets her so much about the presence of the family on the beach. Arguably, it is the recognition of the mundaneness of life and the contrast between the innocence of her first love and the ugliness of their life ("they were all resigned to each other's daring and ugliness," ibid.). Quite literally, the appearance of the family in the picture that the narrator has painted in her mind alerts her to the fact that life is not the idyllic scenery she wishes it to be. Once the strangers have left again, the narrator feels "victimized" (ibid.: 79) by the sight of their leftovers – an unfinished bulwark and the shapes of their wet bodies in the sand – and starts to cry, bemoaning the loss of her own innocence. After this encounter, nothing seems the same to her, and she does not return to the beach again ("That was my last morning on the beach," ibid.: 80) The magic of her childhood and the dreamlike experience of her first, innocent love are all marred by the sight of the bathers, as if they were the "examples of what was to come [that] showed themselves to me" (ibid.).

If compared with Anderson's "I Want to Know Why", the general idea as well as the outcome of the two stories are the same: An initially innocent, young protagonist has an experience that corrupts his/her idealized notion of love and life, introducing him/her to the ways of the grown-up world. In Welty's story, however, this insight is presented much subtler and less portentous: It does not need an idealized, heroic figure who then turns out to be as bad and 'impure' as the other adults; neither does the protagonist go on a journey that takes him far away from the protected world of his childhood. In "A Memory," the mere confrontation with the loud, ugly family on the beach changes the narrator's knowledge of the world – they are the "representatives of a world hitherto unknown" (Freese 1986: 52).

Michael Kreyling (1999: 25) has referred to "A Memory" as one of Welty's 'threshold stories', oscillating between dream and waking. As a threshold story, it "eschews traditional narrative in favor of nonchronological disturbances, conceives of character as psychological rather than physical, and responds more clearly to its status as a work of art by bringing allusion, reference, controlled patterns of imagery, and other aesthetic aspects of the *work* into play in the fashioning of the whole" (Kreyling 1999: 25). Laying on the beach and enjoying the drowsy feeling that comes with extensive sun exposure, the narrator is present in two worlds at the same time, the world of her dreams and the contrastive reality of the loud family. By fusing these two worlds, the story "invites readers to forge connections between parallel narratives, the narrative of young love and the narrative of initiation into the physicality of sex and love, death and decay of the body" (ibid.: 28).

In both "A Visit of Charity" and "A Memory" Welty depicts youthful female characters in borderline situations that challenge their very knowledge about what life is, confronting them with rather dreadful "examples of what was to come" in life. What is more, by focusing on 'typically female' aspects of the initiation process, both stories are excellent examples of the genre of stories of female initiation as outlined by Elaine Ginsberg (1975) and Ina Bergmann (2003; 2011): In "A Visit of Charity," the emphasis is on the process of aging as it affects female identity. The story highlights and problematizes social conceptions of aging women, for example by describing the old ladies in animal terms. Therefore, the story can also be read as a critique of the institutionalization of old age in American society as a result of the increasing temporalization of biography, and the presentation of the cantankerous elderly ladies as society's locked away contrasts sharply with the youthful mobility of the protagonist. Similarly, in "A Memory" youthful innocence and love of life are also contrasted with the decay and disillusionment of the world of adults. In both stories the female initiates involuntarily catch a glimpse of adult life that challenges their very life knowledge, just as it urges the reader to reflect on how this knowledge is culturally construed, not least in the form of stories.

Throughout the 20th century, and well into the new millennium, the story of initiation has thrived as one of the most productive subgenres of the short story. While the theme of initiation has proved to be a rather stable anthropological constant, the cultural contexts and instantiations of the theme have changed significantly with the respective societal transformations. A form dedicated to the moment of epistemological uncertainty rather than solution, the story of initiation has thus served as a medium in which socio-cultural notions of life as a temporal project are being critically reflected.

A good case in point for both the continuing productivity *and* its malleability is Junot Díaz's short story cycle *Drown*, published in 1996. In its opening piece, "Ysrael", Díaz narrates the story of two brothers who are stuck in their transcultural life world, which is marked by "poverty and a fraught relationship to a father"

(Perez 2007: 105) who is conspicuously absent. The story is told by Yunior, the nine-year-old autodiegetic narrator, who relates in retrospect how he used to spend his summers together with his older brother Rafa at their aunt and uncle's in the 'campo', i.e. the Dominican countryside, while their mother and father worked in a chocolate factory in Santo Domingo and in New York, respectively. Ysrael always wears a mask to conceal his disfigured face because "when he was a baby a pig had eaten his face off, skinned it like an orange" ("Ysrael," 4). Although only a child with a terrible fate, Ysrael has become a kind of bogeyman in this part of the country: "He was something to talk about, a name that set the kids to screaming, worse than el Cuco or la Vieja Calusa" (ibid.: 4) Like "el Cuco" and "la Vieja Calusa", two mythical monsters from Latin American folklore, Ysrael embodies the people's irrational and exaggerated fears.

Focusing on one particular day, the story culminates in an encounter between the two boys and Ysrael at the end of which the brothers overpower Ysrael and pull the mask off him in order to catch a glance of his mutilated face. Here is the narrator's shocking description of the sight, creating what Renate Brosch (2007) would refer to as the result of 'configurative reading', i.e. the strong, lasting visual image that evokes an affective stance on the part of the recipient and dominates his or her memory of this story:

> His left ear was a nub and you could see the thick veined slab of his tongue through a hole in his cheek. He had no lips. His head was tipped back and his eyes had gone white and the cords were out on his neck. He'd been an infant when the pig had come into the house. The damage looked old but I still jumped back and said, Rafa, let's go! Rafa crouched and using only two of his fingers, turned Ysrael's head from side to side. ("Ysrael," 14)

The horrid scene at the end of the story centers on the powerful visual image of Ysrael lying motionless in the dirt, and Rafa cruelly turning his head in order to examine the terrible scars that the pig has left in his face. Building up to this final moment of revelation – the revelation of Ysrael's 'real' identity by pulling off his mask –, the sight of the boy's badly disfigured face is not only the climax of the story's action, but arguably the reason for the narrator to tell the story in the first place. Moreover, it leaves many questions to the reader: Is Ysrael dead? What caused the unabashed violence with which the twelve-year-old (!) Rafa beats up Ysrael? Is it, as Richard Perez suggests, that the "elaborate scars of Ysrael's face represent the internal damage that Rafa carries from his father's abandonment. His father is the ruthless pig, a cannibal, leaving his devoured children to meet the world alone" (2007: 109)?

To the best of my knowledge, Díaz' memorable story has so far not been read as a story of initiation, yet it shares many of the characteristic features of the genre as outlined by Freese (1999c: 184): The initiate is, of course, Yunior, who undertakes a journey leading him from innocence (or ignorance) to experience and confronting him with the hitherto unknown world. His journey quite typically begins early one morning ("the roosters were screaming," "Ysrael," 6) when his aunt and uncle, or *tío* and *tía* – the representatives of authority – are still sleeping, and the journey comes much to the narrator's surprise: "I kept expecting Rafa to send me home and the longer we went without speaking, the more excited I became." He is accompanied or rather guided on this journey by his brother Rafa, whose role in the initiation process seems somewhat ambiguous. Rafa may be best described as both the mentor and tempter figure at the same time: In absence of their father, who lives in 'Nueva York' in order to support the family, it is Rafa who introduces the protagonist to the secrets of life: "He was handsome and spoke out of the corner of his mouth. I was too young to understand most of what he said, but I listened to him anyway, in case these things might be useful in the future." (ibid.: 4) In this passage Rafa almost appears as a surrogate father to whom the narrator looks up with reverence and admiration. Although he is too young to understand the full meaning of Rafa's words, he is aware that these words refer to an unknown world beyond the narrator's knowledge. However, Rafa is also the one who tempts Yunior to meet Ysrael and thus drives him towards the recognition of the ugliness and brutality of life, represented by Ysrael's face: "That's something we got to check out. I hear it's bad" (ibid.: 5).[5]

Moreover, like in "I Want to Know Why" and many other (male)b stories of initiation, sexuality plays an important role in Díaz' story. Again, it is Rafa who introduces the narrator to the world of adult sexuality, although he is still a child himself: "He'd take the campo girls down to the dams to swim and if he was lucky they let him put it in their mouth or in their asses. He'd done La Muda that way for almost a month before her parents heard about it and barred her from leaving the house forever." (ibid.: 3) What might strike readers as a particularly precocious and perverted sexuality is in fact a 'normal' part of the boys' reality: Rafa tells

5 This ambiguity of Rafa's role in the initiation process is also reflected by the narrator when he talks about their brotherly relationship, which changes according to the respective environment: "In the Capital Rafa and I fought so much that our neighbors took to smashing broomsticks over us to break it up, but in the campo it wasn't like that. In the campo we were friends." ("Ysrael," 3)

boastful stories about "tetas and chochas and leche"[6] (ibid.: 3) and teenage girls who got pregnant, while Yunior listens, internalizing his brother's notions of sexuality just like Rafa must have learned it from his 'mentors'. On their bus ride to Barbacoa, a stranger sits next to Yunior, and when he spots a stain on Yunior's shorts offers his 'help': "He spit in his fingers and started to rub at the stain but then he was pinching at the tip of my pinga through the fabric of my shorts. He was smiling. I shoved him against his seat. He looked to see if anybody had noticed." (ibid.: 8-9) This unobserved act of sexual harassment of a nine-year-old boy in a public place amidst other people is as shocking as the other depictions of sexuality in the story.

Maybe the most important element that characterizes Diaz' story as a story of initiation, however, is the final 'shock of recognition' already hinted at in the passage above. For Yunior, who tells this story retrospectively, the sight of Ysrael's mutilated face coincides with the moment of his initiation, a moment that is marked by the sudden realization of a hitherto unknown reality and that arguably changes his life forever, although the story remains silent about the concrete effects on his later life. One may argue that the epiphanic moment of the story reveals a knowledge about the oppressed history of the Dominican people: "The epiphany of the face reveals that beneath the mask lies [sic] – individual, familial, and colonial – mutilatons [sic], forcing one into new dimensions with oneself and with the world." (Perez 2007: 110) What Yunior sees on this day is not only the mangled face of a child, but the brutal reality of a country in which poverty drives people to extremes: parents who neglect their children because they have to work long hours and seek jobs in the U.S.; people who are exploited by the Western world whose wealth they ensure; children who act like little adults, with a premature, perverted sexuality, and who have to learn how to stay alive in a harsh environment at the age of nine. In such a society, the story seems to suggest, the romanticized Western concept of childhood does not apply: initiation happens at a very young age, and its consequences are as brutal as they are final.

In this context, the ripping off of Ysrael's mask becomes a metaphoric act, the "disillusioning discovery" (Freese 1999c: 184) that typically reveals the discrepancy between appearance and reality in stories of initiation and stands at the core of the story's epistemological process. Ysrael's violent unmasking thus symbolizes the transition from innocence to experience for Yunior. It is important to note in this respect that Ysrael's mask resembles those of the *lucha libre* wrestlers, and

6 Whereas *tetas* hardly needs any translation at all, according to the *Urban Dictionary* *chocha* translates as 'pussy' and *leche* – meaning 'milk' in standard Spanish – as semen.

that it therefore carries strong cultural meaning as well. In this context, it is significant that the narrator's first encounter with Ysrael coincides with the dropping of leaflets from a plane, advertising a particularly important wrestling match ("Ysrael," 4). *Lucha libre* is an enormously popular form of free-style wrestling in the Spanish-speaking parts of South and Middle America characterized by the spectacular, high-flying maneuvers of the *luchadores* as well as their colorful masks, which conceal the fighters' real identities. The defeated wrestler's loss of the mask is regarded as the ultimate insult – especially in so-called wager matches (*luchas de apuestas*) –, as Mark Bondurant (2004: n.p.) explains:

> To wear it is to defy the opposition, to deny them your identity and assume the traits symbolized by the mask itself. To lose it is to be forever humbled before your foe, and to be exposed as being too human. The moment of unmasking is the point of highest dramatic tension in Lucha Libre; it is conducted with an air of respect and dignity fitting the instant of ultimate revelation.

Rafa's violent act against the social misfit Ysrael flouts the ethical practices and codex of of *lucha libre* wrestling. There is neither respect nor dignity in his brutal humiliation of his 'opponent', as Rafa breaks the rules of the game both by using an illegal weapon (the Coca Cola bottle) and by ripping off completely his opponent's mask. The Coca Cola bottle – probably the most striking image of United States capitalism and cultural imperialism – therefore symbolizes the corruption of Dominican cultural values through the absent-present hegemonic American society. It becomes symptomatic of the cultural context the story hones in on, representing the detrimental "after-effects of a Caribbean economy brutalized by postcolonial relations wherein life's sweets are unevenly distributed to others" (Perez 2007: 106).

This cultural reference to *lucha libre* and its infiltration or contamination by American values thus complicates "Ysrael" as a story of initiation, since it poses questions about cultural identity in addition to the personal initiation of the narrator. Lyn di Iorio Sandín suggests that "in many contemporary U.S. Latino/a works of fiction, the violent death of a double character [...] represents ambivalence about U.S. Latino/a identity, an ambivalence most often resolved through violence and the 'killing' off of the character associated with the Hispanic origin" (2007: 15). Hence, Ysrael becomes a typical scapegoat and his – at least metaphorical – death stands as the ultimate symbol for Yunior's initiation into the harsh reality of Dominican-American migrants, preparing him for his 'new life' in the United

States, which is also the stuff for the subsequent stories in *Drown*.[7] However, the fact that "the autobus was heading for Ocoa, not for home" ("Ysrael," 15) suggests that Yunior's initiation is not completed – the initiate is not to reenter society yet, his journey must continue.

Tracing the generic development of the story of initiation in America, Freese (1999c) discriminates between various aspects of the initiation process in different stories, from Hawthorne's "My Kinsman, Major Molineux" to Anderson's "I Want to Know Why" to Oates's "How I Contemplated the World..." If the representation of the protagonist's initiation in Hawthorne's story is dominated by a theological aspect and Anderson's by a psychological one, we might argue that what is most important in "Ysrael" is a postcolonial aspect. The story's central question, we might ask with Richard Perez, is the following: "What is it in Ysrael's mutilated face they need to see?" (Perez 2007: 105) In other words, what is the 'lesson in life knowledge' that derives from this sight for the narrator Yunior? As Richard Perez puts it somewhat awkwardly: "Interestingly, to see, hear, and touch are important conduits of knowledge that the story becomes increasingly aware of." (Perez 2007: 106) The story's life knowledge unfolds on many different layers, integrating questions of ethics, personal and collective identity, as well as culturally specific norms and rules for living together.

* * *

As the foregoing examples have shown, the story of initiation has emerged and thrived as a preeminent subgenre of the modern short story form in America. Concerned with a crisis moment – the existential moment between innocence and experience or knowledge – in the life of its protagonist, the story of initiation stands metonymically for the short story in general, and for the ways in which it handles knowledge in particular. Stories of initiation demonstrate how the short story revolves around life-changing experiences and turning points, and how the acquisition of life knowledge becomes a key element in these stories, both at the story and discourse level as well as at the level of reception. The short story's aesthetic setup provides an ideal medium for presenting human life not as a consistent sequence of episodes and chapters (i.e. the life-course model), but as a fragmented

7 Although there is some evidence for Ysrael's death (e.g. Rafa's cold remark that the doctors "aren't going to do shit to him."), the story remains ambiguous about whether Rafa really killed Ysrael or not. This question, however, strikes me as marginal, since it does not have an effect on the interpretation of the scene as a symbolic killing of the Latino identity.

narrative that requires the reader to construct meaning by combining two modes of knowledge, story and projection. The next two chapters will explore how similar aesthetico-epistemological patterns are at work in stories that give shape to another life phase: the 'story of midlife crisis' and the 'story of unlived life' as representative subgenres of the short story which embody cultural notions of the precariousness of existence in adulthood/maturity.

9. Midlife Crisis as Turning Point for the 'Mature Moderns':

John Cheever's "The Country Husband"

> Life is a vexatious trap; when a thinking man reaches maturity and attains to full consciousness he cannot help feeling that he is in a trap from which there is no escape.
> (Anton Chekhov)

It is impossible to fully understand the 20th-century American short story without taking into account the inestimable role of one of its major sites for publication: *The New Yorker*. Founded in 1925 by Harold Ross and his wife Jane Grant, *The New Yorker* intended to address a decidedly metropolitan audience and their socio-cultural life worlds (see Boddy 2010: 37). From its very beginnings, the magazine included non-fictional writing as well as fiction, poetry, and other genres like cartoons or satire. Very soon, the magazine became the unrivaled forum in the US for many of the most important short story writers of their time, including James Thurber, John O'Hara, Eudora Welty, Vladimir Nabokov, J.D. Salinger, John Updike, Donald Barthelme, Joyce Carol Oates, and Alice Munro, to name but a few of the magazine's favorite authors. To have a story published in *The New Yorker* often meant the beginning of a successful career, and numerous acclaimed writers have commented in interviews on their many ineffective attempts and their struggles with the magazine's fiction editors, who are notorious for their rigor and fastidiousness. Whether or not it is justifiable to speak of a distinct *New Yorker*-style, the impact of the magazine on the course of the short story since the late 1920s is largely undisputed. As Kasia Boddy avers, the magazine "grew steadily in circulation, advertising revenue and influence throughout the 1930s and 1940s and by mid-century, it had become 'a totem for the educated American middle and upper-middle classes'" (2010: 37).

The nation's preeminent forum for short fiction, *The New Yorker* has also significantly contributed to the launching and disseminating of certain thematic preferences and aesthetic ideals that have become the trademark of some of the most important short story writers of the 20th-century, and has thus influenced the development of the genre as such.[1] By "preferring stories to be grounded in recognisable aspects of contemporary life" (Boddy 2010: 39), for example, the magazine has favored the (sub-)urban realism of John Updike, John Cheever, or Raymond Carver over the more allegorical and fantastic writing of, say, Flannery O'Connor (see ibid.: 37). *New Yorker* stories, even in the surrealist version of Donald Barthelme, are usually marked by a distinct, recognizable connection to the life-world of their middle-class metropolitan readers, reflecting their social and cultural standards, often in a rather satirical and self-deprecating manner. As Thomas Leitch succinctly remarks, particularly the stories of the generations of O'Hara, Cheever, and Updike "worked by chastising the social and cultural pretensions of an upscale milieu that somehow survived every revelation that destroyed so many of its fictional scapegoats" (1997: 145).

One of the main outlets for short fiction in the 20th century, the *New Yorker* thus exerted a tremendous influence on the development of the North American short story that includes not only the favored subject matters and formal choices, but also the ways in which short stories are the product of a particular zeitgeist and collective literary sensibility. Like the Iowa writer's workshop, which brought forth many masters of the short story from Flannery O'Connor to ZZ Packer and thus 'institutionalized' the genre, the *New Yorker* also contributed to the collective notion about what constitutes a good short story. The 'typical' *New Yorker* story is the product of a literary community "generated by a moment of interaction between editor[s], author[s], genre, and culture, rather than by an isolated author" (Levy 1993: 118). It is in this sense that the stories, essays, and other texts published in the magazine become representative examples of the discourse about 'American life' in the 20th century – at least as far as a white and dominantly male middle-class environment is concerned.

Given this enormous popularity of the magazine and its influence on the self-fashioning of well-heeled Americans, it is not surprising that *The New Yorker* has recently been used by historians as a source to study the lives and attitudes of the

1 On '*New Yorker*-type stories' and their influence on contemporary American short-story writing see Levy (1993: 118-20) and particularly Leitch (1997) who offers a very detailed and well-researched account of the magazine's history, its politics and aesthetics, its role in defining what a short story is, as well as the different stages in the development of the *New Yorker* short story.

American (upper) middle class in the mid-20th century (see Boddy 2010: 40). By 1950, *The New Yorker* had become an important public site of discourse in which cultural notions of what it means to live a 'good life' were negotiated and life models were both reflected and invented (see Levy 1993: 118). The magazine's fictional and non-fictional contributions have arguably shaped the collective consciousness and affected cultural notions of the life course, models of behavior, lifestyles, and the values and norms of generations of middle-class Americans. More particularly, many of the recurrent themes of *New Yorker* stories pertain to what one could call the middle-aged anxiety of 20th-century Americans, i.e. the "social and psychological difficulties attributed to middle age, specifically the anxieties attending the recognition of oneself as belonging to a supposedly mature generation" (Dawson 2009: 253).

John Cheever, easily one of the most prolific and critically acclaimed American short story writers of the 20th century, is one of the figureheads of this 'type' of story. Alongside his long-time friend and literary rival John Updike, Cheever has cultivated to a great degree what is frequently called the *New Yorker* style, although he himself refused this label for its obvious artistic limitations.[2] Like John O'Hara and especially Updike, Cheever is most famous for his meticulous literary portraits of the (white Anglo-Saxon) American middle-class, depicting life in suburbia with its very peculiar shallowness, absurdity, and the latent unhappiness and human drama that pervade it.[3] His stories often deal with what James Warren aptly calls "moment[s] of heightened moral consciousness" (2001: 201), situations which seem to appear out of the blue and which are brought about by the "grueling pace and pressures" (ibid.: 200) that underlie modern life in the mid-20th-century, middle-class United States. In the typical Cheever story, there is a "low-keyed repetitiveness of suburban sadness" (Boddy 2010: 45), and particularly a mourning of the loss of youth: "Cheever shares with Fitzgerald a luxuriant melancholy about lost youth and a rueful admiration for futile attempts to stop time." (ibid.: 49)

First published in *The New Yorker* in the November issue of 1954 and decorated with the O. Henry prize for the best short story one year later, "The Country Husband" is a typical Cheever story in many respects, and one that arguably stands

2 Cheever has published more than two thirds (141 of 180) of his short stories in *The New Yorker* (see Warren 2001: 199).

3 Cheever himself, however, had a more universalist understanding of his stories, as Scott Donaldson (2002: 141) reminds us: "The stories were not *about* suburbia, Cheever would insist: they were about men and women and children and dogs who happened to live there."

out as one of his finest achievements, although it is probably less popular than "The Enormous Radio" or "The Swimmer."[4] Like many other of Cheever's characters, the protagonist Francis Weed is clearly one of those 'fictional scapegoats' which epitomize the middle-class neuroses but are ultimately sacrificed in order to maintain the lifestyle of the upscale milieu. With its explicit, masterful treatment of the protagonist's struggle with what Chekhov has called the 'vexatious trap' of adult life, "The Country Husband" represents a subgenre of the short story dealing with the social-psychological phenomenon of the midlife crisis, thus epitomizing the genre's focus on life-changing experiences and turning points.

More importantly, however, as I would like to argue in the following, Cheever's story – as a representative of many other stories of that kind that have filled the pages of *The New Yorker* over the past decades – engages in the production and dissemination of a highly age-, class-, and gender-specific 'life knowledge' insofar as it constructs and popularizes the very concept of 'midlife crisis' among a predominantly WASP readership. The story's theme, if broken down to its most basic elements, resembles the prototypical narrative that underlies the concept of midlife crisis in Western societies, understood as the period of self-doubt and desperation that frequently befalls individuals, especially men, in the third quarter of their life, and that is usually associated with a certain discontent regarding the professional situation as well as a profound unhappiness in private life. One could argue, therefore, that Cheever's story stands at the peak of a socio-historical development that had begun some decades earlier as a response to the social upheavals of modernism. As Melanie Dawson maintains, middle age as a distinct generational category in the life-course model (and in literature) emerged in the 1920s-30s, when the "mature moderns" struggled with "adjusting cognitively and emotionally to their dispossession of youth": "Whereas younger adults could look to the vital experiences of courtship, job-seeking, marriage, procreation, and initial success, the mature moderns, who had their crucial decisions about life decades earlier, appear set in patterns that are cast as mundane and unfulfilling." (2009: 254) From this vantage, middle age and its accompanying life crises are the symptoms of a socio-psychological reality, namely the "fragmentation, discontinuity, and performativity of modern life" and particularly the "recognition that life is passing one by" (ibid.: 255).

The *Oxford English Dictionary* defines a midlife crisis as "an emotional crisis of self-confidence or identity that can occur in early middle age, associated with the idea that one is growing old or that life is passing one by; also in extended

4 According to Donaldson (1995: 133), Vladimir Nabokov listed "The Country Husband" as his personal favorite of all American short stories.

use." Interestingly enough, the term or rather concept 'midlife crisis' itself was only coined in 1965 by the Canadian psychoanalyst Elliott Jacques, and thus a good decade after the publication of Cheever's story. Jacques begins his pioneering essay by conceding that there are several 'critical phases' in the course of the development of individuals, and that one of these critical phases occurs around the age of 35. In the following, I will analyze how Cheever's story already stages the cultural phenomenon of the midlife crisis long before it emerged as a concept in the social sciences, and argue that this exemplifies the short story's cultural work in reflecting and shaping a certain life knowledge, particularly with regard to the temporality of life that is aesthetically foregrounded in 'moments of truth'. Linking an individual, fictional story to a wider social phenomenon, Cheever's story exemplifies the short story's intricate interrelation with other forms and discourses of cultural, but also (social-)scientific life knowledge.

"The Country Husband" is set in the locale that Cheever is best known for – the prototypical suburbia as the new American 'countryside', as the title ironically suggests. Shady Hill is a commuter town in the New York area, a place of (pseudo-)colonial mansions and pleasant front gardens, cocktail parties and tennis matches, retriever dogs, and bird-feeding stations. Portraying the middle-class life in Shady Hill with all its peculiarities and curious details, "The Country Husband" supports James Warren's claim that Cheever is "essentially a realist writer of manners" (Warren 2001: 200): What we find in the story is a minute, beautifully stylized depiction of life in an American suburb, with all its typical stock characters, events, and props. Stylistically, the story is an apt example of a central ambiguity in Cheever's writing, namely the ambiguity between ironical distance and a deep sympathy for the characters' existential struggles and their motivations. At times, the narrator seems to mock the grotesque artificiality and superficiality of life in Shady Hill, as in the following passage:

> The Weed's Dutch Colonial house was larger than it appeared to be from the driveway [...] The largest part of the living room centered on a fireplace. On the right were some bookshelves and a piano. The room was polished and tranquil, and from the window that opened to the west there was some late-summer sunlight, brilliant and as clear as water. Nothing here was neglected; nothing had not been burnished. [...] The hearth was swept, the roses on the piano were reflected in the polish of the broad top, and there was an album of Schubert waltzes on the rack. ("The Country Husband", 326)

The large living room is merely a decorum, emptied of any actual 'living' and instead putting the fetishes and status symbols of middle-class life on display. Although the narrator describes the composed order of the Weed's domicile with some ironic distance, indicating how surface and appearance are eventually more important than substance, however, he never betrays his characters by divulging them to the readers' contempt or ridicule. The circumstances of their lives might seem odd to the reader – especially a present-day reader –, but their feelings, actions, and moral decisions in these situations are utterly comprehensible.[5]

What underlies "The Country Husband" as well as numerous other of Cheever's stories is therefore the sometimes tragic and sometimes comic attempts of the characters in their struggles to come to terms with their middle-class existence. As James Warren put it:

> The corollary of Cheever's notion of an abiding moral foundation for human existence is that the grueling pace and pressures of modern life often cause people to lose touch with that foundation. Their struggles to understand their position and gain or regain balance and a measure of happiness are the central concern of a number of his best stories. (2000: 200)

Temporalization and the "grueling pace and pressures of modern life" are the major themes of Cheever's story, and we can see once again how the short story functions as a medium that, because of its aesthetic-epistemological setup, lends itself particularly well to addressing these issues. In this respect, "The Country Husband" can be regarded as a quintessential expression of its writer's "deepening dissatisfaction with modern life" (Donaldson 2002: 201). Cheever's heartfelt contempt for modern America's materialism, its bigotry and ethical decay, and its "excessive mobility and rootlessness" (ibid.) surface fiercely in this story.

The story has been equally criticized and hailed for the complexity and diversity of its plot and themes. It begins with the depiction of the emergency landing of an airplane in which Francis Weed, the protagonist, travels home from a business trip. Although Francis had been in heavy weather before, the narrator reveals that "he had never been shaken up so much" ("The Country Husband," 325), thus already alluding to the existential crisis that Francis is going to live through. Children start to cry, the cabin lights go out, and all the adult passengers "saw in their minds the spreading wings of the Angel of Death" (ibid.). However, the catastrophe is averted as the emergency landing succeeds: "Nothing happened," (ibid.: 326) and so Francis takes the train to New York, almost as if nothing really hap-

5 In a similar vein, Scott Donaldson (1995: 136-7) remarks that Cheever "does not demand that we identify with Shady Hill's Johnny Hake or Cash Bentley or Francis Weed, but he does expect us to care about what happened to them, for in their particular distress they take on a measure of universality."

pened. When Francis comes home to tell his friends and family about this terrifying experience, however, no one listens to him as they are absorbed by their own business: His friend and colleague, Trace Bearden, hears the story but remains unperturbed, since "Francis had no powers that would let him re-create a brush with death" (ibid.). Weed's wife and kids, who "[n]ine times out of ten" (ibid.: 327) would greet him with affection at his return, are completely "absorbed in their own antagonisms" (ibid.): While the smaller children tussle with each other, his wife Julia is too immersed in her household routines to recognize her husband's despair. At the dinner table, Francis even "says loudly that he has been in a plane crash and that he is tired" (ibid.), but still nobody pays attention to him. His oldest daughter is engrossed in her *True Romance* magazine (which makes Francis go at her, since he despises such trivial readings); his youngest son keeps crying for no apparent reason and despite his father's promises of an exciting story ("Daddy was in a plane crash this afternoon, Toby. Don't you want to hear about it?" ibid.: 328). Upset by so much familial neglect, Francis then admonishes his wife for not preparing an earlier dinner for the children, thereby escalating the whole situation, with everyone drifting away from the battlefield and Francis escaping to the garden to have a cigarette.

The next day, the Weeds are invited to one of the frequent parties at the Farquarsons. When they get home after the party, Francis waits in the car to take the babysitter home and is stunned when instead of the expected old Mrs. Henlein a young and beautiful girl named Anne Murchison walks out of the door. Still upset by the plane crash and the following lack of interest displayed by his friends and family, Francis immediately falls in love with the girl – a prototypical American beauty – and is even kissed by her after driving her home. When Francis gets home, Julia and the children are asleep and he indulges in sweet dreams about the babysitter, "crossing the Atlantic with her on the old *Mauretania* and, later, living with her in Paris" (ibid.: 333). On the following morning, the dreams are all gone but what remains is the feeling that he "had been bitten gravely" (ibid.). The girl has shattered the seeming security of his home: "His spirits were feverish and high. The image of the girl seemed to put him into a relationship to the world that was mysterious and enthralling." (ibid.) When he is on the way to work the following day, he watches a passing train and sees an "unclothed woman of exceptional beauty" (ibid.: 334) sitting at one of the windows, "combing and combing her hair" (ibid.). This sight fills him with enthusiastic feelings of sexual desire and youth, and for a moment he breaks out of the narrow confines of his orderly middle-class life, insulting an old lady who squabbles about some curtains she had bought a few days ago and now wants to return since they don't match her living-room windows.

With "his appetite for life" (ibid.) thus quickened, Francis feels rejuvenated and liberated from the dullness of his life and the onerous burdens of Shady Hill: "The autumnal loves of middle age are well publicized, and he guessed that he was face to face with one of these, but there was not a trace of autumn in what he felt." (ibid.: 334-5.) He dreams about the girl who brings "back into his life something like the sound of music" (ibid.: 334), but at the same time he is concerned that anyone might find out and condemn him for this moral misbehavior. Nobody in Shady Hill, it seems to him, has ever committed a crime like that before, in fact "there had not even been a breath of scandal" (ibid.: 335). Just in the moment when he brushes aside those concerns and kisses Anne Murchison, he is found out by Gertrude Flannery, a girl who is known for her forays into other people's houses. After this incident, Francis more than ever indulges in his reveries and gradually loses his grip on reality, even more so when he finds out that Anne Murchison is engaged to a young (and, according to Francis, imbecile) lad from Shady Hill.

The would-be affair leads to a deep rupture in Francis's life. When his wife one day accuses him of acting selfish, wrecking "anyone's happiness" (ibid.: 340) and so putting at stake the life they had struggled so hard to achieve, Francis loses his temper and slaps her in the face. In the argument that follows, Julia Weed threatens to leave her husband, accusing him further of not loving her. However, after he repeatedly begs her not to leave, she gives in to him rather easily: "'I guess I'd better stay and take care of you for a little while longer', she said." (ibid.: 342) The next morning, Francis sees "the girl" on his way to work and follows her across the platform and through the cars of the train and shouting her name. When he reaches the girl, however, he is surprised to find that it is not Anne Murchison, but "and older woman wearing glasses" (ibid.: 343). Soon after this, his secretary tells him that she won't work for him any longer, and Francis realizes that his life has come to a serious crisis: "He was in trouble. He had been lost once in his life, coming back from a trout stream in the north woods, and he had now the same bleak realization that no amount of cheerfulness or hopefulness or valor or perseverance could help him find, in the gathering dark, the path that he'd lost." (ibid.: 344)

The story ends after Francis has decided to see a psychiatrist in order to get his life together again. As part of the therapy, Francis builds a coffee table, finding "some true consolation" (ibid.: 345) in the "holy smell of new wood" as well as the simple forms and arithmetic of his woodwork. Apparently, everything has gone back to normal: Francis is happy again, his children are crying, his neighbor is shouting at the squirrels in the bird-feeding station. It seems that all traces of Francis's midlife crisis have dissolved again; "[h]is near-brush with death brought him close to the temptation of truly great dreams, but now his restlessness is cured," as Harold Bloom (2004: 74) remarks.

There are two central events that trigger Francis' midlife crisis and at the same time identify it as a typical phenomenon of modern life: (1) the near plane crash that causes Francis to question his composed, dispassionate middle-class existence in Shady Hill and (2) the subsequent party at the Farquarsons, where the shell-shocked Francis recognizes the Norman woman whose public punishment he had witnessed during his time as a soldier in WWII (and it is after this reencounter that he sees Anne Murchison for the first time). This bleak scene is staged rather graphically in the story by means of a flashback: Under the gaze of the gathered town community, the mayor of Trenon reads out the accusation and sentence, and soon after this a "little man with a gray mustache" ("The Country Husband," 330) begins to shave the woman's skull, before she is made to take off her clothes. When the prisoner stands naked and bald before the crowd, the women "jeered" (ibid.) whereas the men remain silent. The jeering only "ended gradually, put down by the recognition of their common humanity" (ibid.: 331). With these war-memories coming back to him, Francis all of a sudden feels removed from his family and his seemingly carefree life in Shady Hill. As the narrator relates, their lives are based on their "tacit claim that there had been no past, no war – that there was no danger or trouble in the world" (ibid.). The horrid memory of the woman's public chastisement at once disrupts the artificial peace of Weed's Shady Hill existence, triggering his identity crisis.

Apart from their function as drivers of the plot, these two events have an important symbolical function as they contextualize "The Country Husband" in the distinct life-world of post-WWII-America. Whereas the plane crash signals the pace, uprootedness, and unpredictability of modern life as well as America's belief in technological progress and the vulnerability thereof, the war episode represents the deep feeling of unsettledness and epistemological skepticism that marks modern life in the 'age of anxiety' and that still overshadows the material affluence of the 1950s American economy. As Susanne Rohr has pointed out, American literature of this era is marked by a rather pessimistic tone:

> the crisis of individual identity; the ensuing feeling that the individual's actions are devoid of significance or meaning; a profound philosophical uncertainty concerning the true nature of man as a result of the most recent and deeply disturbing, if not traumatizing historical events […] and the fear that the sense of historical continuity that had hitherto provided reliable orientation had vanished, leaving the individual vulnerable and adrift. (2011: 274)

Taken together, the near plane crash and the war episode symbolically allude to the modern origins of the midlife crisis as a concept in the human life-course: one the one hand, the acceleration of life and the changing conception of the human life-course model, and the traumatizing historical events of the war that have produced a deep and profound uncertainty. Of course, it is no coincidence that Francis is confronted with his own past and the things in his life that he would rather forget about during a cocktail party, a locale that embodies the lifestyle of the 1950s American middle-class better than anything else: This is the occasion at which which the middle-class celebrates itself and its material achievements. In the fatal security of the party, the Second World War emerges as an uncanny presence that underlies Francis' (and everybody else's) life in Shady Hill. At first, Francis only recognizes a certain familiarity in the Farquarson's new maid without being able to specify on where or when he had seen her before. As the narrator relates, Francis' memory "was something like his appendix – a vestigial repository" ("The Country Husband," 330), and he has been extraordinarily successful escaping his past. Francis becomes the embodiment of cultural amnesia, a figure of a modern America that wants to forget, a new version of Jay Gatsby. It is only when he asks Nellie Farquarson about their new maid that he realizes where they had met before: now it dawns on him that this is the woman he had seen at the end of World War II in the Norman city of Trenon, where she had been publicly chastised for having lived with a Nazi commandant.

The woman is the ghost from his past, haunting Francis in his burnished, tranquil home. As Francis remembers the woman from Normandy, he knows right away that there is no place for such memories in Shady Hill:

> He could not tell anybody. And if he had told the story now, at the dinner table, it would have been a social as well as a human error […] In the recorded history of human arrangements, this extraordinary meeting would have fallen into place, but the atmosphere of Shady Hill made the memory unseemly and impolite. (ibid.: 331)

In the constructed idyll of Shady Hill, no such human tragedies are tolerated, and so Francis' involuntary memory goes unnoticed by the other partygoers including his wife; nothing disturbs the pleasant, demonstratively happy atmosphere. Only Francis is left "feeling languid; it had opened his memory and his senses, and left them dilated" (ibid.).

What is striking, however, is that the repressed memory becomes the trigger of Francis's midlife crisis, thus implicitly pointing to the cultural specificity of the very concept of midlife crisis. It is only in a society marked by material affluence, loss of meaning and significance, and a collective suppression of the past that such radical crises can emerge. What is at stake for Francis is nothing less than the meaning of his life. His crisis is essentially a crisis of values. The circumstances of this crisis are to a great extent culturally and historically specific insofar as they are brought about by the social framework of the American upper middle class in the middle of the 20th century. What Cheever's story depicts, then, is as much a fictionalized individual story as it is a recording of a socio-cultural pathology. It seems that the very concept of the midlife crisis – as well as the story of midlife crisis as the literary manifestation thereof – are inextricably intertwined with the socio-cultural background that produced it.

One might even go so far as to argue that "The Country Husband" is a formative story that shaped the very concept midlife crisis, because it employs – or rather introduces – the narrative patterns that have been associated with middle-aged discontent ever since. First, stories of midlife crisis are typically concerned with a character's personal or private crisis, which, however, resonates with the public sphere and is imbued with socio-cultural meanings. Above all, Francis Weed's crisis results from the recognition of an (at least felt) irrelevance or even wastefulness of his life, brought about by some unexpected and disquieting incidents in the private sphere that have, however, deep social-historical roots and ramifications. Second, stories of midlife crisis typically feature a male protagonist in his 40s who leads a 'successful' life with material wealth and a seemingly intact social network. Third, the crisis itself is usually triggered by some life-turning incident ('significant incident'/'significant event', see Nünning 2012), i.e. the protagonist is involved in an incident that disrupts the tranquility or order of his life. In the narrative framework of stories of midlife crisis, this incident is clearly marked and thereby identified as the turning point, as in the opening paragraph of "The Country Husband": "To begin at the beginning, the airplane from Minneapolis in which Francis Weed was traveling East ran into heavy weather." ("The Country Husband," 325) Fourth, as a consequence of this upheaval, the protagonist comes to question his entire life, including his family and job situation, and seeks acknowledgement and recognition in this dramatic period of self-doubt. Fifth, the pattern of the midlife crisis narrative usually involves extra-marital affairs and sexual 'adventures', especially with younger partners, or at least a fantasizing about it. Here, Cheever's story can be seen as the prototype of the narrative of the middle-class suburban husband who seeks a loophole from his confined existence by indulging in fantasies (more than the reality) of having an affair with a beautiful young girl (we may think of Sam Mendes' and Alan Ball's *American Beauty* (1999) as a more recent instantiation of that pattern).[6] Finally, the crisis is temporarily limited, i.e. it must lead to a new constellation, either in form of a turning point or breach, or the restoration of the status quo (which is the case in Cheever's story).

In the context of the American society of the 20th century, the narrative of the midlife crisis has arguably become a dominant pattern to make sense of the changing socio-cultural climate and the many transitions in the private and working lives of middle-class Americans. In the fictional literature since the 1920s, at least, one can find evidence for this: "So pervasive is the narrative pattern of middle-aged discontent that few middle-aged figures escape the crippling effects of recognizing themselves as inhabiting generational categories." (Dawson 2009: 269) Literature, and particularly the short story has significantly contributed to the proliferation of these narrative patterns, but it arguably also plays an important part in scrutinizing and coming to terms with the social-psychological implications of middle-aged discontent and the notion of a midlife crisis.

The example of "The Country Husband" shows how and why midlife crisis narratives go far beyond the mere personal discontent of an individual. As Cheever's story suggests, the social phenomenon of the midlife crisis as well as the narrative conventions that created it must be understood as a symptom of an accelerated society. As Cheever's story serves to demonstrate, the narrative pattern of the midlife crisis is deeply entangled with late capitalist, postwar societal concerns, particularly with a blatant tension between moral values and traumatic experiences on the one hand, and fast economic growth and material wealth and abundance on the other. Moreover, Weed's midlife crisis is essentially depicted as the upshot of a desynchronization of the different temporal dimensions of life in the late modern US-American society, in which the increasing acceleration of his everyday work life stands in stark contrast to the artificial, tranquil world of Shady Hills. As a symbol of this desynchronization, the plane (and the near crash of it) causes a severe adjustment disorder for the story's protagonist, especially through his deliberate suppression of the past, implied in Weed's involuntary memory of the castigated French woman. The 'grueling pace' and neatly structured sequences of everyday life in the artificial world of Shady Hill do not allow for any historical perspective, which would fundamentally jeopardize the constructed idyll of Suburbia.

Cheever's stories were hugely popular during the 1950s to 1980s, and their publication in *The New Yorker* has arguably contributed to their wide cultural significance in terms of their impact on the lives of their readers. The story analyzed

6 Other typical behavioral patterns include the abuse of alcohol and a heightened consumerism.

in this chapter, "The Country Husband," served to illustrate how the short story – with its focus on crisis and turning point – works as a medium in which not only historically and culturally specific notions, and particularly the temporal patterns and sequences of life, are being made visible and negotiable. The story moreover demonstrates how literary 'life knowledge' is always bound to specific life-worlds, the models and ways of life and living together of a particular group, in this case the white American middle-class during the post-war era. Literary-historically speaking, "The Country Husband" can be seen as the culmination of a larger development in modern American literature, marked by the proliferation of dissatisfied, socially and psychologically troubled middle-aged characters. The proliferation of such characters, becoming more prominent since the 1920s, can be regarded as a direct upshot of the rise of youth culture, as Melanie Dawson has reminded us: "Their anxieties about ageing [...] reveal middle-aged characters' inability to come to terms with their generational positions during an era when age-specific categories and the behaviors linked to them became visible as a basic and observable element of modern culture." (2009: 253) With their emphasis on the moment of (mid-)life crisis in which these culturally induced anxieties and age-consciousness are brought to the surface, stories of midlife crisis engage in the cultural negotiation of life knowledge insofar as they explore the effects of modernization on the individual in general, and the life-patterns and temporal compartmentalization of life in particular. As "The Country Husband" shows, sometimes such literary life knowledge even predates and premediates the knowledge of other – in this case social-scientific discourses – by providing the narrative form through which a society comes to terms with its historical traumas, temporal practices, and time regimes.

10. Stories of 'Unlived' and Secret Lives:

Nathaniel Hawthorne, Sherwood Anderson, Henry James, and James Thurber

> Sighing I said to myself: What have I done in this world? I was created to live, and I am dying without having lived.
> (Jean-Jacques Rousseau, *Reveries of the Solitary Walker*)

It is a hallmark of literary fiction in general that it can provide us with an opportunity to imagine alternative lives which differ, to a greater or lesser extent, from our actual ones. As a matter of fact, this is part of the literary-anthropological explanation of why we read (and need) fiction: it allows us to transcend the confines of our comparatively narrow existences – to extend our selves as it were – by means of our imagination, a process that is enabled by the aesthetic structure of the text (see e.g. Iser 1989). By means of a more or less complete immersion into a literary text, readers are granted the privilege and potentially self-expanding experience of imagining a second, third, etc. life for themselves. From this vantage, all fiction is about 'unlived life' insofar as it makes this experience possible for the reader.

What the phrase 'stories of unlived life' in the heading of this chapter is supposed to signal, however, is something slightly different, namely the explicit thematization and literary staging of a 'life unled'. The idea of unlived life is a common theme in modern literature (see Engelberg 1989; Miller 2007; Hart 2011). As Engelberg (1989) contends, it became a widespread cultural phenomenon and literary motif in the 19th century. In its typical form it is presented as the belated, sorrowful recognition of a character that he or she has missed out on the opportunities of life and has therefore failed to achieve self-actualization – hence the title of Engelberg's book-length study of such narratives, *Elegiac Fictions*: Where elegies express the lamentation for the dead, in stories of unlived life it is the protagonist who bemoans his own impending death in light of the realization that he has never actually *lived* his life.

One might say that the life knowledge inherent in such stories of unlived life is a self-knowledge *ex negativo*: By realizing the void or meaninglessness in their lives, the tragic heroes of such narratives not only set up an example of what it means to 'waste' one's life due to false beliefs, wrong expectations or the lack of courage. By experiencing what it means to make the wrong decisions in life or to shy away from them at all, readers can potentially live through these situations and draw their own conclusions that may (or may not) be of use to them in similar situations in their own lives. But stories of unlived life also explore what it means – and how it feels – to become aware of this when it is already too late. Quite ironically, life knowledge in stories of unlived life is an untimely, even unwanted knowledge that does not seem to be of any help for the protagonists. Yet it may be useful to the reader as a kind of anticipatory knowledge, a warning even, providing the possibility to transfer the epistemological import of the story into the reader's own life narrative.

As a slight variation of this theme of *unlived* life, stories of *secret* life (or double lives) also deal with unfulfilled potentials, desires, and socio-cultural repression, and thus with the social power over life. More than stories of unlived life, however, stories of secret life tend to focus more or less explicitly on the tension between the individual and society, especially reflecting on how living in a modern society can forestall self-actualization and the sense of a 'fulfilled' life. When literary characters revert to secret lives, this often means that they cannot live out their potential 'actual lives' due to societal restrictions and role expectations. However, the protagonists of stories of secret life not necessarily consciously realize the shortcomings and wasted potentials of their 'actual' lives. Quite often, in fact, stories of secret life actually rely on the very tension between the protagonist's lack of understanding or knowledge and the presentation of his or her life through the transmission of an extradiegetic narrator, as in the example James Thurber's "The Secret Life of Walter Mitty".

Despite this distinction, it is hardly possible to neatly separate stories of unlived life from stories of secret life in terms of terminological or taxonomic precision. In fact, what stories of unlived and secret lives share in common is the potential to narratively instantiate the question of what constitutes a good, meaningful life by presenting dissuasive counter examples. Whereas in stories of unlived life the protagonists tend to be deprived of the 'good life' altogether, in stories of secret life such a good life takes place 'behind the back' of society. The epistemological value of these kinds of stories as genres that reflect and produce something like life knowledge resides in their function as thought experiments. They invite readers to imagine the unlived or secret life of a character and to compare this to their own, actual lives as well as the many unlived lives that may or may not exist in the readers' imagination.

An early example and influential model of a short story that centers on the motif of unlived/secret life is Nathaniel Hawthorne's "Wakefield" (1835). For no apparent reason, Hawthorne's eponymous character deserts his wife and, as the narrator relates, "took lodgings in the next street to his own house, and there, unheard of by his wife or friends, or without the shadow of a reason for such a self-banishment, dwelt upwards of twenty years" ("Wakefield," 1298). What is probably most remarkable about this story is that throughout the years of his absence from home, Wakefield beholds the life he decided not to live from only a short geographical and emotional distance. He "moves around a street corner and becomes a mere spectator of the life he might have lived" (Ruland/Bradbury 1992: 150) until one evening he enters his house "as from a day's absence, and became a loving spouse until death" ("Wakefield," 1298). As a variation of his literary predecessor Rip Van Winkle, Wakefield is away from home for twenty years before he returns, and like for Rip these years seem like a mere day to him. Yet whereas Rip's hiatus from his life is involuntary and results from supernatural powers, Wakefield consciously decides to go into hiding and become an observer of his life.

As a story of secret life, "Wakefield" expresses a number of universal themes, but also culturally specific notions of increasingly modern forms of life. As Ruland and Bradbury noted, the story is representative of Hawthorne's interest in the "complexities of isolation and the haunting need for the community of the human heart" (1992: 150). The motif of the unlived/secret life, therefore, serves to reflect on what it means to lose contact "with the warm flow of human life" (ibid.). Wakefield's experience of isolation and the narrator's extensive reflections thereof are intricately connected to the life-world in which the story takes place: the modern city, in this case London. Ingo Berensmeyer and Martin Spies point out that Wakefield's solitude "is not that of the hermit, the solitary person living apart from the rest of mankind for religious reasons; it is made possible by 'the crowd' [...], a completely new situation that Hawthorne's story explores" (2011: 115). In the context of the dawn of the modern city, "Wakefield" can be seen as an early literary representation of the anxieties of modern life as such, especially concerning the detrimental effects of anonymity and a loss of social contact that accompany the process of urbanization. The story therefore not only reverts to the notion of estrangement and alienation in the wake of American modernization that had also been the subject of Irving's "Rip Van Winkle", but it also foreshadows the fate of Melville's Bartleby (and with that the inexorable urbanization that led to the triplication of the population of New York in the two decades that lie between the publication of "Wakefield" and "Bartleby").

What is particularly interesting about the presentation of the theme or motif of the unlived or secret life in Hawthorne's piece is the strong presence of the narrator, who not only depicts Wakefield's fate as a 'twice-told tale' based on a newspaper report, but also indulges in copious comments and speculations about the motivations and reasons for the protagonist's strange behavior. What causes this man to stop living his life for twenty years? Or, in the words of the narrator: "What sort of man was Wakefield?" ("Wakefield," 1299) These questions no doubt stand in the center of the narrator's attention, since its outline, the 'bare facts' of the story, is told in just one paragraph:

> In some old magazine or newspaper, I recollect a story, told as truth, of a man – let us call him Wakefield – who absented himself for a long time, from his wife. The fact, thus abstractedly is not very uncommon, nor – without a proper distinction of circumstances – to be condemned either as naughty or nonsensical. Howbeit, this, though far from the most aggravated, is perhaps the strangest instance, on record, of marital delinquency; and, moreover, as remarkable a freak as may be found in the whole list of human oddities. The wedded couple lived in London. The man, under presence of going a journey, took lodgings in the next street to his own house, and there, unheard of by his wife or friends, and without the shadow of a reason for such self-banishment, dwelt upwards of twenty years. During that period, he beheld his home every day, and frequently the forlorn Mrs. Wakefield. And after so great a gap in his matrimonial felicity – when his death was reckoned certain, his estate settled, his name dismissed from memory, and his wife, long, long ago, resigned to her autumnal widowhood – he entered the door one evening, quietly, as from a day's absence, and became a loving spouse till death. (ibid.: 1298)

After this expositional summary, the major part of the story is devoted to a meticulous analysis of Wakefield's case, introduced by the narrator's invitation to the reader to ponder the question of what drove "poor Wakefield" to such extremes: "If the reader choose, let him do his own meditation." (ibid.) This, of course, is exemplary of Hawthorne's dictum to instruct rather than merely move the reader; it is an explicit incitement to investigate the moral psychology that underlies this peculiar story, and thus to read it on an allegorical level – or, as we might say, as a story of theoretical and practical life knowledge. Throughout the story, the narrator reminds and encourages the reader to find answers to the questions the story poses: "We are free to shape out our own idea [...]" (ibid.: 1299), "Let us now imagine [...]" (ibid.) etc. Hawthorne thus deliberately presents this story as a kind of literary thought experiment, emphasizing the hypothetic air of the narrative. It is on the reader to imaginatively explore the moral implications of the story's scenario. As the narrator concludes in the final paragraph: "He has left us much *food for thought*, a portion of which shall lend its wisdom to a moral, and be shaped into a figure." (ibid.: 1303, emphasis added, M.B.)

Knowledge, or what the narrator calls 'wisdom' and 'moral', is thus the ultimate goal of Hawthorne's literary thought experiment, which features a protagonist who becomes the signum or 'figure' of this knowledge. Wakefield embodies the perils of his time; he serves as a literary emblem to denote a central dilemma and a moral conflict of modern life in which, paradoxically, the individual is, at the same time, fully adjusted to and fully alienated from society:

> Amid the seeming confusion of our mysterious world, individuals are so nicely adjusted to a system, and systems to one another, and to a whole, that, by *stepping aside for a moment*, a man exposes himself to a fearful risk of losing his place forever. (ibid.: 1303, emphasis added, M.B.)

The somewhat enigmatic story of Wakefield's unlived life, then, mainly serves to point at something beyond itself, and that is the acceleration, alienation, and isolation of life in modernity. As a result of the increasing speed of life, Hawthorne suggests, the modern individual is trapped and, ultimately, doomed to keep pace with the speed of life. There is no time to 'step aside for a moment', or else the individual will suffer from isolation and social exclusion – which in the end amounts to an unlived or secret life. Strange and unbelievable as this story may seem, as an allegory of modern life it brings to the fore the effects of the temporalization of modern life. It is in this sense that "Wakefield", just like Irving's "Rip Van Winkle" and Fitzergerald's "Benjamin Button", engages in the reflection and production of a 'life knowledge' that is deeply embedded in, and responds to, the social and cultural reality of its time.

Hawthorne's remarkably modern story of unlived/secret life may help us to shed further light on the question of how literary texts, and especially short stories, engage in the cultural negotiation and production of life knowledge. Of course, the theme or motif of unlived life is not the exclusive domain of the short story genre but in fact a common subject of modern literature in general. Robert Frost's poem "The Road Not Taken" (1915), for example, famously stages the lyric persona's rueful reflection on the alternative road he might have taken in his life, thus dwelling on the widespread conceptual metaphor of life as a journey. It is conspicuous, however, that Frost's poem employs a strong narrative structure: The speaker relates how "[t]wo roads diverged in a yellow wood," and how he, after some reflection, decided for the less traveled one. The final stanza then presents the moral of the poem: "I shall be *telling* this with a sigh/ Somewhere ages and ages hence:/ Two roads diverged in a wood, and I –/ I took the one less traveled by,/ And that has made all the difference" (emphasis added, M.B.). The theme of alternative life thus seems to rely on a narrative structure, mainly because it requires a temporal sequence as well as a contrasting of at least two temporal layers, i.e. the time of the telling and the time of the events ("Somewhere ages and ages hence"). Only the passing of time can reveal the *difference* between the real and unlived life, leading to a reflection of the decisions and circumstances that separated one from the other. At the same time, it is the narrative act – the *telling* of a life in retrospect – that only produces these decisions and differences.

Sherwood Anderson's "The Other Woman," first published in 1920 and later selected by John Updike and Katrina Kenison as one of the *Best American Short Stories of the Century*, presents a variation on the theme of the secret life as presented in Hawthorne's "Wakefield" insofar as its main character is also tempted into leaving his old life behind and start a new one, but eventually decides to go back to his wife-to-be. Written by Anderson "partly with my tongue in cheek" (qtd. from Modlin 1992: xii), this "subtly humorous" (ibid.) story is also a 'twice-told tale' as it employs a frame narrative in which the narrator explains that he has heard the story directly from a friend of his: "He began to talk and told me the tale I am now about to set down." ("The Other Woman," 18)

"The Other Woman", in its depiction of a 'slice of life', is a direct sequel to Anderson's most famous story collection. The publication of *Winesburg, Ohio* in 1919 received very mixed reviews. Whereas some critics condemned Anderson's stories as equally formless, amoral and 'dirty', others were enthusiastic about their liberating effect on the bulk of the American short story. Those who appreciated Anderson's art especially praised his handling of 'slices of life' that replaced the plot-centered and formulaic craft that had dominated American short-story writing at the beginning of the 20th century. Anderson himself has often talked about his intention to write stories about 'human beings living their lives' and thereby bring the short story closer to 'real life'. Whereas the short story since Poe was primarily conceived as a concocted form that produces a certain 'unity of effect', Anderson championed the idea that perhaps "it is so called merely because it contains a maximum of life in a minimum of space," as one contemporary critic put it (Fagin 1927: 272). The notion was that through these characters' lives one could perceive the changes in the 'inner life' of America.

The story relates the happenings of what the narrator describes as the most eventful week of his friend's life. In the days before his marriage with the daughter of a judge, the protagonist, a young and celebrated poet, becomes attracted to a married woman ten years older than himself, who works in her husband's small cigar shop. His feelings and desire for the 'other woman' grow so strong that eventually he solicits her to leave her husband and live with him, and the feeling is mutual. On the very same night she comes to his apartment and the protagonist takes her in his arms, standing in the dark of his room and feeling "happy and strong" (ibid.: 23). After this brief, exalted moment, however, his longing for her suddenly ebbs away: "she went entirely out of my mind," (ibid.: 24) and so he marries his fiancée, explaining that "after that evening I never thought of the other woman at all" (ibid.: 25). The secret meeting with the tobacconist's wife thus turns out to be a turning point for the protagonist (if not for the poor woman). Only now, after this sobering experience, he is committed to his fiancée: "To tell you the truth I had come down off my perch. The spirit of the other woman did that to me." (ibid.)

What are we to make of this brief story of 'marital delinquency', to borrow a term from the narrator of "Wakefield"? Apart from the misogynistic tendency that characterizes many of Anderson's works – the women in the story appear merely as vehicles for the male protagonist's egotistic vanities and self-fulfillment – "The Other Woman" story touches a key theme of modernity: People have to make choices that fundamentally influence the further course of their lives, or as the protagonist puts it: "It is one thing or the other with me." (ibid.: 24) Each life lived usually implies other, unlived lives. Sometimes, as in this case, the unlived life can become a somewhat haunting presence: As the protagonist confesses, from time to time "the feeling of her comes sharply into my body and mind" (ibid.: 25). Although he is keen to emphasize that he is "in love with my wife" (ibid.: 18), he can hardly conceal the ambiguity of his decision to marry her, and not the other woman. "I will think that for an hour I was closer to her than I have ever been to anyone else," (ibid.: 26) he admits at the end:

> Then I will sleep and when I awake in the morning it will be as it was that evening when I walked out of my dark apartment after having had the most notable experience of my life. What I mean to say, you understand, is that, for me, when I awake, the other woman will be utterly gone. (ibid.: 26)

Focusing on just one evening in the main character's life, Anderson's story draws on the momentariness of experience as a hallmark of modern life. In the short hour of this secret encounter, he seems to be closer to the truth or meaning of his life than in all the years before or after. Quite paradoxically, the 'most notable experience' of his life is also ultimately detached from his life, since it happened outside its social and moral confines. For one brief instant, the protagonist has overcome the loneliness of his existence – a common theme in Anderson's work –, yet this experience does not connect to his life: with the other woman, an alternative life has revealed itself to him but is 'utterly gone' in the end.

While their plot tends to be highly compressed (as in both Hawthorne's and Anderson's 'narratives'), the focus of stories of unlived/secret life usually lies on the level of the narrative *discourse*. In this respect, the notion of crisis and turning point, as described earlier, is crucial: What stands at the center of these stories are the reflections on the alternative possibilities in life, as the recognition of the 'road not taken' usually comes to characters in brief, elusive moments and does not last for very long. In Sherwood Anderson's "The Other Woman," the protagonist and intradiegetic narrator refers to this as the occasional feeling that "comes sharply into my body and mind" (ibid.: 25). The short story thus focuses not on the life that the protagonist has chosen to live, but on the brief moments in which he comes to question his decision and ponders on the alternatives that may have led to an entirely different life: Stories of unlived and/or of secret lives are primarily concerned with the lives we *don't* live, yet they dwell on this idea in order to reflect on the lives we *do* live.

Another, slightly different variation of the secret-life theme can be found in James Thurber's iconic "The Secret Life of Walter Mitty," which soon after its first publication in *The New Yorker* in 1939 became one of the most popular and best-known modern American short stories. Despite the general tendency towards an ironical distance between the narrator and the central character that characterizes all of the stories of unlived/secret life discussed above, Thurber's is clearly the most openly comic one. The story's eponymous hero is such a ludicrous, memorable figure that he has entered the English language as a synonym for a "a commonplace unadventurous person who seeks escape from reality through daydreaming" (*Merriam-Webster Online*). To act 'Walter Mittyish' is to abandon oneself to imaginary secret lives rather than actually achieve self-actualization in real life.

Thurber's story is made up of four reveries (and a fifth one on the way at the end of the story) of the middle-aged Walter Mitty, interspersed with the dull reality in which Mitty accompanies his wife on one of her weekly trips into town. As Mitty makes his way through the town, running errands for his wife and buying trivial things like overshoes and dog biscuits, he dips into one imaginative adventure after the other as he dreams up for himself all the things he could be: a daredevil pilot of a Navy hydroplane, a skilled surgeon, a defendant gangster in a courtroom, and a bomber pilot in the Second World War. These wild fantasies or 'secret lives', of course, contrast sharply with the drabness of his real life, thus producing the story's comic effect. In his dreams, he is an intrepid hero, admired and feared by other people; in real life, he is a pitiable henpecked husband. Mitty's daydreams resemble those of a child: they are triggered by the actual events and the mundane actions he performs in reality, like driving a car (pilot), putting on gloves (surgeon), hearing a newsboy shouting "something about the Waterbury trial" (gangster), and the pictures of bombing planes in an old newspaper (bomber pilot).

The story is told from the perspective of a heterodiegetic narrator, deploying Walter Mitty as the focalizing subject during the depiction of his daydreams: "'We're going through!' The commander's voice was like thin ice breaking." ("Walter Mitty," 34) The first sentence of the story directly catapults the reader into one of Mitty's imaginary adventures. The dream is then abrubtly interrupted, for Mitty as well as for the reader, by the protagonist's wife's exclamation, "Not so fast! You're driving too fast!" (ibid.), followed by the narrator's description of the actual scene: "Walter Mitty drove on toward Waterbury in silence, the roaring of the SN202 through the worst storm in twenty years of Navy flying fading in the remote, intimate airways of his mind." (ibid.)

Emphasizing the contrast between Mitty's actual life and his counterfactual, imagined lives, the story adds up to an ironic depiction of the superfluous, consumerist and ultimately hollow reality of the American middle class that should later become the trademark of writers like John Updike and John Cheever (and a major theme for the *New Yorker* story, as discussed in chapter 9). The Mittys' life is a life of meaningless trivia in which appearance is more important than essence, as the frequent use of brand names (e.g. 'Kleenex', 'Squibb's' etc.) suggests. The emptiness of his real life is humorously contrasted with the daringness of the daydreaming Mitty. For example, after fashioning himself as a cool, relentless contract killer in front of a jury, Mitty is asked by the clerk about the special brand of the requested puppy biscuits. Mitty, the "greatest pistol shot in the world" replies that "It says 'Puppies bark for It' on the box" ("Walter Mitty," 36) – the absurdity could hardly be more pronounced.

Unlike his literary predecessors Hawthorne and Anderson, Thurber thus employs the motif of the 'secret life' mainly as an ironic comment on the life world of its middle-class readers. Whereas in the earlier examples the existential, inner conflict of the modern individual is presented as an effect of the urbanization and individualization as well as the temporalization of life, Thurber's story casts the contrast between the dullness of mid-century, middle-class life and the protagonist's fanciful reveries which resemble scenes from Hollywood movies of that era.

In this sense, Walter Mitty appears like a modern American Don Quixote, a tragicomic hero whose aggrandized visions of himself finally result in an inability to separate reality from imagination.

LIFE KNOWLEDGE AS DEFERRED SELF-KNOWLEDGE: HENRY JAMES'S "THE BEAST IN THE JUNGLE"

Henry James, whether in his long or short fiction, is of course a rather obvious source in search of literary knowledge. It is no coincidence that his works stand in the center of many interrogations into 'literature and knowledge', whether in Martha Nussbaum's *Love's Knowledge* or in Michael Wood's *Literature and the Taste of Knowledge*, to name but two of the most prominent ones. James – like his brother William, yet with a different approach – was preoccupied with epistemological questions, and consequently many of his texts explore the preconditions and limits of human knowledge. In *What Maisie Knew* (1897) and *The Wings of the Dove* (1902), for example, he delves into the different meanings of the words 'knowledge' and 'know', examining what it means if characters *see* more than they *understand*, or know more (or less) than they are aware of (see Wood 2005: 13-36). With regard to the knowledge in question here – life knowledge – it is particularly interesting that Wood (ibid.: 19) observes in James a "semi-intransitive sense of 'know', where the word seems almost synonymous with life." In the following, I will attempt to shed some light on the relationship between life and knowledge in one of James's short stories, namely "The Beast in the Jungle." In this story, James provides what is arguably one of the most compelling literary instantiations of the theme of unlived life in literary history.[1]

Particularly within the context and conceptual framework of this study, Henry James's "The Beast in the Jungle" is a remarkable story in many respects.[2] Over 40 pages long, it is a rather long short story, and in fact many critics have therefore referred to it as novella. James himself preferred the terms 'tale', 'nouvelle' or sometimes even simply 'short things' (see Scofield 2006: 78-9; Cooke 2011: 172). In contrast to his modern American successors, however, James's 'short things' are comparatively long (and sometimes also long-winded): They share little of the

1 Cf. Engelberg (1989: 130), who states that the story is "not one of James's most accomplished stories, [but it] is nevertheless the most nakedly self-conscious analysis of the 'too late' motif".

2 For an excellent general discussion and contextualization of James's story, see Cooke (2011). For essays that deal explicitly with the story's notion of 'unlived life', see Miller (2007) and, more critically, Goodheart (2003).

narrative economy and linguistic terseness of, say, Hemingway's early short stories, and James is surely much more renowned as a novelist than as a short story writer. As Simon Cooke (2011: 172) notes, compared to the massive critical attention his novels received, James's short stories have been "somewhat sidelined" by literary critics. However, James himself valued the story form because it made it possible for him to cover a wider range of topics and experiment with a variety of perspectives. By 'doing' short things, James believed, he could "touch so many subjects, break out in so many places, handle so many of the threads of life" (qtd. in Scofield 2006: 79). In this sense, one could say that James' short stories are somehow even more 'modern' than his novels, since they emphasize the multitude and the "increasingly fragmented and various experience that characterizes the experience of a modern world" (Cooke 2011: 173).

If Hawthorne's "Wakefield" represents the genre of the story of secret life, "The Beast in the Jungle" is probably the purest example of a story of 'unlived life', exploring the unknown (and unknowable) by imagining an alternative yet eventually elusive life. John Marcher, the story's protagonist-as-"ultimate narcissist" (Engelberg 1989: 129), is so obsessed with the idea that something mysterious and important will happen to him – leaping at him like a beast in the jungle – that he is paralyzed and virtually unable to actually *live*. It is his deepest sense that he is "being kept for something rare and strange, possibly prodigious and terrible, that was sooner or later to happen to [him]" ("Beast," 39).

The very idea of an 'unlived life' is based on a paradox, since life, of course, cannot be 'unlived' in any literal sense. What it expresses, however, is the notion that life can be led wrongly or incompletely, that 'life is not lived to the fullest'. This is arguably an essentially modern theme, since the idea of unlived life did probably not occur to people from pre-modern, traditional societies: Only with the modern project of individualization and a temporalization of the life course could the idea of an 'unlived life' emerge. In the sense that he represents the modern individual's struggle for a meaningful life, Marcher can thus be regarded as one of the prominent literary victims of modernity, trapped in the vast multitude of possibilities and identities: "Waiting to experience life more deeply than most people, he pretty much experiences nothing." (Silber 2009: 99) Life, in James's story, is metaphorically depicted as a jungle in which people have to be alert at all times in order to fend off wild creatures, if only imaginary ones. The 'beast' in the jungle of John Marcher's life, as it turns out, is merely an expectation, a result of the protagonist's misguided notion of what life is and how it needs to be led. This, of course, is the tragic irony of the story: Marcher's misconception of life denies him the possibility of actually living a fulfilled life.

Against this backdrop of life in modernity, "The Beast in the Jungle" is essentially a story about the detrimental effects of an obsession with 'life knowledge', or a story of meta-life knowledge: Marcher is convinced to the extent of obstinacy or even lunacy that he *knows* what awaits him in his life. As Michael Wood argues, James often employs a 'semi-intransitive' use of the word 'know', which becomes almost synonymous with life itself (2005: 19). But is knowing really the same as living in this case? Or is it not rather that knowing forecloses any kind of living and vice versa? In fact, the story can be read as a thought experiment on the question of whether life and knowledge are mutually exclusive, and to what extent the meaning of life can be known in the present moment – or whether it always and inevitably relies on storytelling as a belated act of meaning-making.

The semantic field of 'knowledge' dominates the entire story. The following passage – with no less than five occurrences of the verbs 'to know' and 'to understand' – is instructive in this regard:

> He knew how he felt, but, besides knowing that, she knew how he *looked* as well; he knew each of the things of importance he was insidiously kept from doing, but she could add up to the amount they made, understand how much, with a lighter weight on his spirit, he might have done, and thereby established how, clever as he was, he fell short. ("Beast," 45)

The 'he' referred to in this passage is John Marcher, 'she' is May Bartram, the unfulfilled love of his unlived life. Above all, the passage reveals the story's central conflict between some obscure, misleading knowledge of life and the actual practice of living one's life. But it is also representative of the awkward interaction between the two: there is a constant misapprehension as to how they feel and what they know, or believe they must know. Knowing stands in direct opposition to doing or living: What he *might have done* is foreclosed by his preoccupation with what he *knows* about the "things of importance" in his life. Marcher's life knowledge is delusive, it turns out to keep him from actually living his life, but it, rather cruelly, also keeps May Bartram from living hers. Here, James admirably stages the tension between, and even incompatibility of, knowledge and life, emphasizing that life cannot be 'known' and 'lived' at the same time. It is in this sense that Marcher's 'unlived life' is the direct result of his 'insurmountable desire' to *know* life.

The fact that Marcher's tragically unfulfilled love to May Bartram – and their 'unlived life' as a couple – is based on the 'bond of knowledge' that connects them further adds to the story's marked irony. John Marcher is an extremely close-lipped character, and the only person who knows about his 'fate' is May Bartram. This, however, does not lead to an intimate relationship; he sees her "as a mere confidante." (ibid.: 42) Quite sadly, his innermost conviction forestalls a relationship with May, although, as the narrator informs us, the "real form it should have taken on the basis that stood out large was the form of their marrying." (ibid.: 43) Obsessed by the idea that the "crouching beast" awaits him, he mock-heroically decides that he should not be "accompanied by a lady on a tiger-hunt. Such was the image under which he had ended by figuring his life" (ibid.: 44).

The story's relative length, as several critics have pointed out, is a necessary structural result of the central idea of 'unlived life'. In this regard, "The Beast in the Jungle" illustrates James's aestheticist conviction that form and content are inseparably intertwined. Admitting the reader intimate insights into the consciousness of the main character, the story almost painfully reenacts the tragedy of Marcher's life, making his experience available for the reader. The story's aesthetic structure is crucial for the life knowledge it imparts, or as Cooke aptly puts it: "The form performs the apprehensive, long, suspenseful wait for the great event that is to mark the protagonist's experience, deferring the reckoning for some six chapters." (Cooke 2011: 176) The story's marked eventlessness, along with its relative and somewhat excruciating length, is therefore a formal necessity for the view of life it expresses.

What is important on a formal level for the story's treatment of the theme of 'unlived life' is therefore, once again, its temporal dimension. Unlike so many other short stories, "The Beast in the Jungle" does not focus on one decisive moment in the protagonist's life, but "stretches out, like a short story wanting to be a long story, or a *Bildungsroman* truncated into a tale" (Cooke 2011: 176). The heterodiegetic narrator follows Marcher (and Bartram) through the "interval of years" ("Beast," 34), from the day they first met as young people to their old age (or in May's case even death). This long-scale temporal perspective, of course, is crucial for the representation of the idea of a missed life. The story's basic temporal structural principle is that of compression, yet it focuses not on what happened in those years but on the very absence of any important events. A lifetime is presented in just 40 pages, and while the reader watches Marcher through the decades, he becomes aware of the vacuity and wastefulness of this life. As the years pass, Marcher's life seems to stand still: "Something or other lay in wait for him, amid the twists and turns of the months and the years, like a crouching beast in the jungle." (ibid.: 43-4) Like Fitzgerald's "The Curious Case of Benjamin Button," James creates the effect of a time-lapse. Whereas Fitzgerald, however, uses this narrative technique to render visible the grotesque effects of the life-course model in modernity, James deploys this technique in order to intensify and narrativize the notion of the unlived life.

If one takes a closer look at how James structures the story spatially and temporally, two metaphors stand out. The story's guiding spatial metaphor is clearly that of 'life is a jungle'. At least since the publication of Kipling's *Jungle Book* and Conrad's *Heart of Darkness* a few years prior to "The Beast in the Jungle," and continued with Upton Sinclair's *The Jungle* only a couple years later, the jungle emerged as a prominent trope in the Western literary and cultural imaginary of the early 20th century, the archetypical space of the human psyche and the increasing obscurity, but also the dangers and cold fascination of modern life. As Michael Lundblad argues, in the modernist "discourse of the jungle, the behavior of 'real' animals comes to represent 'natural' human instincts" (2013: 4), influenced by Darwinian thought as well as Freud's work on sexuality and the human psyche. The spatial metaphor of life as a jungle in James's story, however, arguably also serves to produce a decidedly modern view of life as something that cannot be fully *known* or charted. The "epistemology of the jungle" (ibid.: 31) in James's story thus not only expresses modernist notions and social anxieties of hetero- and homosexuality (as several James scholars have argued), but also the very unknowability of life, the undomesticated and unruly disparity between life and knowledge that fuels James's narrative.

At a temporal level, the story's main chronotope, to borrow Mikhail Bakhtin's term, is that of 'life as a day'. It is in "the late afternoon of his life, the time at which for people in general the unexpected has died out" ("Beast," 53) that Marcher begins to ponder on the temporality of his life:

> Since it was in Time that he was to have met his fate, so it was in Time that his fate was to have acted; and as he waked up to the sense of no longer being young, which was exactly the sense of being stale, just as that, in turn, was the sense of being weak, he waked up to another matter beside. (ibid.)

The sudden realization that he is no longer young unsparingly brings to the fore the passivity and vacuity of his life. Time is capitalized here, I would like to suggest, to emphasize that Marcher has not been able to capitalize *his* time: To live in time means to act in time, which is exactly what Marcher has failed to do. As Joan Silber astutely remarks:

> Quite a lot of fiction looks at wasted, ruined, and unled lives (often more intriguing than well-led ones), but what is especially striking in this story is that it holds up to the light the entire question of what 'wasted time' is. What Marcher has missed, in the end, is an essential privilege of being human, not only the experience of love but the will to imagine another consciousness. (2009: 100-1)

The idea of 'wasted time' is inextricably intertwined with John Marcher's inability to live in the present, which, as we have seen, is a direct result of his obsessive desire to know his life. After May Bartram's death, Marcher's perspective on life changes fundamentally. Where he used to project the meaning of his life into the future – waiting for the beast to reveal itself –, he now has to live with the certainty that it has already sprung without him recognizing it:

> The change from his old sense to his new was absolute and final: what was to happen *had* so absolutely and finally happened that he was as little able to know a fear for his future as to know a hope; so absent in short was any question of anything still to come. He was to live entirely with the other question, that of his unidentified past, that of his having to see his fortune impenetrably muffled and masked. ("Beast," 65)

What remains the same after this absolute transition from his "old sense to his new" is that life, for Marcher, does not happen in the present. Living in the future for the biggest part of his life, he is forced to live in the past for what remains of his years. In the story's sixth and last section, May Bartram's grave becomes the powerful if somewhat dramatic metaphor for his unlived life, which he now bemoans with the same kind of self-absorption that characterized his younger years: "The open page was the tomb of his friend, and *there* were the facts of the past, there was the truth of his life, there the backward reaches in which he could lose himself." (ibid.: 68) It is not so much May's death but the failure of his own life that Marcher bemoans. He now wanders around "with his hand in the arms of a companion who was […] his older, his younger self" (ibid.), looking back on his life that seemed unfulfilled at the time, but now turns out to be the only life he had. Only then, that is after this painful realization, he is able to 'settle to live', "feeding all on the sense that he once *had* lived, and dependent on it not alone for a support but for an identity" (ibid.). Now that the beast "had stolen away" (ibid.: 65), he is bereft not only of his life, but of his very identity, of the "'real truth' about him" (ibid.: 44).

On the discourse level, James's deliberately plot-less story explicitly thematizes life knowledge in so far as it poses deep epistemological questions: What can human beings know about their fate? How does such knowledge, or the lack thereof, affect people's behaviors and attitudes towards life? To what extent are life and knowledge incompatible terms? The narrative perspective of the story, its transmission through a heterodiegetic narrator, is therefore arguably at least as important as the actual story. The narrator, as Eugene Goodheart observes with some clarity, is "inside his [Marcher's] consciousness without absolutely identifying with it" (2003: 121). With Marcher being the center of consciousness, the narrative control lies still with the narrator. Through this, the readers "are able to see both the powers and the limitations of his consciousness" (ibid.). And while the entire story is interspersed with the narrator's comments throughout, the limits of the Marcher's consciousness become particularly apparent in the closing pages, when the story's life knowledge is made explicit by the narrator.

Even though the story depicts a quite long period of time instead of a brief situation, it centers around the 'moment of truth' that comes to Marcher in the 'evening' of his life. This is what the narrator works up to throughout the whole tale. When the story eventually culminates in a kind of epiphanic moment – the 'short story effect'–, the insight is rather painful, at least for Marcher. The final revelation is brought about when Marcher, visiting May's grave once again, sees a "middle-aged man apparently [...] in mourning" ("Beast," 68). He at once recognizes the man's deep despair and comes to ask himself: "What had the man *had*, to make him by the loss of it so bleed and yet live?" (ibid.: 69) The answer to this question comes as an insight that is as plain as it is hurtful: "Something [...] that *he*, John Marcher, hadn't" (ibid.), namely a passionate and fulfilled life: "No passion had ever touched him, for this was what passion meant; he had survived and maundered and pined, but where had been *his* deep ravage?" (ibid.: 69-70)

The story's theme of the disparity between life and knowledge is thus presented by the narrator as the protagonist's eventual acquisition of self-knowledge. This self-knowledge is comparative, in that it is the process of comparing oneself to another person which brings out the climactic recognition in Marcher (see Miller 2007: 129). Only by seeing the stranger and comparing this man's mourning to his own, Marcher becomes aware of the void in his life. In a similar way, one could argue, James's story provides its readers with an opportunity to compare their lives to that of Marcher and thereby engage in self-reflection. In an imaginative act, the story allows the reader to cast his own life narrative against Marcher's, thus obtaining a sense of their difference and triggering a process of self-observation (see Fluck 1999b: 240). In this way, the story potentially creates a practical knowledge of how to live: by initiating and guiding a reflection of one's own life, or what Renate Brosch calls 'projective reading'.

In the final paragraph, the story's life knowledge is made even more explicit by the narrator, who now sums up the whole tragedy of Marcher's life. The passage is worth quoting at length here:

> He had seen *outside* of his life, not learned it within, the way a woman was mourned when she had been loved for herself: such was the force of his conviction of the stranger's face [...] It hadn't come to him, the knowledge, on the wings of experience; it had brushed him, jostled him, upset him, with the disrespect of chance, the insolence of accident. Now that

the illumination had begun, however, it blazed to the zenith, and what he presently stood there gazing at was the sounded void of his life. […] This was the awful thought, the answer to all the past, the vision at the dread clearness of which he grew as cold as the stone beneath him. Everything fell together, confessed, explained, overwhelmed; leaving him most of all stupefied at the blindness he had cherished. The fate he had been marked for he had met with a vengeance – he had emptied the cup to the lees; he had been the man of his time, *the* man, to whom nothing on earth was to have happened. That was the rare stroke – that was his visitation. So he saw it, as we say, in pale horror, while the pieces fitted and fitted. ("Beast," 70)

The narrator not only presents the reader with this epiphanic moment in which the secret of Marcher's life is finally and tragically (yet with almost comic overtones) revealed to him. He even has a very practical, moral piece of advice to offer to the reader: "The escape would have been to love her; then, *then*, he would have lived" (ibid.). What Marcher was striving for all his life is presented in a sudden "horror of waking": "*this* was knowledge, knowledge under the breath of which the very tears in his eyes seemed to freeze. […] That at least, belated and bitter, had something of the taste of life." (ibid.: 71) Referring to Marcher as '*the* man of his time', he suggests that Marcher's fate is representative of his era: he is a modern individual agonized by his individuality.

As the foregoing analysis has revealed, "The Beast in the Jungle" is decidedly and quite explicitly a story of life knowledge, it is *ex negativo* a story about how to live.[3] Presenting the reader a rather dreadful example of an 'unlived life', the story's life knowledge slowly unfolds over the course of the story, making the reader aware of the complicated relationship between knowledge and life. Certainly, the story's 'moral' could be "boiled down to the cliché: 'live life to the full'" (Cooke 2011: 178). What the story does, however, is to instantiate this cliché, adding depth and substance to it, and thereby turning it into a rich and subtle reflection on the question of how to live. Many commentators have searched for the hidden meaning in this story, arguing for instance that it is a story about

3 In her story "The Fulness of Life" (1897) Edith Wharton also, and even more explicitly, examines the notion of an unfulfilled life by pointing to the epistemological dilemma that underlies the very notion of the fulfilled life. As in James's story, the protagonist only realizes too late – in the moments *after* her death, in fact, when she has entered the "wide vista of light" of the afterworld – that she has not lived her life to the fullest, and that, while actually living her life, she has not even known what this means: "I have never known […] that fulness of life which we all feel ourselves capable of knowing" ("Fulness", 13-4).

James's unfulfilled love to Fenimore Woolson or his repressed homosexuality. I agree with Goodheart (2003: 127), however, that an "interpretation of *The Beast in the Jungle* should begin once we recognize what is plainly in sight" – and that are, first and foremost, its insights into the complicated relation between life and knowledge.

* * *

The theme or motif of unlived/secret life remains a prominent one in short fiction throughout the 20th century. Henry James, e.g. in *The Ambassadors*, "The Jolly Corner," "Daisy Miller," and "The Middle Years," undertook several attempts at exploring unlived lives and the motif of 'too late'. "The Middle Years," for example, reflects more explicitly on the tensions between life, knowledge, and literature, as is revealed in the protagonist Dencombe's disarmingly frank insight that it "had taken him too much of his life to produce too little of his art" ("The Middle Years," 214). Now that he has perfected his art, he wishes for an extension of his life, something that even the young physician Doctor Hugh, a glowing admirer of Dencombe's art, cannot give him.

Other stories in which the motif of unlived/secret life features to a certain degree include Sherwood Anderson's "Mother," Eudora Welty's "Old Mr. Marblehall," Hemingway's "The Snows of Kilimanjaro" and "The Short Happy Life of Francis Macomber," as well as Alice Munro's "Walker Brothers Cowboy" and "Meneseteung". By exploring 'unlived lives', these stories delve into the "moral psychology of counterfactual narratives" (Miller 2007: 118), thereby reflecting, producing, and disseminating a knowledge of what it means to live a fulfilled life. In so doing, these stories can be regarded as representations of Nadine Gordimer's notion that "each of us has a thousand lives and a novel gives a character only one" (qtd. in Hunter 2007: 2). The short story genre, with its formal and thematic preference for brief, significant moments and disruptive encounters provides a preeminent outlet in which such cultural notions of alternative lives have been expressed and shaped. As they respond to the wider processes and patterns of modernization, these stories aesthetically instantiate the challenges of introspection as well as well as the burden of decision-making that an increasingly modernized, temporalized, and differentialized society has imposed upon individuals.

11. Gerontophobia, Ageism, and the Wisdom of Later Life in Stories of Aging:

Willa Cather's "Old Mrs. Harris" and Eudora Welty's "Old Mr. Marblehall"

> [A]ge remains an undertheorized site of difference in cultural studies. (DeFalco 2010: xv)
>
> Every society creates symbols, images, and rituals that help people live meaningfully within the limits of human existence. Meanings of aging and old age are inevitably linked to these cultural forms that symbolize life's meaning.
> (Cole 2006: xxx)

In the chronology of the life-course model, old age is the final stage of life; and it is also the final category in my discussion of the short story as an organon of life knowledge. Like all other stages of life, age is to a great extent a social and cultural construct, a discursive phenomenon. This, of course, is not to deny the irrefutable fact that people do (still) age biologically, even in spite of all the inventions and strategies in biomedical gerontology and life extension science of recent years. To conceive of aging as a social phenomenon simply means to acknowledge the fact that "the experience and cultural representation of human aging help to constitute its reality" (Cole 2006: xxi). As Margaret M. Gullette (2004) succinctly put it, we are "aged by culture".

The notion of old age as the final stage of human life is thus not simply a natural fact, but largely depends on culturally viable representations, models, and meaning-making processes. Definitions and images of 'age' always reveal what societies expect from their old (see Abels et al. 2008: 8). Moreover, in differentiated modern societies there is never just one definition or image of age, but a plurality of definitions, and these definitions depend very much on the respective social area in which they are formed (law, politics, economy, health system, etc.). Hence, the specific logics of these social systems also determine their respective semantics of age: From a biomedical perspective, for example, age is primarily defined in terms of health care, diseases, etc. Economic and political perspectives on age focus on issues of retirement, pensions, or poverty. As Thomas Cole therefore reminds us, "[a]ging and old age are certainly real, but they do not exist in some natural realm, independently of the ideals, images, and social practices that conceptualize and represent them" (Cole 2006: xxii).

Consequently, modern sociology, especially the theory of social inclusion, regards age not as a universal anthropological constant, but as a social category that determines the characteristics and patterns of behavior of old people and turns them into a self-contained social group. Moreover, 'age' as a distinct stage in the human life course is often considered as a social problem or a response to a problem. In this light, the life phase of old age exists precisely because it allows to give an answer to a societal set of problems (see Saake 2008: 242). As a social problem age emerged in the wake of the modern differentiation of society and the paradigm of efficiency and accomplishment. As a unifying category, age is therefore considered as an essentially modern invention that results from the differentiation processes in modern societies. According to Saake (ibid.: 249), the invention of 'age' is basically a product of three historical conditions, namely (1) the modern use of collective singulars (such as 'history', 'civilization', 'progress'), (2) the demographic change in the 19th century, and (3) the modern grief about the loss of consistent, homogeneous descriptions of society.

From a cultural studies-oriented perspective, the narratives, metaphors, and images that shape the social category of age come into sight. In his insightful study, *The Journey of Life*, Thomas Cole traces the perception and social construction of human lifetime and the process of aging in middle-class American culture, beginning with the notions of age that the first European settlers brought with them. As Cole suggests, the history of aging in America is characterized by a continual devaluation of old age that lasts well into the recent past. Until the Middle Ages, life in Western cultures was understood as an endless circle, represented in motifs of the 'wheel of life', which convey the notion of daily life as an eternal cycle only broken by death (see Cole 2006: 17). Aging was largely seen as a mysterious yet crucial part of life and of the eternal order of things. In seventeenth-century Europe, this idea had been more or less fully replaced by the model of the life course, iconographically represented as a staircase of life, with each step constituting a distinct stage or age of life (ibid.: 5). In Puritanism, age and maturity were still honored, since it was regarded as the final stage in the "pilgrimage to

God and final judgment" (ibid.: 48). Particularly, old age was connected with the idea of a 'review of life', i.e. the retrospective assessment of one's life as the ultimate means towards reconciliation and redemption.

This Calvinist ideal of aging and old age as well as the images of life's ages and the 'journey of life', as Cole (ibid.: 67) argues, "persisted well into the nineteenth century," before they were replaced by the 'dualist vision' of aging in Victorian America, "splitting later life into sin, decay, and dependence on the one hand, and virtue, self-reliance, and health on the other." (ibid: 91) The Victorians believed that everyone could potentially live independently and healthily even at an old age – those who suffered from illness, poverty, or frailty were punished by God for their sinful, immoral life (ibid.: 140). This dualist view of old life, Cole maintains, "remained powerful through the 1920s," as the Victorian ideal of 'civilized' old age was propagated in self-help manuals that instructed people how to maintain their health, proper character, activity, and usefulness as well as to cultivate their inner or spiritual life and thereby to resist decay and deterioration (ibid.: 146).

With a fundamental revision of the stages of life and the beginning of a valorization or even glorification of youth, 19th-century America displayed an increasing "hostility toward old age – suggesting that old people are seen as powerful impediments to progress, unwelcome reminders both of the oppressive weight of the past and of humankind's inevitable weakness and dependence" (ibid.: 83). Although by 1850 still far more people died under the age of fifteen than at the age of sixty, old age was increasingly associated with death (ibid.: 88). Here, and not in the Puritan heritage, are the roots of America's preference for youth. Since the mid-19th century, there has been a tendency in America to view aging and age as one of life's problems that needs to be solved by the means of science and technology, and not as an integral and meaningful part of life.

This trend was furthered in the late 19th and early 20th century, which saw health reforms and scientific dreams of prolongevity or even a life without death (e.g. Charles Asbury Stephens, or Elie Metchnikoff's theory of aging as a chronic disease). In an "atmosphere of deep hostility to the organic processes of decline and death" (ibid.: 178-9), America and Western modernity in general began a downright "war on old age" (ibid.: 181). Moreover, the religious and moral implications of old age gave way to a supposedly neutral scientific view: "On both sides of the Atlantic, modernist culture repudiated the rigid moralism and the static, obsolete imagery of the ages-of-life motif." (ibid.: 192) The institutionalization of gerontology and geriatrics in the early 20th century finally "helped complete the long-term cultural shift from conceiving aging primarily as a mystery or an existential problem to viewing it primarily as a scientific and technical problem" (ibid.: 195). As Cole therefore concludes, "[l]ike other aspects of our biological and social existence, aging has been brought under the dominion of scientific management, which is primarily interested in *how* we age in order to explain and control the aging process" (ibid.: xx-xxi).

But whereas, in the past years, especially the social sciences have increasingly addressed the interplay between biological and social factors that influences our knowledge and understanding of old age, relatively little attention has yet been paid to the ways in which these notions are also culturally shaped. Nevertheless, aging and old age have always figured prominently in literature. World literature is replete with characters who grow, or are, old: Methuselah, King Lear, "Rip van Winkle," and Santiago, the protagonist of Hemingway's *The Old Man and the Sea*, to name but a few of the most famous literary old men.[1] By creating these and other characters, literature has arguably contributed immensely to the construction and dissemination of images and narratives of old people and has therefore helped to define 'age' for the better or worse. A closer analysis of literary representations of old people can shed light on the culturally prevalent notions of age. At the same time, however, literary texts also often complement or undermine these notions and provide alternative versions, thus constituting an imaginative counter-discourse (Zapf) to gerontophobic views and concepts of aging. As Rosalie Baum states,

> Literature has [...] been influential in forming current views of aging. It has done so by acting as a mirror to culturally accepted views of aging and to the underlying assumptions of those views. But it has also done so by investigating those views, by testing new concepts of aging, and by inventing different paradigms for meaningful living in the last stages of life. (Baum 1999: 89)

Literature can thus broaden our perspective and respond to questions like: Is there a *meaning* or *significance* of age? If so, what does it mean to grow and be old? Who defines what age is, and according to which norms and criteria? What is part of the social practice of 'doing age'? What values, qualities, virtues, attitudes, and practices are associated with old age (e.g. wisdom, experience, authority, uselessness, disorientation, cowardice, etc.)? Is old age primarily an engineering problem that needs to be solved, as some positions in the social and biomedical sciences seem to suggest?

---

1 Interestingly enough, as this list already suggests there are much less famous old women in literature – a fact that says a lot about our societies' conception of the intersections between age and gender.

* * *

According to the cultural history of aging in America presented by Cole, the early decades of the 20th century witnessed the eventual shift from religious and moral towards scientific and technological concepts of old age. In the following, I will therefore look at two exemplary texts from this period to explore in how far the short story is entwined with such shifting cultural notions about age and ageing, and how the formal-aesthetic setup of the short story with its heightened temporality provides a privileged medium in which these shifting notions can be expressed. My two main examples are Willa Cather's "Old Mr. Harris" (1932) and Eudora Welty's "Old Mr. Marblehall" (1941). While these stories differ significantly with regard to how they deal with the question of old age and an emerging ageism in American culture, they also represent the tension between modern and anti-modern tendencies in the American literature of the first decades of the 20th century. While Cather's is a sentimental story that hearkens back to Victorian notions of age by endowing old age with moral and spiritual values, Welty's grotesque story can be read as a subtle critique of modern America's changing conceptions of age and a parable for the power of the (literary) imagination. Their main characters are also very different: Where Cather's female character serves as a literary example for a good, fulfilled life and a cautioning against the marginalization and incapacitation of the old, the male protagonist in Welty's piece constitutes more a protagonist-as-metaphor, a symbol for the changing perception of age and an emerging gerontophobia in the American society. It is in this tension field between cultural and socio-economic conceptions of old age, modern and anti-modern tendencies, as well as gendered notions of old age that my reading of Cather and Welty addresses specifically the question of the generic constitution of life knowledge: What does the short story 'know' about the construction processes that define age as the end-of-life phase in the (modern and postmodern) American society? Where does literary knowledge about ageing exceed the statistical and systems theoretical knowledge of the social sciences? How does literature, how do short stories, contribute to the formation of images and discourses of (old) age?

Being quite a long story of about 50 pages and divided into thirteen sections, Willa Cather's "Old Mrs. Harris" from her collection *Obscure Destinies* demonstrates that clear-cut generic distinctions are inherently problematic. With its many characters, little episodes as well as the broad social perspective it offers, the story does not conform to the conventional slice-of-life model of the (modern) short story and appears almost like a 'condensed novel'. This closeness to the novel is not very surprising, since Cather's literary reputation rests almost entirely on her novels, most importantly perhaps *My Ántonia* (1918). However, throughout her career Cather was almost equally devoted to the short story, with three collections published during her lifetime and one more collection appearing posthumously in 1948 (see De Roche 2006: 39). In "Old Mrs. Harris," as in all of her short fiction, Cather is miles away from the formal and thematic innovations of her modernist contemporaries Anderson, Fitzgerald, Faulkner, and Hemingway. As Harold Bloom notes, she "appears [...] to have no aesthetic affinities with her younger contemporaries" (1985: 1). As a matter of fact, Cather is much more indebted to Henry James whose aestheticism and formal ideas, as presented in "The Art of Fiction," she shares (see also Müntefering 2010: 54-5).

In "Old Mrs. Harris," Cather depicts the domestic life of a rather poor yet virtuous and industrious family in Colorado, probably at the turn of the 20th century. Like so many other of Cather's stories and novels, it is a 'frontier narrative' that deals with the settlers' experiences in the West and the fates of European immigrants in the late 19th and early 20th century. The story's material, thus, is a crucial part of what made it so successful: it is in stories like "Old Mrs. Harris" that Cather wrote into public consciousness the 'obscure destinies' and otherwise unnoticed lives of the immigrant communities in the Midwest and West (see Roche 2006: 40). Thus portraying the life and survival of a pioneer community in the early days of the state of Colorado, and depicting the coexistence of different social and ethnic groups, the story provides a good example of what Ottmar Ette (2009) has called literary *Überlebenswissen* and *Zusammenlebenswissen*, i.e., a knowledge of how to survive and live together in a given society. What is more, through its focus on the contributions of women, but also by complicating the history of a region through presenting it from different angles and perspectives than the dominant historiographical ones, Cather may also be regarded as a literary forerunner to more recent short-story writing by women authors, notably the works of Alice Munro.

While the story may draw a rather nostalgic, romanticized image of the life of the settler generation and their traditional, conservative norms and values, it nevertheless succeeds to function as a counterpoint to the modernist project, especially where the modern perception of age and aging people is concerned. Published in 1932, the story shares none of the radicalism and modern exuberance of the works of her contemporaries. Even much more directly than Sherwood Anderson, whose modernism is always accompanied by a nostalgic longing for a lost harmony, Cather's moral vision as well as her social attitudes appear "altogether archaic" (Bloom 1985: 2). In Cather's story about old Mrs. Harris, age is not described as an impediment of progress or an organic process of decline, but as a reminder of the old values and ways of life. In this sense, age has an intrinsic meaning and pragmatic value in the story.

Together with the family of her daughter Victoria, the story's eponymous character lives in Skyline, Colorado, after spending most of her life in Tennessee. Two years before the story sets in, the Templetons – Victoria and her husband Hillary, their daughter Vickie and the twins Albert and Adelbert – had moved westward in order to find a better future. Although they have managed to ensconce quite well in their new environment and have made friends in the neighborhood, the Templetons still struggle with the harsh reality in the West. Particularly the elderly lady has some trouble adjusting to this altogether different life: "Mrs. Harris was no longer living in a feudal society, where there were plenty of landless people, glad to render service to the more fortunate, but in a snappy little Western democracy, where every man was as good as his neighbour and out to prove it." ("Old Mrs. Harris," 288) Being raised in the 'old order' of the genteel South, the social fabric of the new American democracy proves a great challenge for the old lady.

As the narrative unfolds, Cather's story stages the generational and cultural conflicts in the family as well as in the town community of Skyline that arise from the different lifestyles as well as the different expectations and views of life.[2] As suggested in the title, the focus is primarily on Mrs. Harris, the representative of the old generation: Although she misses her Tennessean home, her neighbors, her garden and yard, her apple and lemon trees, she had "never thought it possible" (ibid.: 271) not to follow the family on their westward journey. Mrs. Harris believes that old women "were tied to the chariot of young life, and had to go where it went, because they were needed" (ibid.). Her understanding of the societal role of old people, hence, is essentially connected to the traditional social order of the south, which demanded from the old that they subordinate their own needs and wants to the good of the family, yet granted them a crucial, if somewhat hidden role: Managing their daughter's households, they usually kept in the background from where they ruled and "ordered life to their own taste" (ibid.: 287). They willingly "left the front porch and the parlour" to the young generation and "spent most of their lives in the kitchen and pantries and back dining-room" (ibid.). Mrs. Harris thus represents the traditional social order in which the elderly were mostly invisible but had their fixed place in the family and the social life of the town. She holds on to the agrarian values of the South that privilege the well-being and prosperity of the family over the personal wants of the individual, especially women.

Fully embracing her new role, however, offers Mrs. Harris rich opportunities to become a meaningful part of the whole rather than an impediment: As the good spirit of the Templeton family, she is the one who reads to the boys, takes care of

2 In this respect, Cather's story can be likened to Katherine Anne Porter's short stories, particular her 'Miranda Stories.'

the family cat, clothes and feeds her grandchildren, and rocks the baby to sleep. The children seem to be the only ones not jaundiced by her age; they adore her and want to be in her lap when they are sick: "They had no physical shrinking from her because she was old." (ibid.: 289) And when Vickie, her granddaughter, is admitted to the University of Michigan, Mrs. Harris asks the neighbors, Mr. and Mrs. Rosen, for the money to pay the school fees. She endures all hardships, afflictions, and the vanities and selfishness of her daughter and granddaughter and selflessly devotes herself to the well-being of the family, even to the extent of complete self-denial:

> Indeed, she ceased to be an individual, an old woman with aching feet; she became part of a group, became a relationship. [...] The tired, solitary old woman Grandmother had been at daybreak vanished; suddenly the morning seemed as important to her as it did to the children, and the morning ahead stretched out sunshiny, important. (ibid.: 290)

Physically and mentally declining, she feels tired and solitary even to the point of evanescence, yet her sense of duty and loyalty compels her to act in favor of her family. In the house, her presence is more tolerated than welcome: "Mrs. Harris and her 'things' were almost required to be invisible." (ibid.: 272) Even when she realizes that her end is near, the old lady tries hard to conceal this fact from everyone in order not to become a burden. For the present-day reader, such a life may appear utterly tragic, since it does not concur with modern notions of self-realization, fulfillment, and happiness in life – Mrs. Harris is certainly no "golden girl". Her subjectivity is straitjacketed by the gender and age roles the society inflicts upon her.

According to the assessment of the heterodiegetic narrator, however, Mrs. Harris's life is a meaningful life of fulfillment and happiness, despite all the deprivation and limitations she has to endure. The humanist, compassionate narrative voice describes the old lady in extraordinarily positive terms: "She had the kind of quiet, intensely quiet, dignity that comes from complete resignation to the chances of life." (ibid.: 263) In order to support this affirmative, sympathetic perception of the old lady, the narrator also incorporates the perspectives of other characters in the story and relates how they think of old Mrs. Harris. A case in point is the neighbor Mrs. Rosen, a Jewish-German immigrant, who admires the impressive "kind of nobility" that radiates from the old lady: "an absence of self-consciousness, vanity, preoccupation – something absolute" (ibid.: 265). Despite all she has to endure in the austere conditions of her life, "the old lady looked happy" (ibid.).

This altogether positive image of Mrs. Harris is also reflected in the presentation and semanticization of the narrative space, particularly the small chamber in which the old lady lives. The narrator's first description of the room is instructive in this respect:

> A corner of the room was curtained off with some black-and-red-striped cotton goods, for a clothes closet. In another corner was the wooden lounge with a thin mattress and a red calico spread which was Grandma's bed. Beside it was her wooden rocking-chair, and the little splint-bottom chair with the legs sawed short on which her darning-basket usually stood, but which Mrs. Rosen was now using for a tea-table. (ibid.: 264)

This meagerly equipped, "hideous, cluttered room" (ibid.) already tells the reader a lot about Mrs. Harris's character and her life. While there is hardly any trace of comfort or even luxury, the high-spiritedness of the old lady turn the room into an agreeable habitat. Making a virtue out of necessity, she creatively uses whatever is there to make her room homely. The wooden lounge and the thin mattress tell of the hardships and physical strenuousness of her life, yet the rocking-chair and the tea-table signify its simple pleasures. At the end of the story, when Mrs. Harris is about to die, she is glad that Mrs. Rosen is away to Chicago and that she therefore does not find out about Mrs. Harris's "little secrets," that is the many blemishes and inconveniences of her life, mirrored by the objects in her room: "how hard her bed was, that she had no proper place to wash, and kept her comb in her pocket; that her nightgowns were patched and darned. Mrs. Rosen would have been indignant." (ibid.: 312-3)

From today's perspective, Cather certainly fails in providing a vision of old age that does not revert to pre-modern role models for aging women, which are essentially based on self-denial, subordination, and a relentless work ethic. As Alfred Kazin remarked about Cather's traditionalism already in 1942, it "was a candid and philosophical nostalgia" and had "given her the conviction that the values of the world she had lost were the primary values, and everything else their degradation" (1995 [1942]: 251).

However, in contrast to the modern tendency of defining old age as a problem of life and old people as a burden of the society, Cather's story offers an ultimately more positive and affirmative vision of aging which is marked by virtue, self-reliance, experience, and wisdom rather than decline, poverty, and frailty. Despite its nostalgic shortcomings, the story reveals an ethics of aging that is hard to refute, even for present-day readers. In a crucial passage at the end of the story, this 'life knowledge' is made explicit by the narrator:

> Thus Mrs. Harris slipped out of the Templetons' story; but Victoria and Vickie had still to go on, to follow the long road that leads through things unguessed at and unforeseeable. When they are old, they will come closer and closer to Grandma Harris. They will think a great deal about her, and remember things they never noticed; and their lot will be more or less like hers. They will regret that they heeded her so little; but they, too, will look into the eager, unseeing eyes of young people and feel themselves alone. They will say to themselves: 'I was heartless, because I was young and strong and wanted things so much. But now I know.' ("Old Mrs. Harris," 314)

Although one may criticize this passage for its somewhat over-emphatic, didactic tone, it provides a good example of how literary writing can "absorb its audiences in its work and its medium-specific forms of attention to life" (Eldridge 2009: 1). First and foremost, life is understood in narrative terms here, and it needs to be told in order to become meaningful. As a metanarrative comment, the passage also interprets the foregoing story and generalizes about its implications for the following generations. Employing what Cole (2006) has identified as the main metaphor of the life course ('life is a journey'), the story projects the old lady's fate to the following generations who still have to 'follow the long road' at whose end Mrs. Harris has already arrived. Moreover, the life-as-journey metaphor is quite literally reflected in the family's migration toward the unknown territory of the West. Like life itself, the journey held in store many obstacles and impediments, many things "unguessed at and unforeseeable," all mastered with dignity by old Mrs. Harris. In this sense, Mrs. Harris's individual life story therefore also represents the collective experience of the settlers who shaped the American nation in the 19th and early 20th century.

Cather's story explicitly puts into question her contemporaries' penchant for youth. Old age is not only described as the inevitable final reality of human beings, but as a valuable yet ambiguous state of insight and regret, of wisdom and disillusionment. In the story, this seems to be the ultimate truth about old age: "their lot will be more or less like hers". Quite paradoxically, then, the final insight of the story will come too late for both Victoria and Vickie. Once they will have reached the last stage of their lives, they will share the knowledge of life that grandma Harris possessed, but there will be no possibility to turn back time and act differently. The final recognition – "now I know" – is ultimately reserved for the old. As a story about the cultural perception of old age and the social roles of elderly women, in "Old Mrs. Harris" Cather creates a positive image of aging that serves as a reminder to the cultural need for the kind of (gendered) life knowledge that comes with old age. Although she remains trapped in the social expectations and her own notion of 'how to be old', Mrs. Harris possesses the wisdom that comes with age, i.e. "an expert knowledge system in the domain of fundamental life pragmatics (life planning, life management, and life review)" (Baltes et al. 1990, qtd. from Munson Deats/Tallent Lenker 1999: 7). In a nation that had always been, and became even more obsessed with youth with the advent of modernism, Cather reminds the reader of the futility and foolishness of any attempt to ignore old age and abandon its resources.

Rosalie Baum (1999: 93) has observed that one characteristic of literary representations of aging female characters in 20th-century American fiction is that they are often misunderstood by the other (and younger) characters, even when they manage to live a meaningful and happy life. According to her, stories of aging women are therefore marked by a tension "between an elderly woman who sees herself living a satisfying and meaningful life and a world that sees little value in her life" (ibid.). Old Mrs. Harris is no exception to this, at least in the beginning of the story. While she holds together the family without them really noticing, the old woman has to endure many hardships herself. Particularly her self-absorbed daughter Victoria "accepts her mother's sacrifice without ever seeing it as such" (De Roche 2006: 41). In the end, however, many of the story's younger characters – including the twins, or the neighbor Mrs. Rosen – do appreciate Mrs. Harris's endearing personality and her achievement in the family and community. The story thus works decidedly against an objectification and pathologization of old age in cultural discourse, emphasizing the value of old people and especially women.

So, what about the story's life knowledge and its potential for a projective reading? Interestingly enough, Cather's compassionate story about the life of old Mrs. Harris has been suggested on the reading list of the "Literature, Arts, and Medicine Database," an internet page of NYU's school of medicine that provides a resource of literature as well as film, video, and art for teaching in medical humanities (http://litmed.med.nyu.edu). In a paper held at the 49th annual Willa Cather Spring Festival in Redcloud, Nebraska, in 2004, Marjorie Sirridge, a professor of medicine and medical humanities and contributor to the above mentioned database, writes about what makes "Old Mrs. Harris" a valuable teaching resource for her. Sirridge states: "[I]n my teaching of medical students, I was seeking literature that could illustrate the important issues which affect most human lives, and thus help students understand better the needs of their patients. This story proved to be an ideal choice." (2004: n.p.) Although doctor-patient relationships do not figure at all in this story about generational conflict and the 'long road of life', Sirridge finds in it a great value for the education of prospective physicians. In medical training, stories have become an important addition to scientific knowledge: "scientific knowledge of the human being is necessary, but in the end it only serves to enable the medical practitioner to heal the patient or provide palliation for his ailment. Stories are generally a central factor in the doctor-patient relationship, particularly when anamnesis is concerned." (Meuter 2009: 254) In this context, Sirridge's affirmative comment on Cather's story, it seems, implies at least one felicitous definition of literary life knowledge: *a knowledge about the important issues that affect most human lives and that therefore has a significance and urgency beyond the realm of the mere aesthetic.*

And although, of course, we need to be very careful about instrumentalizing literature for didactic purposes, literary critics would arguably be well advised to engage more decidedly in the exploration of the models and styles of life immanent in literary texts and provided by literary experience (see Gaskill 2008) and communicate their knowledge in an interdisciplinary discourse. Such an approach must not be understood as the only or even dominant approach to literature, but as a valuable addition to the "hermeneutics of suspicion" (Felski 2008: 1) that fosters only skepticism and that prevails in current debates in literary and cultural studies. From such a perspective, literary studies and life sciences do not need to be mutually exclusive, but instead can together provide a more complex knowledge of life. As John Dewey writes in *Art as Experience*:

> Tangled scenes of life are made more intelligible in esthetic experience: not, however, as reflection and science render things more intelligible by reduction to conceptual form, but by presenting their meanings as the matter of a clarified, coherent, and intensified or 'impassioned' experience. (Dewey 2005 [1934]: 302)

* * *

Eudora Welty's "Old Mr. Marblehall," published in her first short story collection *A Curtain of Green* (1941), stands in stark contrast to "Old Mrs. Harris," sharing nothing of Cather's nostalgic view on the main character's life or of its compassionate, philanthropic narrative voice. In fact, the narrator of Welty's story draws a rather negative and grotesque image of its eponymous character, an image that resonates ambivalently with the increasing age anxiety and gerontophobia that characterize the modern age in America (see Cole 2006). If Cather's narrator solicits the reader to understand the meaning and importance of the life portrayed in the story and to empathize with her aging character, "Old Mr. Marblehall" is an example for the ways in which Welty allows the narrators to "stand between the reader and her story's characters" (Pollack 2008 [1997]: 265). Whereas the life knowledge presented by Cather therefore largely conflates with the narrator's perspective on old Mrs. Harris's life, Welty's story is much more indirect, less didactic and much more polyvalent with regard to the question of what might be learned from such a story.

Mainly recognized as a southern regionalist writer in the tradition of Robert Penn Warren, William Faulkner, and Katherine Anne Porter, Eudora Welty's short stories pertain to the most ambiguous, suggestive, and disquieting prose fiction writing in American literature. They often resemble dreamlike sequences, depicting quirky yet believable characters and incorporating diverse mythical elements.[3] "R.P. Warren has noted […] that in Welty's stories the logic of things is not the logic of ordinary daylight life," Charles May (2002: 70) reminds us, agreeing with Warren that the power and suggestiveness of Welty's writing stem from her ability to render meaningful the most "trivial realistic details" (ibid.). In a similar vein, Martin Scofield praises Welty's "feeling for the odd and the outlandish within ordinary settings (village, town, and family life), where the oddity is revelatory of some central human impulse or condition" (2006: 174). Welty's style is often described as a well-balanced mixture of realism and lyricism (cf., for instance, Burt 2004, and Weston 2010, who refers to this as "lyric/realist technique"), demonstrating a keen sense for the basic ingredients of a good, well-made story as well as an elaborate aesthetic formalism.[4] This mingling of realist storytelling and a lyric compression of language can also be regarded as the source of Welty's "modernist indirection" (Burt 2004: 562), i.e. her ability to suggest many things "behind the surface of narration" (ibid.: 561), connecting her to other modernists like Virginia Woolf, James Joyce, and Ernest Hemingway.

Warren's widely noticed essay on Welty, referred to by Charles May in the above quote, famously identified 'love and separateness' (most strikingly perhaps in "A Still Moment") and 'innocence and experience' as the central themes in Welty's work. As Ruth Weston puts it, "Welty most often develops the theme of Love and Separateness in terms of human relationships, especially the tensions between individuals and family or community, and of the risks inherent in the bonds of love and in breaking those bonds" (2010: 277). Similar to Sherwood Anderson, the protagonists in Welty's stories are often tragically separated from other individuals, 'trapped characters' who struggle with their own lives and are unable to communicate their feelings and desires. In "A Curtain of Green," for instance, Mrs. Larkin bemoans the loss of her beloved husband by growing an

3 Cf. Kreyling (1999: 34): "Long-standing interests in Greek and Roman mythology and the Grimm folktales clearly shape some stories."

4 Scofield even goes so far as to argue that "[m]ore than any other American short story writer of the twentieth century, Welty's sensibility is that of a poet" (2006: 174).

almost impenetrable garden of flowers that works as a kind of bulwark to separate her from the rest of the town ("they found her place in the garden, as they might have run their fingers toward a city on a map of a foreign country, located her from their distance almost in curiosity, and then forgot her," "A Curtain of Green," 108). R.J. Bowman, the protagonist of her first published story, "Death of a Traveling Salesman" (1936) seems even more forlorn and isolated on his trip through the "desolate hill country" ("Death," 119) of rural Mississippi. When he seeks help from a somewhat outlandish local couple after his car has crashed into a ravine, he – at least for a moment – finds relief from his "almost inaudible life of heartbeats and dreams that came back, a life of fever and privacy, a delicate life which had left him weak to the point of – what? Of begging" ("Death," 123). Bowman has literally driven his life into a one-way road; there is neither return nor turning point. Strangely enough, however, he gains a glimpse of someone else's fulfilled life, namely the life of the woman and her husband who dwell in the remote country hut. When the salesman dies in the end of the story, he is as alone as anyone could possibly be: "He covered his heart with both hands to keep anyone from hearing the noise it made. But nobody heard it." ("Death," 130) Although the reader has known the salesman's destiny from the very beginning of the story, the salesman himself "understands nothing of why he has been given just this fate, and in this respect he is exactly like us when we think about our own lives," as David Mikics pithily remarks (2013: 187).

Welty's own intention in *A Curtain of Green* was to depict brief everyday situations which reveal something deeper about the characters' lives. As she wrote to Ford Madox Ford, these stories were not meant as "exciting stories", but "only come from the complexity and the burdens of poverty or love or grief I have tried to describe through some incident or moment in people's lives" (qtd. from Kreyling 1999: 10). "Old Mr. Marblehall" perfectly illustrates Welty's poetic sensibility, her interest in the frailty of human relations and human life, and her capability to defamiliarize the familiar.[5] Usually, the story is read as a typical exponent of Welty's "'monstrous' stories" (Kreyling 1999: 19), i.e. stories which feature "a strong first-person narrator, figures of physical or sexual 'abnormality', sketchy and rapid brushstrokes of composition, and a soupçon of mythological or psychoanalytic imagery" (ibid.: 19-20).

5 Eunice Glenn praised the story for its interweaving of "fantasy and surface reality" (1988 [1947]: 471). According to Glenn, the story's eponymous hero has "lost the power to distinguish them [i.e. fantasy and reality, M.B.]," and therefore they "become one and the same thing" (ibid.) at certain points in the story.

"Old Mr. Marblehall" is quite a peculiar story about an eccentric pensioner whose life virtually begins after his sixtieth birthday: "Old Mr. Marblehall never did anything, never got married until he was sixty." ("Marblehall," 91) Given the lethargy that dominated his (untold and thus unknown) life for six decades, it is all the more remarkable that Marblehall is now leading a *double* life: Married to two different women and having a son with each of them, it is as if he wants to make up for the life he missed. To the community of his hometown Natchez, Mississippi, – the cultural and historical environment in which this and many other of Welty's stories are deeply embedded –, the old man hardly exists at all, which is also why nobody finds out about his secret second life: "He is just like other people to them. He could have easily danced with a troupe of angels in Paradise every night, and they wouldn't have guessed." (ibid.: 93)

The narrator's quirky descriptions of Marblehall's parallel families contribute to the surreal, phantasmagorial atmosphere that pervades the story. Whereas the first wife "looks remote and nebulous" (ibid.: 91) with her "electric-looking hair and curly lips" (ibid.) and sings in a "voice that dizzies other ladies like an organ note, and amuses men like a halloo down the well" (ibid.: 92), the second wife is described by the narrator as "really worse than the other one" (ibid.: 94), looking "like funny furniture" (ibid.) and screaming at her neighbors.[6] Similarly, the second son is "just like the first one" (ibid.: 95), who is described by the narrator as looking "quietly and maliciously absurd" with his "sparse Japanese hair, tiny little pearly teeth [and] long little wilted fingers" (ibid.: 92). The story ends on an enigmatic note, suggesting that none of Marblehall's wives – and lives – are real, but that Marblehall might have dreamed all of this up, probably in an extension of his appetite for the "*Terror Tales* and *Astonishing Stories*" (ibid.: 95) he devours as his bedtime reading: "Old Mr. Marblehall! He may have years ahead in which to wake up bolt upright in the bed under the naked bulb, his heart thumping, his old eyes watering and wild, imagining that if people knew about his double life, they'd die." (ibid.: 97)

Some critics have commented on the perplexity that the story produces with its peculiar merging of dream and reality, resulting from Marblehall's vivid imagination that enables him to escape the bleak reality of his uneventful life, or even a "life of general failure" (Davis 1972, n.p.). In this light, the protagonist's name can be read as a reference to an opera song by Alfred Bunn, titled "I Dreamt I

6 Kreyling (1999: 24) has suggested that whereas Marblehall's uptown wife bears a close resemblance to the neurasthenic woman in Eliot's *The Waste Land* and the mythological Medusa-figure, his other wife, with her witch-like appearance, "comes from folklore, not from highbrow art poetry or classical mythology."

Dwelt in Marble Halls", establishing the connection between the story's titular character and the dreamer in Bunn's libretto (cf. Davis 1972). Such a reading indeed seems plausible, especially given that the name Marblehall chooses for his second life – Mr. Bird – further suggests that he takes imaginative flight to escape his dreary life and "soar above the everyday world of man's existence" (ibid.).

While this blending of dream and reality, imagination and fact, would already render "Old Mr. Marblehall" an interesting example for the ways in which short stories create imaginative spaces that question our knowledge and perception of everyday life and our notions of what constitutes a good or fulfilled life, such a reading neglects what strikes me as the pivotal element of the story, namely the protagonist's age: it is not simply about Mr. Marblehall, but *old* Mr. Marblehall. In the following, I would therefore like to discuss Welty's story with regard to two main foci: 1) as a literary representation of later life, i.e. of what Cole (2006: xviii) calls the "Fourth Age" or "old old"; and 2) in terms of its presentation of the theme of the double life, which is arguably employed in order to defamiliarize the familiar and thus reflect on the portentousness of the mundane. More particularly, I will focus on the question of how Welty's story stages old age between the normal and the 'abnormal' or pathological, critically reflecting on contemporary notions of aging and particularly the tendency to normalize images of old age and elderly people and to see aging as "a problem rather than part of a transcendent reality" (Cole 2006: 211). In this sense, there exists a striking parallel between Fitzgerald's "The Curious Case of Benjamin Button" and Welty's piece, as both stories deliberately alienate real-life images of old age and disconnect it from prevailing cultural conceptions of the human life-course. Whereas Fitzgerald achieves this effect by inverting his protagonist's normal biography and thus desynchronizing the underlying biological, chronological, and social temporalities, however, Welty isolates old age from the other stages of life altogether. Thus uncoupled from the modern life-course regime, old age no longer gains its meaning and importance as the well-deserved withdrawal from economic activity, but defies any meaningful integration or interpretation.

In his influential study titled *Geriatrics* (1915), Ignatz Leo Nascher introduced the term of geriatrics, which only decades later came to serve as the common name for this new field of healthcare. In the introduction, Nascher presents – perhaps somewhat surprisingly for a present-day reader – what for him is the common view of old people in the United States at the beginning of the 20th century: "Their appearance is generally unesthetic, their actions objectionable, their very existence often an incubus to those who in a spirit of humanity or duty take upon themselves the care of the aged." (qtd. in Cole 2006: 211) The culturally prevailing attitude towards the aged in the early decades of the 20th century thus essentially marginalizes and discriminates old people as useless, as they become a burden to their family and the society at large. Some sixty years later, David Fischer (1978) still identified gerontophobia as the predominant attitude of Americans toward old age and the aged, brought about by the increasing urbanization and industrialization that marginalized old people as economically useless and led to the cult of youth in modern America.

It is against this background that "Old Mr. Marblehall" appears as a story that is closely entwined with the gerontophobic discourse of its time, and thus entwined with cultural life knowledge and forms of life. In the first paragraph of Welty's story the narrator describes the eponymous character in words that seem to echo – if not mock – Nascher's description:

> You can see him out taking a walk. Watch and you'll see *how preciously old people come to think they are made* – the way they walk, *like conspirators*, bent over a little, filled with protection. They stand long on the corners but more impatiently than anyone, as if they expect traffic to take notice of them, rear up the horses and throw on the brakes so they can go where they want to go. That's Mr. Marblehall. He has short white bangs, and a bit of snapdragon in his lapel. He walks with a big polished stick, a present. That's what people think of him. Everybody says to his face, "So well preserved!" Behind his back they say cheerfully, "One foot in the grave." He has on his thick, beautiful, glowing coat – tweed, but he looks as gratified as an animal in its own tingling fur. You see, even in summer he wears it, because *he is cold all the time*. He *looks quaintly secretive and prepared for anything*, out walking very luxuriously on Catherine Street. ("Marblehall," 91, emphases added, M.B.)

Literally parading the old man in the story's initial paragraph, the narrator firmly establishes an ironic distance between him- or herself and the protagonist right from the beginning. Marblehall is indeed represented here as an 'unesthetic' or even grotesque sight, looking like a strange animal in his furry coat and walking luxuriously, secretively, and conspiratorially along the streets of Natchez. With his white hair, bent posture, polished stick, and the snapdragon (a flower whose seed resembles a human skull) in his lapel, the old man is introduced as the ultimate other, an almost devilish creature. This description of Marblehall strongly resonates with Nascher's remarks, especially with his use of the term 'incubus' to describe old people. An incubus is usually defined as "a feigned evil spirit or demon (originating in personified representations of the nightmare) supposed to descend upon persons in their sleep, and especially to seek carnal intercourse with women" (*Oxford English Dictionary Online*). In the story, Marblehall's body not only becomes the "dominant signifier of old age" (Woodward 1991: 10) and thus a sign of decline and deformation; his representation as an evil spirit also echoes with the gerontophobic descriptions that we find in Nascher's text. Paradoxically, the figure of the old man even becomes a sexual threat to society: As an incubus, he is the incarnation of a cultural fear of old age, descending upon younger women in their sleep and producing freakish children with them.

But who is this narrator that can hardly conceal his or her contempt for Marblehall and in fact for all elderly people ("you'll see how preciously old people come to think they are made")? Like Faulkner in "A Rose for Emily" – another story about the perception of old age in the post-bellum Southern society –, Welty employs a communal narrative voice that contains all of the curiosities, assumptions, and prejudices of the town community. Given the narrator's profound and intimate knowledge of the town's social structure and its gossip, it seems safe to claim that the narrator is part of the community he talks about (cf. Kreyling 1999: 23). Throughout the entire story, the narrator not only comments extensively (and derisively) on Marblehall's life, but also relates what the other community members think and say about him: "Behind his back they say..." ("Marblehall," 91), "Everybody passing by thinks..." (ibid.: 93), "He could die, for all they care" (ibid.), "Nobody cares" (ibid.: 96), etc. Perhaps even more importantly, the narrator frequently and directly addresses the reader, inviting her to share the view of old Marblehall as a burden of the community.

One could interpret the narrator's descriptions of Marblehall's strange looks and behavior as well as the speculations about his double life as primarily a strategy of social othering: Marblehall's appearance (his "short white bangs", his inadequate clothing, etc.), his psychological disposition as well as his social behavior (his impatience and craving for recognition) all stigmatize him as a social other, an outlandish individual, a devilish presence in the cultural subconscious. In fact, there is a certain paradox in the story, concerning the community's perception of and behavior towards Marblehall. Although the town's community would prefer to ignore him altogether, he somehow "commands attention because having married for the first time at age 60 and, worse, having a six-year-old son, he is a jarring contradiction of the dry, dusty decrepitude which society ascribes to the old" (Loughman 1980: 183-4). Hence, it is not his appearance *per se* that provokes the narrator's contempt, but Marblehall's refusal to accept the role and behaviors that society holds in store for him (and for all elderly people).

In her introduction to *A Curtain of Green*, Katherine Anne Porter has praised Welty for her ability to portray the grotesques of southern life and southern society and thereby set the tone for further critical evaluation of her work (cf. Kreyling 1999: 9-10). Comparing Welty's use of grotesque characters to that of "painters of the grotesque" who "make only detailed reports of actual living types observed more keenly than the average eye is able of observing" (Porter 1979: xxi), Porter calls Welty's characters "little human monsters", even though she is quick to add that they are "not really caricatures at all, but individuals exactly and clearly presented" (ibid.). This notion, somewhat mildly rejected by Welty herself (cf. Kreyling 1999: 9), clearly foregrounds the outlandish appearance of stories like "Old Mr. Marblehall" and underlines the visual quality of Welty's stories by linking them to other art forms such as painting.

The grotesque in "Old Mr. Marblehall" serves as the main literary technique that allows Welty to establish a connection to her contemporaries' perceptions of old age and elderly people as demonic, and to expose and subvert these perceptions. Employing highly grotesque characters, a morally, factually, and psychologically questionable (and therefore unreliable?) narrator, as well as a rather unrealistic, 'larger-than-life' plot, Welty magnifies certain aspects of human life and living together: the self-absorption and inattentiveness of society toward older people's lives, the cruelty, hypocrisy, and "vindictiveness" ("Marblehall," 93) with which people talk about them ("He could die, for all they care; some people even say, 'Oh, is he still alive?'", ibid.), and particularly the loneliness and marginalized position of elderly people. As Celeste Loughman rightly points out in one of the very few discussions of the story that take into account the aspect of senescence, "the satire in 'Old Mr. Marblehall' is directed principally at an undiscerning society which can offer its old only indifference or ridicule" (1980: 184).

On a more abstract level, the story can also be read as an allegory of time – human time, lifetime – , and thus of a crucial element or rather measure of human life that can never be fully known or understood. However, it is by no means clear what time *means* for Marblehall. On the one hand, as the title already seems to suggest, time is of the essence for *old* Mr. Marblehall: his life is almost over. The story is an instantiation of Welty's notion about human time as an essentially narrative phenomenon, something that finds its purest expression in storytelling:

> The events in our lives happen in a sequence in time, but in their significance to ourselves they find their own order, a timetable not necessarily – perhaps not possibly – chronological. The time as we know it subjectively is often the chronology that stories and novels follow: it is the continuous thread of revelation. (Welty 2003 [1983]: 68-9)

But Welty also introduces a very specific concept of subjective time here. Spending the first sixty years of his life in a curious state of non-existence, Marblehall somehow has to make up for his past failures and the stupor of his old life by living two lives at the same time. Most notably, this temporal dimension of human life finds expression in the idea of 'storing up life':

> Nobody cares. Not an inhabitant of Natchez, Mississippi, cares if he is deceived by old Mr. Marblehall. Neither does anyone care that Mr. Marblehall has finally caught on, he thinks, to what people are supposed to do. This is it: they endure something inwardly – for a time secretly; they establish a past, a memory; thus they *store up life*. He has done this; most remarkably, he has even multiplied his life by deception; and plunging deeper and deeper he speculates upon some glorious finish, a great explosion of revelations ... the future. ("Marblehall," 96, emphasis added, M.B.)

Storing up life is what people are supposed to do, or so Marblehall thinks, and whereas this passage suggests that he tries to compensate for the passiveness and vacuity of his old life by 'storing up' and even multiplying his own life, the reader soon learns that the opposite is also true: quite paradoxically, Marblehall lives a double life in order to get it over with. In expectancy of the "glorious finish," the "great explosion of revelations," Marblehall doesn't cherish the moment, but is entirely focused on the future. The "*Terror Tales* and *Astonishing Stories*",[7] which he reads in bed scare his wife "to death" (ibid.) but somehow seem to delight the old man. However, it is not as if he regards reading as another source to multiply his own life by imagining the lives of other people. For him, reading is not an activity that allows for what Harald Weinrich (2007: 22) has so aptly called a transfer of compressed (or 'stored up') lifetime ("hochverdichtete Lebenszeit"), i.e. an aesthetic experience that allows the reader to acquire and transfer the lifetime stored in a literary work into her own life. Quite on the contrary, for Marblehall reading is a way of *killing* time:

> Mr. Marblehall doesn't feel as terrified as all that, but he reads on. He is killing time. It is richness without taste, like some holiday food. The clock gets a fruity bursting tick, to get through midnight – then leisurely, leisurely on. When time is passing it's like a bug in his ear. ("Marblehall," 95)

The ending of the story, then, arguably undermines the notion of a life that can be doubled or multiplied, and therefore denser and less wasteful of its most essential resource, namely time: "But he still has to kill time, and get through the clocking nights. Otherwise he dreams that he is a great blazing butterfly stitching up a net;

7 For Glenn, Marblehall's literary predilection is evidence for his "soul obsessed with terror" (1988 [1947]: 471).

which doesn't make sense." (ibid.: 97) Why is Marblehall killing (life)time? What does the narrator suggest when he/she states that the clock "gets a fruity bursting tick" or that time passing is "like a bug" in old Marblehall's ear? Is the passing of time something positive or negative in this story?

While these metaphors are ultimately ambivalent, contributing to the story's hypnagogic atmosphere that has puzzled so many readers, in the end Marblehall's double life is exposed to be as futile and meaningless as the life unlived in his first sixty years. Perhaps, the image of the extraordinary old Mr. Marblehall is created only to emphasize that all heightened expectations about the *meaning* of life, about what people are supposed to do – "establish a past, a memory" –, are misleading: "You will think, what if nothing ever happens? What if there is no climax, even to this amazing life? Suppose old Mr. Marblehall simply remains alive, getting older by the minute, shuttling, still secretly, back and forth?" ("Marblehall," 96)

In the end, emphasized by the narrator's explicit reader addresses, the story thus overtly turns into a kind of thought experiment, confronting the reader with existential questions about nothing less than the meaning of (later) life in the context of a hostile, self-absorbed, and overtly ageist society. However, the story's life *knowledge*, if there is any, is ultimately opaque and puzzling, and in this sense it is typical of the modernist preoccupation with everyday life and its mystification. "[I]t is quite possible," Thomas Leitch (1989: 133) writes, "to challenge the character's, and the audience's, assumptions about the world without substituting any more-authoritative knowledge, so that such stories constitute not a form of knowledge but a challenge to knowledge, that is, a way of debunking assumptions which are not really true." (ibid.) The mode of challenging or 'debunking' epistemological certainties, which Leitch describes as a characteristic 'rhythm' of the modern American short story, certainly is at work in Welty's story, thus going far beyond the scope of its own fantastic plot, and evoking in the reader questions that concern his or her own life. And while the story does not offer any direct answers to these questions, it nevertheless hints at modernist notions of the tension between social time regimes and the subjective temporality of individual lives.

12. Understanding Life Retrospectively in Stories of Remembered Life:

Willa Cather, William Saroyan, Russell Banks, Anthony Doerr

> Narrative falsifies because, in fact, most of what we do is unknown, unremembered and unap-preciated. [...] Narratives are dreams of com-memoration and relative immortality, both of which life denies to most of us.
> (Malcolm 2011: 98)

In the last years the complex and dynamic relationship between literature and memory has become a dominant concern in literary and cultural studies. A whole plethora of studies explore how fictional literary texts as well as non-fictional (or semi-fictional) genres like biography and autobiography engage in culturally situated processes of reflection, negotiation and production of individual and collective memories, shaping the very concepts, metaphors, and narratives by which people make sense of their past in order to create identities. This research draws on a wide range of interdisciplinary memory research in order to explain how such 'fictions of memory' aesthetically deal with the ways in which human memory works (see Basseler/Birke 2005), but also how memory as a dynamic cognitive-cultural complex works, to a significant degree, with the same principles and strategies of selection, causation, and narrativization as literary storytelling. If we are prepared to accept the major claim of this research field, namely that, as Paul John Eakin (1999) has famously put it, 'our lives become stories', then it already becomes obvious how far fictions of memory also serve to impart a certain cultural life knowledge based on the principles of retrospective storytelling and meaning-making.

Whereas most studies on literature and memory focus on the novel as the predominant genre of memory (see, e.g., van Gorp/Musarra-Schröder 2000; Humphrey 2005), short stories have been largely neglected or even outright dismissed in this context. There is, however, a great number of (American) short stories that deal with "memory's fragile power" (Schacter 1996), examining how memories shape identity and the very notion of a coherent life, from Katherine Anne Porter's "Old Mortality" to Eudora Welty's "A Memory" and Ernest Hemingway's "The Snows of Kilimanjaro" to Alice Munro's "The Bear Came Over the Mountain," to name but a few. Sometimes, these 'memory stories' serve as a kind of preparatory studies for longer works, as is arguably the case with some of Faulkner's stories or Toni Morrison's only short story, "Recitatif," a magnificent piece in which she develops themes of memory that would later figure in her novels, especially *Beloved* and *Jazz*. In this and other cases, the short story form provides a vehicle for an experimental handling of memory beyond the more established 'memory genres' such as epic, historical novel or family chronicle (see Humphrey 2005). A case in point would be Anthony Doerr's recent short-story cycle *Memory Wall* (2010a), in which memory provides the key theme and motifs that bind together the volume's seven stories, spanning several generations and decades as well as continents to explore both the ubiquitous power and frailty of memory.

Despite the generic preference for brief revelatory moments and 'slices of life' there are also numerous short stories which depict large time spans, often to the extent of an entire lifetime, in order to approach life from a temporal distance as it were. In what I would like to call 'stories of remembered life', life is evaluated in retrospective – either by a protagonist (as autodiegetic narrator) or a heterodiegetic narrator –, usually leading to a certain insight and formulating an explicit or implicit life ethic that may be shared or at least considered by the reader. What a life *means* and what constitutes a *meaningful* life can only be judged with the benefit of hindsight, and thus retrospectively: "Life can only be understood backwards; but it must be lived forwards," in the words that are commonly attributed to Kierkegaard.

In this respect, of course, stories of remembered life bear a close relation to biographical and autobiographical writing. In the foreword to *Aging and Biography*, James Birren, one of the pioneers of the discipline of gerontology in the United States, asks why there is such a "surge of interest in autobiographies, diaries, and other personal narratives," only to provide a first tentative answer right away: "I think it is due to a belief by researchers, scholars and the informed public that something important has been left out of our scientific knowledge-generating system in its studies of adult change and aging." (1996: ix) Stories work in ways that science does not and in fact cannot explain, providing an important extension to the methodology of scientific research regarding the understanding of aging both as an anthropological constant and as a social-cultural construct. Whether aging is assessed in positive or negative terms largely depends on the narratives that are told. To study the "inside experience of life" revealed in and through stories means to get "beyond the slings and arrows and the laboratory measurements and what our cells and tissues tell us about time" (ibid.). Birren thus emphatically ascribes a certain knowledge to life stories that is not available to other discourses, a knowledge that provides "pathways to helping all persons – including the helpless and hopeless – heal the bruises of life" (ibid.: x). As a gerontologist, Birren is primarily interested in the pragmatic uses and functions of narratives within the practice of healthcare. By interpreting lives and creating meaning of and in life, and by responding to the life circumstance and structures in a given historical period and society, fictional as well as non-fictional life stories can "provide research with a rich source of new insights into human aging" (ibid.: x).

Literary stories, with their rich and complex narrative structures and their interweaving of social and individual plots, can offer us multiple insights into the ways in which we understand life retrospectively. In this chapter, I will explore how particularly short stories, with their great degree of narrative compression and their emphasis on the temporality of human life, often connect the idea of a remembered life with old age, and thereby emphasize and shape the very notion of 'life as narrative': the idea of reminiscence, biographical work, and the storied aspects of aging, and the culturally specific idea of 'life review' (see Butler 1963; 1980), and especially the understanding that this process constitutes a kind of socialization through memory (see Kohli 1990; Saake 2008). By looking at the example of Willa Cather's "Neigbhour Rosicky", a very popular story when it first appeared in 1930, one can see how short stories often apply and prefigure biographical storytelling, and how this is used in order to produce a certain life knowledge that transcends the individual life and points toward societal issues, contributing to the cultural repository of stories Americans live by. Cather's story demonstrates how short stories, despite their limited length, can actually handle long-term temporal structures and thereby reflect on the ways in which people ascribe meaning and coherence to certain life events or how they re-examine crucial life decisions by means of narrative remembering.

In its theme and narrative structure, "Neighbour Rosicky" is perhaps the prototypical example of what I call the "short story of remembered life". In short stories of remembered life, i.e. stories in which the life of a character (or characters) is depicted retrospectively, involving a more or less explicit 'memory-effect' (*Erinnerungshaftigkeit*, see Basseler/Birke 2005), and serving to explain and create coherence in this 'storied life'. Stories of remembered life typically feature either an autodiegetic narrator who looks back on his life or, in a variation of this, a heterodiegetic narrator who relates the life of a character or characters in order to highlight certain ethical aspects of the remembered life, as in the case of "Neighbour Rosicky." In contrast to the typical 'slice-of-life' story or the epiphanic story with its emphasis on the single, life-changing moment, stories of remembered life depict life as a temporal sequence of events. The story time exceeds discourse time by many times, which usually involves a relatively high degree of narrative compression. Moreover, stories of remembered life are characterized by the formal aspect that there are always at least two temporal layers of the story: present and past are interspersed, with several flashbacks disrupting the chronological order of the story and creating a 'mimesis of memory' (see ibid.). Frequently, this effect is achieved by alternation of summary *and* scenic narration.

The theme and narrative pattern of the story of remembered life are found frequently in American literature, but also beyond. In William Saroyan's "Resurrection of a Life" (1935), for instance, the narrator recalls scenes from his youth in which he used to work as a paper boy. While the story juxtaposes the narrator's individual memories with the larger plot of world history, and especially the mass annihilation of similar lives and life stories in the first world war, it also foregrounds the momentariness and fleetingness of life:

> Everything begins with inhale and exhale, and never ends, moment after moment, yourself inhaling, and exhaling, seeing, hearing, smelling, touching, tasting, moving, sleeping, waking, day after day and year after year, until it is now, this moment, the moment of your being, the last moment, which is the saddest and most glorious. ("Resurrection," 159)

Despite relating all these memories, remembrance for the narrator only partially, if at all, renders something like a knowledge of life. In fact, life remains an ultimate riddle to him: "All that I have learned is that we breathe, from moment to moment, now, always now, and then we remember" (ibid.: 167). With this unbridgeable gap between the 'now' of living and the 'then' of remembering, life and knowledge remain antitheses, expressed in the narrator's sober recognition: "all that I know is that we are somehow alive" (ibid.).

Recent examples of the story of remembered life include, among many others, Russell Banks's "My Mother's Memoirs, My Father's Lie, and Other Stories" (1986) and Anthony Doerr's "Afterworld" (2010). In Banks's piece the narrator hears and interprets his parents' stories about their past, grappling with the truthfulness of these stories and, even more so, their relevance and significance for his own life. As the narrator remembers and retells these stories, Banks's story turns into a meta-story of remembered life, in which the forms and functions of autobiographical storytelling themselves take center stage: "By remembering, as if writing my memoirs, what the stories of others have reminded me of, what they have literally brought to my mind, I have learned how my own stories function in the world" ("My Mother's Memoirs," 67). Doerr's "Afterworld" introduces the reader to the memories of Esther Gramm, an orphaned Jewish girl who had to flee from her native Hamburg during the Nazi regime. What is striking about Doerr's story is that old Esther's memories are triggered by the epileptic seizures she has suffered all of her life, now bringing back her traumatic, unwanted memories from the time of her *Auswanderung*. Complexly interweaving clinical and historical, individual and collective, generational and cross-generational dimensions of memory and life review, the story stages the long-term consequences and fragile power of such memories, as they affect not only Esther but also her grandson Robert:

> Every hour, Robert thinks, all over the globe, and infinite number of memories disappear, whole glowing atlases dragged into graves. But during that same hour children are moving about, surveying territory that seems to them entirely new. They push back the darkness; they scatter memories behind like bread crumbs. The world is remade. ("Afterworld," 242)

* * *

Against these recent examples of stories of remembered life which question and complicate the interrelation between remembrance, storytelling, and life knowledge, Cather's "Neighbour Rosicky" stands as an affirmative example of the cultural significance of stories of remembered life, as well as of the practical knowledge that can be gained from them. One of Cather's most famous stories, "Neighbour Rosicky" first appeared in the *Woman's Home Companion*, an extremely successful monthly that was published from 1873 to 1957 and reached a circulation peak of over four million during the 1930s. It was also included in her story collection *Obscure Destinies* (1932). "Neighbour Rosicky" is widely regarded as one of her finest achievements in the genre, a "rich portrait of the life of a Czech immigrant who has settled in Nebraska, and a kind of Wordsworthian pastoral [...], with a distinctly elegiac feeling at the close" (Scofield 2006: 104). The story is subdivided into six sections. The first sections begins *in medias res* with Anton Rosicky's visit at Doctor Burleigh's, who tells him that he has a bad heart. In the second part, Rosicky is on his way home from the doctor, and here the narrator describes at some length the Nebraskan landscape that Rosicky loves so much, while this section also foreshadows Rosicky's death when the old man passes the graveyard. Moreover, in this part the reader learns about the Rosickys' marriage and their idea of life, which the narrator implicitly contrasts with the modern *zeitgeist* of expansion and acceleration: "They had been at one accord not to hurry through life, not to be always skimping and saving. They saw their neighbours buy more land and feed more stock than they did, without discontent." ("Rosicky," 240) The third section, then, presents the protagonist's immigrant past and traces his long, eventful journey to Nebraska. Part four depicts in more detail the family situation of the Rosickys and especially the relationship between Anton and his children and grandchildren. The fifth section provides some more details about Rosicky's past, relating further episodes from different stages of his life. In the sixth and final section, the narrator once more emphasizes the old man's kind-heartedness and his compassion, and the story ends on an elegiac note with Doctor Burleigh's memories of Rosicky: "Rosicky's life seemed to him complete and beautiful." ("Rosicky," 261)

Despite the frequent acknowledgement of the story's nostalgia and its sentimental focus on an idealized, pre-modern past, the way in which Cather fictionalizes the concept of life review in order to provide the reader with a kind of generalizable knowledge about what constitutes a good, virtuous life has yet remained largely unnoticed. In the social sciences, psychology, and particularly in gerontology, life review is regarded as a "naturally occurring, universal mental process" (Butler 1963: 66), which is "prompted by the realization of approaching dissolution and death, and the inability to maintain one's sense of personal invulnerability" (ibid.). And while a life review therefore necessarily involves introspection and reminiscence, it is more than a mere remembering of one's life. The dominant functions of the process of life review are the reorganization and integration of one's personality as well as the resolution and understanding of the conflicts of earlier life (Woolf 1998). Moreover, it is essentially a narrative process that can have a therapeutic value, at least for those who assess their lives as successful, and it can thus prepare the individual for his or her own death. "Neighbour Rosicky" not only constitutes a fictionalized example of this process of life review by looking back on the main character's life; it also expands the traditional notion of life review as a process of introspection by involving several perspectives, thus staging it as a communal act and thereby foreclosing psychoanalyst Erik H. Erikson's assumption that life review is "most productive when experienced with significant others" (ibid., n.p.).

In *Love's Knowledge*, Martha Nussbaum (1990: 148) calls the novel the most appropriate form to articulate moral attention and vision and claims that "the novel is itself a moral achievement, and the well-lived life is a work of literary art". Taking Henry James as her prime example, Nussbaum defines novels as "works of moral philosophy" and "paradigm[s] of moral activity" (ibid.) and assesses the "moral contribution of texts that narrate the experiences of beings committed to value" (ibid.: 149). Cather, who was a great admirer of James's style, also exemplifies the way in which fiction can work on the moral imagination, narrativizing life in order to illuminate the ethics as well as pragmatics of life. In her use of the short story form Cather particularly capitalizes on the genre's potential to condense and thus bring into sharper focus certain aspects of life that she found essentially missing from, or detrimental to, the culturally dominant conceptions and norms and values of life in modern, capitalist America.

Regardless of the question of whether or not the story is marred by an antimodern nostalgia and a naïve glorification of the pastoral idyll that already led Granville Hicks, a contemporary critic, to plead "the case against Willa Cather" as early as 1933, I will discuss how the story works on the ethical imagination by fictionalizing and secularizing the notion of life review and introspection in old age. For the Puritans, as Thomas Cole (2006) has argued, the review of one's life was the primary function of age and the final step towards redemption. For Cather, it seems, the primary function of life review is no longer a religious or spiritual one, but a moral one, providing ethical guidance to the younger generations rather than achieving religious or spiritual redemption. Thus, Cather's story can be read to represent a general shift in the concept of life review from a dominantly religious to a secularized version of life review in modern Western societies.

In the story's opening paragraph, Doctor Burleigh, who has a deep affection for the Rosicky family and who they only refer to as 'Doctor Ed', tells Anton Rosicky that he suffers from cardiopathy due to the hard physical labor he has performed throughout his entire life, and that he has to be more careful from now on:

> When Doctor Burleigh told neighbour Rosicky that he had a bad heart, Rosicky protested. "So? No, I guess my heart was always pretty good. I got a little asthma, maybe. Just a awful short breath when I was pitchin' hay last summer, dat's all." ("Rosicky," 231)

The life-threatening diagnosis at the very beginning of the story thus readily identifies Rosicky as a moribund individual: Rosicky, whose life story the reader is about to hear, is already dead at the moment his story is told. Moreover, the doctor's diagnosis of Rosicky's 'bad heart' and Rosicky's own assertion that he has always had a 'good heart' establishes the difference between a knowledge about the mere physiological condition of life, and the question whether his was a good or bad life – and whether it was memorable or not: "The scientific diagnosis is accurate: within the year Rosicky will die. But the story demonstrates how limited that diagnosis is, and how Rosicky does have a good heart in that which matters – the ability to love." (Rosowski 2002 [1986]: 126) Hence, by reflecting on Anton Rosicky's life, and by relating a number of episodes which serve to demonstrate the kind-hearted wisdom of this "very simple man," the story expresses a kind of life knowledge that is deeply embedded in ethical questions and that exceeds the precarious biological process called life.

In order to create a mimesis of memory (see Basseler/Birke 2005), literary texts often juxtapose different temporal layers or levels and thus imitate the way in which past and present are interrelated in human memory. Loretta Wasserman (2002 [1991]: 249) aptly describes "Neighbour Rosicky" as a "picture of the interpenetration of the past and the present, [...] a Bergsonian concept fictionalized": By keeping a balance between the level of the basis narration and the level of flashbacks or analepses, the story creates a strong memory effect, that is a poetics of 'looking back'. The story shifts back and forth between the basis narration, expanding from Doctor Burleigh's diagnosis of Rosicky's bad heart in autumn to his death in the spring of the following year, and various episodes from different stages in Rosicky's life. Some of these episodes date back no longer than a few days or weeks, others, however, go back many years or even decades. And although there is no strict chronological order or temporal logic behind those flashbacks, the episodes tend to 'dig deeper' in Rosicky's past life as the story unfolds. What is rather unusual and innovative about "Neighbour Rosicky" as a fiction of memory and a story of remembered life is the fact that there are at least four character narrators who partake in the reminiscence of old Rosicky's life: the heterodiegetic narrator, Rosicky himself, his wife, and Doctor Burleigh, the family's physician.

First, the story is told by a rather conventional heterodiegetic (or authorial) narrator who relates Rosicky's life with some temporal distance between the events and the telling. Beginning *in medias res* with the scene in Doctor Burleigh's office, the authorial narrator later supplies all kinds of information about Rosicky, his family, and his relation to his neighbors, especially Doctor Burleigh. This alone, however, does not create a very strong mimesis of memory, since literary creation, as Richard Humphrey reminds us, always necessarily involves "an initial reminiscence and a form-giving act of re-collection and re-membering" (2005: 73). In other words, memory is "the stuff that literature is made of" (ibid.), and so the narrator's remembering of Anton Rosicky's life alone does not produce a particularly strong 'memory effect'.

Second, Anton Rosicky serves as a focalizer whenever the story relates how the immigrant came to live in Nebraska, depicting the earlier stages of his life in London and New York. These memoirs, thus, are bound to the consciousness of

Rosicky, and this is what creates the strongest illusion of a memory in "Neighbour Rosicky". In section three of the story, which includes Rosicky's first lengthier reminiscence, the old man recollects how he arrived in New York after his two rather unhappy and grievous years in London: "While he sewed, he let his mind run back over his life. He had a good deal to remember, really; life in three countries." ("Rosicky," 241) Thus staging old Rosicky's memory process, the story relies on the cultural notion of life review: In the final stage of his life, Rosicky is doing the biographical work that ascribes meaning to certain life events, creates coherence, and re-examines crucial decisions. His life is already lived, and now it needs to be storied. The sewing serves as the contemplative activity that triggers Rosicky's recollections, but it is of course also a metaphor for memory: Rosicky, quite literally, sews up his life by looking back on it. The end of the handwork also marks the end of his memory-work: "It was still early when the old farmer put aside his sewing and his recollections." ("Rosicky," 249)

It is no coincidence that Rosicky's strongest, most vivid recollections are connected with the most important, life-changing events in his past. Again, the story emphasizes the difference between the remembering self (old Rosicky) and the remembered self (young Rosicky) to create a mimesis of memory:

> Rosicky, the old Rosicky, could remember as if it were yesterday when the young Rosicky found out what was the matter with him. It was on a Fourth of July afternoon, and he was sitting in Park Place in the Sun. The lower part of New York was empty. Wall Street, Liberty Street, Broadway, all empty. So much stone and asphalt with nothing going on, so many empty windows. The emptiness was intense, like the stillness in a great factory when the machinery stops and the belts and bands cease running. It was too great a change, it took all the strength out of one. Those blank buildings, without the stream of life pouring through them, were like empty jails. It struck young Rosicky that this was the trouble with big cities; they built you in from the earth itself, cemented you away from any contact with the ground. You lived in an unnatural world, like the fish in an aquarium, who were probably much more comfortable than they ever were in the sea. ("Rosicky," 243)

The time of Rosicky's revelation is crucial, too: it is the Fourth of July that makes Rosicky realize how much he has lost his way. Like for so many other Americans before and after him (most prominently, perhaps, Henry David Thoreau, who also started his experiment at Walden Pond on this historical date), the Fourth of July becomes the turning point in his life, literally his very own private day of independence. It is the day when Rosicky leaves behind the materialism and social indifference of his contemporaries, as he recognizes the emptiness and 'unnaturalness' of modern life and makes the decision to "return to the country" and go "farther and farther west" in order to "try his fortune in another part of the world." (ibid.: 244) Here, Cather (though somewhat heavy-handedly) stages Rosicky's life as the prototypical American Dream:

> In this story, [...] she dwells on her version of the American dream – actually the original, Jeffersonian American dream of the yeoman farmer, independent and virtuous. Rosicky has been an American success, we might say, yet he wants for his sons not greater success but goodness and the freedom of personal action. He wants to perpetuate the possibility of virtuous living. (Wasserman 2002 [1991]: 250)

Third, Mary Rosicky, Anton's wife, serves as an intradiegetic narrator when she tells her children how her husband reacted when a hot summer destroyed the year's entire harvest on just one day – the Fourth of July: "I got a mind to tell you a story on him. Maybe you boys can hardly remember the year we had that terrible hot wind, that burned everything up on the Fourth of July?" ("Rosicky," 250) Instead of getting bitter or discouraged like many of their neighbors, the Rosickys had a picnic on that very day, "An' we enjoyed ourselves that year, poor as we was, an' our neighbours wasn't a bit better off for bein' miserable." ("Rosicky," 151)

Fourth, there is Doctor Burleigh who also serves as an important focalizer in the story. His memories of the Rosickys, and especially Anton Rosicky, date back only a few years, but he has an important role in the story since his memories of the title character set the sentimental, nostalgic tone of the story. After Rosicky has left his office in the beginning of the story, Doctor Burleigh, upset by his own diagnosis, remembers how only a year ago he had experienced the Rosickys' heart-felt hospitality and friendliness; there was no other "farm-house where a man could get such a warm welcome, and such good strong coffee with rich cream" ("Rosicky," 233). Burleigh's reflections on Rosicky's life serve to underscore the beauty and ideal of such a life: "Maybe, Doctor Burleigh reflected, people as generous and warm-hearted and affectionate as the Rosickys never got ahead much; maybe you couldn't enjoy your life and put it into the bank, too." ("Rosicky," 236)

When in the end of the story Burleigh comes home from a journey to Chicago, he finds that Rosicky has died, "and for the first few weeks after he got home he was hard driven" (ibid.: 260). And when he passes by the graveyard near the Rosicky's farmhouse where Anton is buried, he stops his car to pause for a moment. In this still moment of contemplation and recollection Burleigh has a kind of epiphany about the very meaning of life and death. All of a sudden, it strikes him that Rosicky "wasn't over there where the red lamplight shone, but here, in the moonlight" (ibid.), and he becomes aware of the authenticity of Rosicky's life, ultimately reflected in the place where he is buried:

> For the first time it struck Doctor Ed that this was really a beautiful graveyard. He thought of city cemeteries; acres of shrubbery and heavy stone, so arranged and lonely and unlike anything in the living world. Cities of the dead, indeed; cities of the forgotten, of the 'put away.' But this was open and free, this little square of long grass which the wind for ever stirred. Nothing but the sky overhead, and the many-coloured fields running on until they met that sky. The horses worked here in summer; the neighbours passed on their way to town; and over yonder, in the cornfield, Rosicky's own cattle would be eating fodder as winter came on. Nothing would be more undeathlike than this place; nothing could be more right for a man who had helped to do the work of great cities and had always longed for the open country and had got to it at last. Rosicky's life seemed to him complete and beautiful. (ibid.: 261)

By integrating several acts of remembrance, Cather's story thus stages Rosicky's life review not as the monoperspectival recollection of the protagonist, but as a collective act of remembrance: Rosicky's life is not forgotten, but remembered as an ideal life by all who knew him well. Anton Rosicky is the embodiment of what Cather – or at least her narrator – consider as a 'good life', and his life is monumentalized in the story. He is described as an extraordinarily kind and friendly man, whose hospitality, politeness, generosity, and good humor show in each and every aspect of his life. Rosicky is always helpful and responsive to the needs of his family and neighbors, an ultimately altruistic human being who "had a special gift for loving people" ("Rosicky," 259).

There are two main metaphors in the story that serve to create coherence in the story of Rosicky's life and thus structure his life review: that of life as a journey and that of the 'seasons of life'. Rosicky's life is presented as the neat succession of the different stages of his journey, which is both a real physical journey from Czechoslovakia to America as well as a metaphorical journey, with each of the stages also representing a stage in the course of his life. As a "lad of eighteen" Anton Rosicky leaves behind his Bohemian home and thus his childhood "with no money and no connexions except the address of a cousin" (ibid.: 248) in London. The travel from Czechoslovakia to London thus represents his coming-of-age. His youth, however, is as short and full of privations as his sojourn in England: He spends only two years in London, sleeping in doorways and not having enough to eat, before he leaves London towards America. This experience of his own lost youth, however, is what makes Rosicky such a passionate and loving father: "Perhaps the fact that his own youth was well over before he began to have a family was one reason why Rosicky was so fond of his boys." (ibid.: 244) If London stands for his short and disadvantaged youth, then New York, the next stage in the journey of his life, represents his early adulthood.

What is probably most striking about the narrator's portrayal of Rosicky's life are the strong, almost normative evaluations derived from it: Anton Rosicky's life is told to exemplify nothing less than the 'art of living', illustrating what it means to live a virtuous, passionate, committed, and ultimately content and happy life. In order to do so, the story draws on the notion and cultural practice of life review as a means to self-understanding and integration of personality, precipitated by the awareness of near death and thus the final life crisis. The outcome of this process of reminiscence has a therapeutic value for Rosicky. Looking back, the old man is content with his life and thus prepared to accept his own death. In one scene, when Rosicky comes home from a visit to his daughter-in-law, he looks at his home, surrounded by fields and the near cemetery: "He stopped by the windmill to look up at the frosty winter stars and draw a long breath before he went inside. That kitchen with the shining windows was dear to him; but the sleeping fields and bright stars and the noble darkness were dearer still." ("Rosicky," 248) As this imagery of darkness and the metaphor of the sleeping fields suggest, Rosicky is satisfied with his life and therefore not only accepts but even cherishes and longs for his own death. But it also goes beyond this, since not only old Rosicky looks back on his life in order to assess it, but also his family and, very importantly, his physician engage in reviewing Rosicky's life in order to find moral guidance. Moreover, the reader's perspective is important as well. Experiencing the collective act of life review, the reader is invited to share the wisdom and thus become a 'neighbor' of Rosicky himself. That the story's view on human life may be marred by its nostalgic tone and its valorization of agrarian values over what Cather regarded as the perils of a modern industrialized society is another matter, yet one that demonstrates how literary life knowledge is always embedded in specific socio-historical contexts.

* * *

Whether in the affirmative version presented by Cather's "Neighbour Rosicky", or in its epistemologically skepticist counterpart exemplified by Saroyan's "Resurrection of a Life", stories of remembered life employ the formal-aesthetic framework of the short story as well as the resulting effects of projective reading to explore the relationship between life, memory, and knowledge. In so doing, life knowledge in these stories is typically staged as a process of individual and collective remembrance and storytelling, often modeled on the cultural practice of life review. As such, the stories of remembered life discussed represent what could be described as an irresistible urge in the last stage of the human life course, i.e. the urge to ascribe meaning to the lived life. At the same time, as especially the analysis of Cather's story has shown, stories of remembered life are not merely the expression of a transhistorical, anthropological necessity, but are deeply embedded in historical conceptions of (old) age as well reflective of the larger social-cultural processes of transformation, in Cather's case the ultimate transformation from a pre-modern, agrarian to a modern America. What all of these stories of remembered life do, to a greater or lesser degree, however, is that they invite the reader to read them projectively, that is to cast these fictional narratives against their own life narratives, and thus to ascribe meaning that transgresses the boundaries of the text.

Coda: The Short Story as Epistemological Fiction

Alice Munro's "What Do You Want to Know For?"[1]

With this final chapter, I return to the beginning of this study to provide one more example of what, to my mind, equips the short story form as an organon of life knowledge. While in the introduction I began my considerations with a cursory reference to David Leavitt's gushing appraisal of Munro's "What Do You Want to Know For?" as a work that taught him "how to live," in the following I will analyze Munro's story itself at some greater length. The story, like many of Munro's works, stands out as a prime example of the short story's epistemological qualities and potential I have described throughout this book, exploiting the genre's capacity to condense issues of theoretical and practical life knowledge in a storied form, and to retroact on the reader's knowledge system. Munro's piece allows me to demonstrate once more the short story's penchant for staging and addressing the ways in which a knowledge of and about life is often narratively configured, but also how the short story genre – both thematically and formally – hinges upon the critical, ephemeral moments in which epistemic certitudes and cultural forms of life knowledge take center stage.

That Alice Munro stands at the beginning and end of this book is no coincidence or mistake, even though she is the only non-US-American author that I discuss at greater length. As a "flagship genre of Canadian literature" (Nischik 2007: 1) the Canadian short story, with its distinct historical development, themes and topoi as well as formal and stylistic preferences, certainly deserves its own critical

1 Parts of this chapter, in an earlier version, have been previously published in Basseler/Nünning (2013).

attention.[2] What justifies the border-crossing (not only) in the context of this study, however, is the fact that the short story in North America, but also the Anglophone short story in general, has become an increasingly inter- or transnational genre. Contemporary debates around the short story are also frequently marked by such globalization, as writers and scholars gather at international conferences, and journals and magazines such as *The New Yorker* become outlets for an increasingly international genre (see also Ibánez et al. 2007: 7).[3] While the inclusion of Alice Munro in this study accommodates this transnational nature of contemporary short story writing in English, it is also justified by the fact that what I have said about the short story as an organon of life knowledge does not stop at the US borders, but arguably characterizes many short narrative forms around the globe, even if the cultural coordinates of what constitutes such life knowledge become different ones.

At least since the past decade Alice Munro is easily among the most celebrated and critically acclaimed contemporary fiction writers in the English language and, as importantly, she is widely acknowledged as one of the most compelling practitioners of the global short story. Munro was awarded with the Man Booker International Prize for her lifetime achievement in 2009 – an accolade that was only reinforced when she received the Nobel Prize in literature four years later, praising her as the 'master of the contemporary short story'.[4] In her conversation with Stefan Åsberg after the Nobel ceremony, Munro emphasized her incentive to write stories which are grounded in the stuff of real life, and thereby cognitively and emotionally move the reader in a way that significantly changes their perspective on life:

> I want my stories to be something about life that causes people to say, not, oh, isn't that the truth, but to feel some kind of reward from the writing, and that doesn't mean that it has to

2 Recently a number of monographs and edited volumes have contributed to a heightened awareness of the significance of the Canadian short story *vis à vis* its North-American neighbor, cf. for instance Lynch/Robbeson (1999), Nischik (2007), and Löschnigg (2014).

3 Compared to the novel, with its strong foundations in the modern nation-state of the eighteenth and 19th centuries, the short story is arguably less concerned with 'big' national(ist) themes, focusing instead on the 'small' realities of everyday life (although collective and individual, private and public, local and (trans-)national issues often overlap in the short story).

4 See the official website of the Nobel Prize, www.nobelprize.org.

be a happy ending or anything, but just that everything the story tells moves the reader in such a way that you feel you are a different person when you finish. (Åsberg 2013: n.p.)

The circumstance that Munro is one of the few authors of international renown whose literary reputation rests entirely on her short stories is often regarded as a kind of oddity: "It is as though Munro is to be considered a great writer *in spite of* the fact that she *only* writes short stories." (Hunter 2007: 165) Her complex and multi-layered stories are mostly set in rural areas of southern Ontario and concern the "brutality and squalor of life on the edge of a small rural community" (Murphy 2009: 42). Focusing on those 'submerged population groups' (Frank O'Connor), Munro's stories render visible a kind of local knowledge of forms and modes of life that is deeply entrenched in the region's history, customs, manners, and mentality. This interest in local history and mentality is, as some critics have pointed out, immediately linked to the literary genre that Munro's literary achievement is so inextricably intertwined with. In her more recent stories, Munro "has begun to use the […] short story to stage an alternative history of Canada's 'settler' past, one that recognizes and accommodates the private life stories of women," as Adrian Hunter (2007: 166) puts it. Particularly her later works are characterized by an open, self-reflexive style that rejects narrative closure and even questions the very possibility of neatly coherent stories (see ibid.).[5] Her stories offer rich and multifarious representations of life and ways of living together in a particular region and society, but they also exceed the mere 'regional' and address universal issues of human life, such as loneliness, loss, grief, love, and friendship.

"What Do You Want to Know For?" was first published in 2006 in the story collection *The View From Castle Rock* and was awarded the O. Henry Prize for short fiction in 2008.[6] It dealsl with an elderly woman's confrontation with a cancer diagnosis and, even more importantly, with the cognitive and emotional uncertainty prompted by this diagnosis. By posing the central, startling question of its title, the story reconstructs the protagonist's quest for knowledge and meta-

5 Carol Ann Howells has applied the somewhat overused term "art of indeterminacy" (1998: 85) to describe this quality in Munro's stories. Adrian Hunter uses the, in my mind, more adequate generic term "interrogative short story" (2007: 176), which is characterized by a "poetics of obscurity and marginality" (ibid.) that opposes or surrenders "the novelistic will-to-knowledge" (ibid.: 176). However, what both Howells and Hunter refer to, despite the slightly different terminology, is the epistemological impetus and formal structure of Munro's short story writing.

6 All page numbers given in the following discussion of the story refer to this publication (see Munro 2008).

knowledge, her desire to know her own life and the lives of her deceased ancestors, triggered by her illness, or rather the diagnosis thereof.

As I will demonstrate in the following, Munro's piece is a paradigmatic example of the short story's epistemological quality and particularly the genre's potential to serve as an organon of life knowledge *vis à vis* the modern life sciences. While Munro draws on the conventions and affordances of the short story form, she at the same time pushes and expands the possibilities of what a short story can look like, and what it can *do*. On the one hand, "What Do You Want to Know For?" renders a highly specific, even idiosyncratic view of life by depicting two weeks in the life of an elderly Canadian woman who travels through the rural parts of Ontario in order to find distraction from an alarming diagnosis. On the other hand, it fuses a number of vastly different discursive perspectives on life, using the literary form of the short story as an epistemological medium in which the very production of life knowledge itself is displayed and reflected.

More specifically, there are six different aspects I wish to elaborate on: (1) the story's focus on crisis and thus on a situation in which life knowledge is challenged and needs to be reassessed; (2) the way in which the story stages and thematizes the complex temporality of human life and thus responds to the question of what it means to live *in time*; (3) the way in which the story foregrounds the act of storytelling as an epistemological process; (4) the story's explicit negotiation of knowledge and meta-knowledge as already suggested by the title, and particularly its response to a pragmatic conception of knowledge ('what for?'); (5) the self-reflexivity of literary life knowledge, i.e. the ways in which Munro's story makes the epistemological process its central theme, stressing both the necessity and the limits and aporias of knowledge for living; (6) the ways in which the story reintegrates different discursive practices and disciplinary approaches to human life, especially medicine, history, and geography, thus linking literature to a variety of discourses and bringing these sectors into a dialogue: "What does literature know about the manner by which other discursive sectors 'know' the world and legitimize their knowledge thereof?" (Angenot 2004: 218)

Dealing with aging and especially with illness and death as phenomena that are culturally ascribed to old age, my analysis of the story also serves to conclude the discussion of the 'stages of life' as they find their expression in the short story genre. In bio-gerontological discourse, illness and death are often regarded as "part of the evolutionary narrative of old age which depicts the aging process as completely devoid of positive meaning" (Hartung/Kunow 2011b: 15). Or, as David Gems puts it:

> Ageing, with its attendant illnesses (and death) is the most terrible thing that many of us will experience; that and witnessing what it does to our loved ones. The evolutionary theory adds insult to injury by telling us that it is a process without any kind of benign function in the cycle of life; moreover, it is, essentially, a form of genetic disease, that everybody has and that is invariably fatal. (qtd. from Hartung/Kunow 2011b: 15)

In Munro's story, the detrimental and ultimately fatal effects of aging on the human body are neither ignored nor euphemized. The narrator's assumed cancer stands in direct relation with her age, and she knows that from now on "[s]uch threats will come and go" ("What," 108). However, as the narrator deals with these unpleasant symptoms of the aging process she assumes agency and takes control of the essentially negative cultural narrative of old age. As the narrator begins to question her diagnosis and embarks on a journey that will reveal to her other, more meaningful aspects of her life, the story succeeds in providing a more positive and less deterministic vision of aging than the one that evolutionary theory or the life sciences may have to offer.

"What Do You Want to Know For?" employs as its homodiegetic narrator a sixty-odd-year-old woman who faces a life crisis after receiving a frightening medical diagnosis. In a routine mammography, a lump has been discovered in her breast:

> There was a lump deep in my left breast, which neither my doctor nor I had been able to feel. We still could not feel it. My doctor said that the mammogram showed it to be about the size of a pea. He had made an appointment for me to see a city doctor who would do a biopsy. As I was leaving he laid his hand on my shoulder. A gesture of concern or reassurance. He is a friend, and I knew that his first wife's death had begun in just this way. (ibid.: 92)

Centering on what seems to be the major event of the story – the diagnosis of probable breast cancer–, this passage already establishes some of the main themes as well as the general mood of "What Do You Want to Know For?". Most importantly, perhaps, it opens up a liminal space between life and death within which the narrator's quest for knowledge, already indicated in the title, takes place. The situation, quite literally in this case, constitutes a life crisis, a crucial "point in the progress of a disease when an important development or change takes place which is decisive of recovery or death" (*OED*). The fact that the doctor's wife has also died of breast cancer not only serves to emphasize the potentially life-threatening consequences of the finding for the narrator, but also hints, in a wider sense, at the vulnerability, finality, and fleetingness of all human life.

The scientific, material evidence of the lump in her breast as revealed by the diagnostic methods of medicine, however, seems curiously detached from the narrator's experience of her own body. Neither she nor the doctor are able to actually feel the lump, even though the mammogram provides them with its visual representation and exact physiological coordinates. Although she *knows* that the lump is there, this knowledge remains theoretical and abstract, it has no direct impact on her own physical, bodily perception. Thus, there is an unbridgeable discrepancy between the 'life knowledge' provided through the representational methods of the life sciences (here mammography) and the narrator's immediate experience. Interestingly enough, the allegedly objective, empirical and unambiguous information about the lump itself cannot close the gap between life and knowledge, but it in fact creates a void in which the very meaning and knowledge of 'life' need to be explored and reassessed.

Quite surprisingly, and perhaps confusingly, the narrator immediately relates the discovery of the lump to an apparently insignificant, unrelated incident that had happened about a year before the diagnosis. On a trip to the rural areas of southern Ontario she and her husband had come across a large, unnatural-looking mound that, on closer inspection, turned out to be a crypt, with "no clues to who or what might be hidden inside" ("What," 91). For one year, the narrator has forgotten about this crypt, but now she feels a strong need to see it again and "find out something about it" (ibid.: 92). However, when she and her husband set off to revisit the crypt they cannot find it immediately:

> We spent three or four afternoons looking for it and were puzzled and disconcerted. But it was a pleasure, as always, to be together in this part of the world looking at the countryside that we think we know so well and that is always springing some sort of surprise on us. (ibid.)

The story here creates a structural parallel between the I-narrator's vain attempts to relocate the crypt and her inability to feel the lump in her breast. Both the methods of modern medicine and their foray into the country reveal unknown secrets to the narrator, leaving her "puzzled and disconcerted".

From the very outset, the story thus centers on a moment of crisis and epistemological disorientation, interrelating her personal life story with the stories that are hidden in the region's past as well as its glacial landscape. Geographical and historical details catch her interest, and one after another she unfolds a number of secrets hidden in this part of the land: The landscape itself, "a record of ancient events" (ibid.), reveals its own geological knowledge, all documented in a special map and a book called *The Physiography of Southern Ontario*. Apart from the "usual roads and towns and rivers" (ibid.: 93), the map also shows various other "things that were a complete surprise to me when I first saw them" (ibid.), especially the moraines, drumlins, spillways and other forms of glacial landscape. At the cemetery where the mysterious crypt is located, the names of the deceased are "nearly all German" (ibid.: 97), testifying to forgotten, or in fact overwritten, chapters of German-Canadian colonial history. More and more intrigued by this knowledge, the narrator visits local town and college libraries and interviews people in the villages to find out more about the history of the cemetery which nobody else seems to be interested in. Quite to her surprise, the stories she encounters even connect to her own family history. She meets people who knew her father and finds comfort and hope in this:

And I am happy to find somebody who can see me still as part of my family, who can remember my father and the place where my parents worked and lived for all of their married lives [...] A place that I seldom drive past and can hardly relate to the life I live now, though it is not much more than twenty miles away. (ibid.: 102)

Just before the fearfully anticipated examination occurs, it is revealed that the lump had been in her breast for years without having significantly changed its shape or size. Relieved, the narrator thus moves on to her daily routines, not without noticing that these will probably not remain entirely unaffected by her recent experiences.

Knowledge, with all its culturally predominant implications and forms, becomes a questionable, fragile good in Munro's story. "What do you want to know for?" provides an unusual approach to knowledge that accounts for and even welcomes the possibility of error and the role of chance. It seems, even, that the very concept of knowledge is under continuous attack by the many mistakes, oblivion, misinterpretation, coincidence and inchoateness that qualify the narrator's life. Frequently, the narrator reflects on this, commenting on the various epistemological problems she has to face:

I thought that the appointment I had was for a biopsy, but it turned out not to be. (ibid.: 95)

It bothered us that we could not find the crypt. [...] Farther north than we had thought – just beyond the boundary of the territory we had been doggedly covering. (ibid.: 96)

(I did not know what cow cabbages were – were they ordinary cabbages kept to be fed to animals or something wild and coarser, like skunk cabbage? And how could they be dug up in such weather, with the ground like rock? There are always puzzles.) (ibid.: 98)

German inscriptions in the old church that are only revealed by a great fire: "Nobody had known, nobody had remembered that the German words were there, until the fire and the cleaning revealed them. They must have been painted over at some time, and afterward nobody spoke of them, and so the memory that they were there had entirely died out." (ibid.: 104)

I ask why nobody had told me about the lump when it first appeared. Oh, she says, they must not have seen it. (ibid.: 108)

The narrator constantly reflects on the limits of her knowledge. Often, these limits have to do with interpretation or rather misinterpretation, as in the case where she misreads the German inscriptions on the tombstones (*"Das arme Herz hienidan/Von manches Sturm bewegt/Erlangt den renen Frieden/Nur wenn es nicht mehr schlagt"* [sic]):

Herz and *Sturm* and *nicht mehr* could hardly be mistaken. But when I got home and checked the words in the German-English dictionary – finding all of them except *renen*, which could easily be a misspelling of *reinen* – I found that the verse was not so comforting. It seemed to say something about the poor heart buried here getting no peace until it stopped beating. (ibid.: 97)

Note how the verse's meaning shifts entirely once the narrator gathers new information, in this case about the exact meaning of the German words. Whereas she had thought that the words would say "something about the heart, the soul, the person buried here being out of harm's way now" (ibid.), the comforting words suddenly seem bleak to her. The passage exemplifies how in this story Munro takes apart, bit by bit, the epistemological certainties and foundations of our lives by showing how brittle, superficial, and unhelpful they can be, especially in moments of severe crisis.

Though never repeated directly in the actual story, the title's question, "What Do You Want To Know For?", becomes the story's mantra, pointing not only to the (non-)usability or (im-)practicality of knowledge, but also to its regimentation, sanctioning as well as hierarchization within society. As the narrator remarks at one point during her research,

It was necessary to learn to read, but not in the least desirable to end up with your nose in a book. If you had to learn history and foreign languages to pass out of school, it was only natural to forget that sort of thing as quickly as you could. Otherwise you would *stand out*. (ibid.: 106-7)

One of the narrator's main concerns, her "appetite for impractical knowledge" (ibid.: 106) and her existential yet ultimately unsatisfiable need *to know*, also serves as a structural element of the story as it metonymically represents the knowledge of literature. This knowledge is always and necessarily tentative, marked by self-reflexivity and openness. Whereas the clinical knowledge provided by the life sciences – the narrator's cancer diagnosis based on medical imaging methods – may be crucial for follow-up medical care and, therefore, for saving her life, it also discloses a void of a different kind of knowledge, a knowledge that can hardly be provided by special disciplines such as radiology, historiography or geography alone. In Munro's story, the event of the upcoming biopsy (or, as it later turns out, the examination preceding the actual biopsy) causes the protagonist to question and reexamine, reevaluate and – quite literally – re-map her life knowledge. It is not the technical knowledge of the life sciences that provides her with what she needs in order to find orientation and comfort. Instead, different and in fact rather marginal, ostensibly insignificant and obscure forms of knowledge become important over the course of the story. From the story's outset the links between the lump in her breast, the geological details hiding beneath the visible surface of the landscape, the region's repressed colonial history and her own family history become apparent at a thematic as well as a structural level, sharing a certain ambiguity and obscurity and thereby emphasizing the acquisition and oblivion of a knowledge that is not immediately accessible. The knowledge in/of the story, however, resides in the making of these connections and, maybe even more importantly, in being aware of the tentativeness of such knowledge. Just as the landscape and history of the region are always in motion, the narrator's body is also subject to constant transformation: "So you have to keep checking, taking in the changes, seeing things while they last." (ibid.: 93)

Structurally speaking, Munro's story draws extensively upon prefigured knowledge in a variety of discursive formations. These formations might best be understood as what Wolfgang Iser (1994: 87) has called the textual 'repertoire' (*Textrepertoire*) of a literary text, i.e. the elements through which it is connected to extra-textual systems of meaning and bodies of knowledge, and whose identification already requires an act of interpretation, based on a broad cultural and linguistic knowledge: The textual repertoire of Munro's short story includes – apart from the mammogram as an example of the representational methods of modern life science – the map of the *Physiography of Southern Ontario* which and investigates the evolutionary history, i.e. the past and present life of the environment of this particular region; the colonial history of the region, which is recorded and stored in many documents across several libraries as well as in the inscriptions and the "Gothic German lettering" ("What," 104); as well as the autobiographical references that connect the short story to Alice Munro's own battle with cancer, which was revealed to the public in 2009.[7] While all these domains constitute different forms of prefigured life knowledge – medical, geographic/geohistorical, historical, religious, and autobiographical –, they are not only incorporated, but also entangled in the aesthetic structure of the story. As in many of her stories, "connection itself is the subsuming theme" (Murphy 2009: 45), rendering problematic the limits, voids and deficits of the compartmentalization of knowledge in highly specialized discourses.

The story thus illustrates the privilege of literature to not be limited to the strict discursive rules of other knowledge formations; literature "specializes in not being specialized" (Ette 2010a: 987). Where specialized scientific discourses necessarily have to reduce 'life' to certain codes, processes, and representational methods, literature can (re-)combine seemingly heterogeneous notions of life and knowledge. Therefore, literature has a "special potential for the reintegration of different areas of cultural knowledge that are kept separate in other forms of discourse" (Zapf 2008b: 850). Following Hubert Zapf, literature can thus be conceptualized as a 'reintegrative interdiscourse' in which diverse kinds of knowledge (political, historical, scientific, philosophical, etc.) are all linked in "ecosemiotic networks of signs that transgress the separations between disciplines and cultures" (ibid.: 865). "What Do You Want to Know For?" perfectly demonstrates such 'reintegration' of knowledge across disciplinary and discursive boundaries: Seen from this vantage point, life is much more than its reductive representation in any highly specialized discourse; rather, it appears as an infinitely diverse, multi-layered, and multi-relational and dynamic formation.

What is more, only in their narrative configuration can all of the historical and present events, agents and objects become meaningful elements of the larger whole that constitutes the narrator's experience of life in a given space and time. Munro's story illustrates the fundamental function of narratives to structure and give form to our lives. Whereas life may appear rather chaotic and arbitrary, "narrative structuring presents awareness with life events and happenings coherently connected together into a storied gestalt" (Polkinghorne 1996: 82). Rather than being neutral 'representations' of life, narratives already configure and shape our

7 The text thus relates to a pre-existent 'reality' and life experience in a very direct, autobiographical manner that is typical of Munro's oeuvre: "To an extraordinary extent, the raw material of Munro's work comes from her life, a fact she readily admits" (Murphy 2009: 41). Without overstressing this autobiographical dimension of the story, it is of course interesting to note that the narrator identifies as Laidlaw (2008: 101) – Munro's maiden name –, thus clearly connecting the story to Munro's own life experiences.

very concept of life. Narrating her experiences allows the narrator to draw formerly disconnected events, people and discourses and fragments of knowledge "into a pattern of things we know about" (Munro 2008: 105), thus making meaning out of a formerly disrupted and disquieting reality. Peter Sloterdijk has recently argued that humans not only rely on their biological immune system to fend off assaults on their physiological and psychological system, but that there are also "socio-immunological" as well as symbolic or "psycho-immunological practices" (Sloterdijk 2009: 20) that contribute to people's well-being and resilience. Whereas socio-immunological practices include, for example, juridical and military aspects, psycho-immunoligical practices comprise all those practices with which humankind, from its early days, has prepared for the many uncertainties and the vulnerability of life. From ancient times on these practices have enabled human beings to cope with their mortality and vulnerability by means of an imaginative anticipation of hardship. And while literary texts like Munro's certainly cannot decrease the vulnerability of life, they arguably fulfill important functions within the cultural systems of 'anticipatory injury processing' ("Systeme zur vorwegnehmenden Verletzungsverarbeitung," Sloterdijk 2009: 22), construing an ecosemiotic network in which life knowledge is produced and negotiated.

In a remarkably complex manner, Munro's story raises a number of quintessential epistemological questions: What kind of knowledge is needed in order to 'understand' and make sense of life? How can we ever be certain that our knowledge is not marred by obliviousness, mindlessness or misinterpretation? And how accurate are our representational models that are employed to encode, store, and decode knowledge? Is the mammogram a truthful representation of the lump in the narrator's breast; and is the map an accurate representation of the landscape? Does the mammogram provide the narrator with any useful knowledge of *how to live*? And, even if it does, what elisions of other types of knowing does this scientific knowledge entail? For example, "What Do You Want to Know For?" explores the temporal dimension of life; this includes not only the time span of individual human lives but also the communicative and cultural memory of social groups – the familial memory, the church history, etc. – as well as the *longue durée* of history and the even longer time of natural history manifested in the landscape and represented in the *Physiography of Southern Ontario.* In so doing, the story presents a very dynamic notion of human life in time, one that transgresses anthropocentric teleology and emphasizes the larger contexts into which individual human lives are embedded.

"What Do You Want to Know For?" underlines both Clare Hanson's claim that the short story is a "vehicle for different *kinds* of knowledge [that] may be in some way at odds with the 'story' of dominant culture" (1989: 6) as well as

Charles May's assumption that ever so often in the short story, an experience is "lifted out of the everyday flow of human actuality and active striving" in order to challenge reality (May 2004: 24). By stressing the momentariness of experience, Munro's story reflects on "human reality in moments that cannot be so easily naturalized" (2004: 17): For the narrator, her cancer diagnosis is a reality that she cannot simply 'naturalize', that is make sense of and integrate into her experience and patterns of knowledge. On the contrary, it keeps her from going on with her life and makes it necessary to re-evaluate and, quite literally, re-map her very understanding and knowledge of life.

* * *

In the foregoing chapters I have attempted to develop a fresh perspective on the genre of the North American short story that acknowledges its cultural work as a medium, or organon, of life knowledge. Broadly speaking, my contention was that due to their thematic, formal, and aesthetic characteristics as well as the reading experience they elicit short stories have a special potential to retroact on their readers' notions and knowledge of life and thereby to shape cultural conceptions of forms of life, life practices, and lifestyles. There may not be, as Richard Eldridge rightly reminds us, any "single path, smooth and bright, for either the achievement of literary value or its transportation into the rest of life" (2008: 7). As I have tried to argue, however, short stories do provide distinct opportunities to aesthetically experience the tension between life and knowledge, manifesting in storied representations of life that invite the reader to explore and thereby transport (or project) the inherent views and knowledge of life 'into the rest of life'. With their increased degree of formal and thematic compression, short stories constitute what one might call a "formally significant attention to life" (Eldridge 2008: 20). As such, short stories serve as a distinctively literary "form of thinking that uses concepts in order to seek orientation in life under forms of emplotment and in order to work through perplexity" (ibid.: 17).

The starting point for my discussions has been the conviction shared by many readers of short stories, namely that they can illuminate and deepen our understanding of life, that they are able to "thicke[n] our sense of the perplexing essence of being human" (Means 2008: 323). And while this notion may smack of esotericism, metaphysics and old-fashioned humanism, I have attempted to theorize, contextualize, and historicize this notion by investigating the epistemological conditions and cultural workings of the American short story from the 19th to the 21st century. Admittedly, such an approach is merely a first, fragmentary and somewhat eclectic step towards a literary and culturally oriented 'science of life' (see

Basseler/Nünning 2013). I am convinced, however, that one task for literary and cultural studies in the 21st century is to engage in the (re-)construction and production of a kind of knowledge that not only speaks to a rather small in-group of literary experts and displays a "self-protecting knowingness" (Rorty 1998: 140), but also contributes to a broader public discourse about societally and culturally relevant issues. The study at hand therefore decidedly answers for a more positive and affirmative approach to literature that inquisitively explores the perspectives on life that literary texts have to offer. This approach is indebted to recent interventions in the field of literary theory and criticism that argue for new modes of interpretation. Exploring forms of 'postcritical reading', this study shares with Rita Felski's observations a

> dawning sense among literary and cultural critics that a shape of thought has grown old. [...] Ideas that seemed revelatory thirty years ago – the decentered subject! the social construction of reality! – have dwindled into shopworn slogans; defamiliarizing has lapsed into doxa, no less dogged and often as dogmatic as the certainties it sought to disrupt. [...] More and more critics are venturing to ask what is lost when a dialogue with literature gives way to a permanent diagnosis, when the remedial reading of texts loses all sight of why we are drawn to such texts in the first place. (2008: 1)

Re-engaging in a dialogue with literary texts rather than reflexively adhering to remedial readings and some, by now rather stale and predictable, "hermeneutics of suspicion" (ibid.) strikes me as one important direction in literary and cultural studies in the new millennium. Bruno Latour, in his remarkable, groundbreaking essay "Why Has Critique Run Out of Steam" argues that "a certain form of critical spirit has sent us down the wrong path" and that a renewed critical mind "is to be found in the cultivation of a *stubbornly realist attitude* [...] dealing with [...] *matters of concern*, not *matters of fact*" (2004: 231, emphasis in the original). One way of restoring such a realist attitude and exposure to matters of concern, to my mind, is to address and critically engage with the life knowledge of literary discourse. As Jörn Rüsen put it in a programmatic essay, the future of the humanities "depends on their capability to produce the kind of knowledge that is needed in order to orientate oneself within the meaning-dimensions (*Sinndimensionen*) of human life, and to stand in for the kind of education (*Bildung*) needed for a competent way of living (*sinnkompetentes Leben*)" (Rüsen 2007: 400, transl. M.B.).[8]

8 The German original reads as follows: "Die Zukunftsfähigkeit der Geisteswissenschaften steht und fällt mit ihren Fähigkeiten, genau das Wissen zu produzieren, das zur Orientierung in den Sinndimensionen der menschlichen Lebenspraxis erforderlich ist, und

The study of literature and culture therefore can and should be more daring to contribute to such a knowledge, especially since literature itself has never ceased to engage in the meaning-making processes needed for *sinnkompetentes Leben.*

The study of short stories, from such a perspective, can provide us with significant insights into the ways in which, by means of certain narrative mechanisms, techniques, and semantics (e.g., life as crisis/turning point), literary genres do engage in the reflection, production, and dissemination of sociocultural 'life knowledge'. Although many critics would agree – at least implicitly – that literature and literary genres can offer the reader valuable and unique insights into the numerous, complexly interwoven dimensions of human life, the question of how and what exactly we can learn from literary fictions remains considerably undertheorized. In this regard, of course, much more critical work is needed than this study could possibly attain. If literary and cultural studies want to play a part in the societal discourse on life knowledge, then what is needed is a collective effort to redress and reconceptualize the interrelations of literature, life, and knowledge.

A major challenge in this study has been to investigate and find evidence for the ways in which literature at large constitutes a powerful tool to "encounter real knowledge along imaginary roads" (Wood 2005: 190), and at the same time ask what characterizes the short story in terms of its epistemological *specificities* and cultural function as an organon of life knowledge. The aim of this study was thus to engage in the broader discussion of 'the knowledge of literature' *and* to substantiate this discussion by looking at the *generic* dimensions of literary (life) knowledge, using the example of the American short story. This approach is based on the assumption that genres are not neutral containers of meaning, but function as "carriers of world view" (Morson 2003: 411) and produce certain "truth effects" (Frow 2010: 72). In this context, the study at hand has attempted to provide a generic perspective on the knowledge of literature – describing the short story phenomenon from various angles, and taking into consideration typical thematic and formal aspects as well as the dimension of reader reception.

The biggest part of this study has thus been concerned with the generic specificity of literary life knowledge, based on the assumption that "knowledge and genre are inescapably intertwined" (Felski 2008: 83). The central aim was to describe the particular kinds of knowledge of and about life that the (American) short story imparts, and thus to develop a theoretical and methodological framework for the text interpretations. In particular, four aspects strike me as crucial in this respect.

---

für die Bildung einzustehen, über die Menschen verfügen müssen, wenn sie sinnkompetent leben wollen."

First, recent developments in genre theory and history have turned away from essentialist, ontological notions of genre and instead conceive of generic forms as interpretive structures and carriers of world view. Accordingly, genres are no longer described as sets of rigid, transcultural and transhistorical formal elements, but as concepts marked by flexible criteria and expressive qualities and thus "offer[ing] frameworks for constructing meaning and value" (Frow 2010: 72).[9] Hence, the short story should not be understood as a mere 'container' of some specific kind of life knowledge, but as a 'field of knowledge' (Dimock 2007) itself which produces and projects a certain view of life in the first place. In other words, the life knowledge that the short story conveys is created through its very generic representation, rather than pre-existing it. This perspective also helps to avoid a naïve mimetic conception of literature as a 'mirror of life', since it stresses the semiotic and communicational particularities of the short story's life knowledge.

Second, the act of reading and the particular *reading experience* that the short story elicits seems crucial for the genre's potential to bring home to the reader a certain sense of life and to work as a productive testing ground for narrative life knowledge. Here, especially Renate Brosch's concept of projective reading has been instructive: short stories enable us to make sense of other stories, e.g. the stories of our own lives, since they force the reader to constantly transgress the boundaries of the text and thus project and expand its meaning. If story is understood as a basic principle of the mind that enables us to create coherence, then the short story provides us with plentiful possibilities for projection.[10] Although stories may stand for nothing else than what they purport to represent, they invite readers to project them onto the macro-narratives of their own lives and thus have the potential to add to the reader's very knowledge and understanding of life.

---

9 I emphatically subscribe to the now dominant notion in short story theory that "[n]othing essential distinguishes a short story from a novel, except the dimensions" (Bonnet 1979: 5).

10 Also see Ibañez et al. (2007: 8), who comment on the cognitivist perspective on the short story: "From the cognitivist point of view, what we experience shapes our concepts and our mind. The literary mind is not a separate kind of mind, it is the fundamental mind, the mind that makes everyday life possible. The story can be considered as a basic principle of mind and every level of our experience is interpreted by means of literary devices which have cognitive and biological grounds. The goal of cognitive investigations is to contribute to situating the study of the short story in a contemporary interdisciplinary dialogue in which many of the relevant disciplines make highly significant theoretical, methodological and empirical advances."

Third, on a thematic level the epistemological quality of the short story and its potential to reflect on, produce, and disseminate life knowledge seems to be related to the genre's perceived focus on moments of crisis and turning point. There is the strong notion in short story criticism that the genre often deals with crucial situations and life-changing events. As Charles May puts it, short stories often reflect on "human reality in moments that cannot be so easily naturalized" (2004: 17). In those moments, life and knowledge seem to be irreconcilably detached: in times of life crisis, knowledge is usually suspended and/or must be reassessed. Short stories often deal with such situations of epistemological uncertainty and thereby unsettle or even debunk perceived knowledge and challenge assumptions about life which might not really be true (see Leitch 1989). But what is more, as a literary genre that tends to dwell on such moments of life-changing significance, short stories engage the question of how people select, structure, and make sense of certain incidents and thus arguably serve as models for the narrative structuring of life. At the end of such moments of crisis and turning point there is often a recognition of great importance: the realization of the futility and emptiness of one's life, an insight into some 'deeper' truth or wisdom, the recognition of missed opportunities or 'unlived life', and so forth.

Fourth, I have described the emergence and development of the short story in North America against the backdrop of the modernization process and the social upheavals of the 19th and 20th century, and particularly the genre's responsiveness to a changed concept and perception of the temporal dimensions of human life that accompanies this process. From the perspective of literary and cultural studies, time is not merely a physical phenomenon or a pre-cultural constant, but a highly cultural, i.e., socially constructed and therefore to some extent arbitrary concept. It is no coincidence, in this context, that the short story became such a foremost genre during modernism with its emphasis on the momentary and the fleetingness of human experience. Thus, it has been my aim to discuss how the short story in America has contributed to collectively shared notions and patterns of time that shape cultural life knowledge to a massive extent: the acceleration and temporalization of life, the notion of everyday time, life time, and historical time, as well as the compartmentalization of life into the distinct life phases of childhood, youth, adulthood, and age.

This study has been an attempt to develop a radically different, new approach to the short story genre that acknowledges its cultural-cognitive work as a medium of life knowledge. While it is my hope that the study will contribute to a further heterogenization and innovation of post-formalist short story theory and criticism in the 21st century, its limits are also obvious. Indeed, much more work needs to be done to further explore the short story as an epistemological genre, both from an historical and a theoretical angle; and in this respect this study can only be understood as a very first step in that process. If, however, as critics like David Shields (2010) have recently argued, conventional narrative forms like the novel, with their emphasis on expansiveness, cohesion, completeness and closure, increasingly give way to shorter and more fragmented forms of storytelling (in literature, but also in the media and other cultural areas), then the question of these forms' epistemological import also becomes more and more important. With their reverence for brevity, narrative compression and temporal finesse, short stories – and recently also their younger siblings: short-shorts (see Basseler 2018, forthcoming) – constitute their own form of literary life knowledge: "In the best short-shorts, the writer seems to have miraculously figured out a way to stage, in a very compressed space, his own metaphysic: *Life feels like this* or at least *Some aspect of life feels like this*." (Shields 2010: 126) In this sense, the study at hand hopefully serves as a first step toward an approach to short (fictional) narratives that explains the role of these texts in the complex and dynamic processes through which readers gain and refine their 'sense of life', which in turn must always be understood as an already culturally prefigured life knowledge.

Works Cited

Abels, Heinz. 2008. "Lebensphase Jugend." In: Heinz Abels et al. (eds.), *Lebensphasen. Eine Einführung*. Wiesbaden: VS Verlag. 77-157.

Abels, Heinz et al. 2008. "Vorwort." In: Heinz Abels et al. (eds.), *Lebensphasen. Eine Einführung*. Wiesbaden: VS Verlag. 7-8.

Abbott, Andrew. 1997. "On the Concept of Turning Point." *Comparative Social Research* 16: 85-105.

Adamson, Jane, Richard Freadman and David Parker (eds.). 1998. *Renegotiating Ethics in Literature, Philosophy, and Theory*. Cambridge: Cambridge UP.

Ahrends, Günter. 2005 [1980]. *Die amerikanische Kurzgeschichte*. Trier: WVT.

Alexander, Henry. 2009. "Reflections on Benjamin Button." In: *Philosophy and Literature* 33.1: 1-17.

Allen, Walter. 1981. *The Short Story in English*. Oxford: Clarendon Press.

Alvarez, Ruth M. 2010. "Katherine Anne Porter." In: Alfred Bendixen and James Nagel (ed.), *A Companion to the American Short Story*. Malden, MA: Blackwell. 256-76.

Anderson, Sherwood. 1992 [1920]. "The Other Woman." In: Charles Modlin (ed.), *Certain Things Last. The Selected Short Stories of Sherwood Anderson*. New York: Four Walls Eight Windows. 18-26.

---. 1994 [1921]. "I Want to Know Why." In: Walton Litz (Ed.), *Major American Short Stories*. Oxford: Oxford University Press. 389-96.

---. 1996a [1919]. *Winesburg, Ohio*. New York: W.W. Norton & Co.

---. 1996b [1919]. "Mother." In: Anderson 1996a. 16-21.

Andringa, Els and Margrit Schreier. 2004. "How Literature Enters Life. An Introduction." In: *Poetics Today* 25.2: 161-69.

Angenot, Marc. 2004. "What Can Literature Do? From Literary Sociocriticism to a Critique of Social Discourse." In: *The Yale Journal of Criticism* 17.2: 217-31.

Arnswald, Ulrich (ed.). 2005. *Die Zukunft der Geisteswissenschaften*. Heidelberg: Manutius.

Åsberg, Stefan. 2013. "Alice Munro: In Her Own Words. Conversation with Alice Munro." https://www.nobelprize.org/nobel_prizes/literature/laureates/2013/munro-lecture_en.html. Last access: November 24, 2017.

Asholt, Wolfgang. 2010. "Neues (in) der Literaturwissenschaft?" In: Wolfgang Asholt and Ottmar Ette (eds.), *Literaturwissenschaft als Lebenswissenschaft. Programm - Projekte - Perspektiven*. Tübingen: Narr. 65-74.

---- and Ottmar Ette (eds.). 2010. *Literaturwissenschaft als Lebenswissenschaft. Programm - Projekte - Perspektiven*. Tübingen: Narr.

Assmann, Aleida. 2006. *Einführung in die Kulturwissenschaft. Grundbegriffe, Themen, Fragestellungen*. Berlin: Erich Schmidt.

Attridge, Derek. 2004. *The Singularity of Literature*. London/New York: Routledge.

Bakan, David. 1971. "Adolescence in America. From Idea to Social Fact." In: *Daedalus* 100.4: 979-95.

Bakhtin, Mikhail, and P.N. Medvedev. 1994 [1928]. "Genres as Ideological Forms." In: Pam Morris (ed.), *The Bakhtin Reader. Selected Writings of Bakhtin, Medvedev, Voloshinov*. London: Edward Arnold. 174-79.

Bakhtin, Mikhail. 2000. "Forms of Time and of the Chronotope in the Novel. Notes toward a Historical Poetics." In: Brian Richardson (Hg.), *Narrative Dynamics. Essays on Time, Plot, Closure, and Frames*. Columbus, OH: Ohio State UP. 15-24.

Balmer, Hans Peter. 2009. "Imagination und Erfahrung. John Deweys ästhetische Theorie." In: Vilmar Geppert and Hubert Zapf (eds.), *Theorien der Literatur*. Vol. 2. Tübingen: Francke. 135-54.

Banerjee, Mita, et al. 2010a. "Introduction." In: Mita Banerjee et al. (eds.), *Living American Studies*. Heidelberg: Winter. ix-xxiii.

--- (ed.). 2010b. *Living American Studies*. Heidelberg: Winter.

Banks, Russell. 2000 [1986]. "My Mother's Memoirs, My Father's Lie, and Other True Stories." In: Daniel Halpern (ed.), *The Art of the Story. An International Anthology of Contemporary Short Stories*. New York: Penguin. 63-68.

Barth, John. 1988 [1968]. *Lost in the Funhouse*. New York: Anchor.

Barthes, Roland. 1980. *Lecon/Lektion*. Trans. Helmut Scheffel. Frankfurt a.M.: Suhrkamp.

Basseler, Michael. 2009. "Literatur - Erfahrung - Lebenswissen. Perspektiven einer pragmatischen Literaturwissenschaft." In: Ottmar Ette (ed.), *Literaturwissenschaft als Lebenswissenschaft. Programm – Projekte – Perspektiven*. Tübingen: Narr. 205-22.

--- 2010. "Methoden des New Historicism und der Kulturpoetik." In: Vera Nünning and Ansgar Nünning (eds.), *Methoden der literatur- und kulturwissenschaftlichen Textanalyse. Ansätze – Grundlagen – Modellanalysen.* Stuttgart/Weimar: Metzler. 225-50.

---. 2011a. "Theories and Typologies of the Short Story." In: Michael Basseler and Ansgar Nünning (eds.), *A History of the American Short Story. Genres – Developments– Model Interpretations.* Trier: WVT. 41-64.

---. 2011b. "Anti-Plot Stories and Stories of Initiation, Sherwood Anderson's 'Mother' and 'I Want to Know Why.'" In: Michael Basseler and Ansgar Nünning (eds.), *A History of the American Short Story. Genres – Classics – Model Interpretations.* Trier: WVT. 171-186.

---. 2017. "Narrative Empathy in George Saunders's Short Fiction." In: Phillip Coleman and Steve Gronert Ellerhoff (eds.), *George Saunders. Critical Essays*. Cham: Palgrave Macmillan, 153-72.

---. 2018. "Short-Short Fiction." In: Paul Delaney and Adrian Hunter (eds.), *The Edinburgh Companion to the Short Story in English*. Edinburgh: EUP [forthcoming].

Basseler, Michael and Dorothee Birke. 2005. "Mimesis des Erinnerns." In: Astrid Erll and Ansgar Nünning (eds.): *Gedächtniskonzepte der Literaturwissenschaft. Theoretische Grundlegung und Anwendungsperspektiven.* Berlin/New York: De Gruyter. 123-48.

Basseler, Michael and Ansgar Nünning (eds.). 2011a. *A History of the American Short Story. Genres – Developments – Model Interpretations*. Trier: WVT.

---. 2013. "Literary Studies as a Form of 'Life Science'. The Knowledge of Literature." In: Ansgar Nünning and Greta Olson (eds.), *New Theories, Models and Methods in Literary and Cultural Studies. Theory into Practice*. Trier: WVT. 189-212.

Basseler, Michael, Daniel Hartley and Ansgar Nünning (eds.). 2015. *Emergent Forms of Life in Anglophone Literature. Conceptual Frameworks and Critical Analyses*. Trier: WVT.

Baum, Rosalie Murphy. 1999. "Work, Contentment, and Identity in Aging Women in Literature." In: Sara Munson Deats and Lagretta Tallent Lenker (eds.), *Aging and Identity. A Humanities Perspective*. Westport/London: Praeger. 89-101.

Baumbach, Sibylle, Ansgar Nünning and Herbert Grabes. 2009. *Literature and Values. Literature as a Medium for Representing, Disseminating, and Constructing Norms and Values*. Trier: WVT.

Baxter, Charles. 1997. "Against Epiphanies." In: Charles Baxter (ed.), *Burning Down the House. Essays on Fiction*. Saint Paul, MN: Graywolf Press. 51-78.

Bayley, John. 1988. *The Short Story. Henry James to Elizabeth Bowen*. Brighton: Harvester.

Beachcroft, T.O. 1968. *The Modest Art*. London: Oxford University Press.

Beck, Ulrich. 1986. *Risikogesellschaft. Auf dem Weg in eine andere Moderne*. Frankfurt a.M.: Suhrkamp.

Bendixen, Alfred and James Nagel (eds.). 2010. *A Companion to the American Short Story*. Malden, MA: Wiley-Blackwell.

Benjamin, Walter. 2006 [1936]. "The Storyteller." In: Dorothy J. Hale (ed.), *The Novel. An Anthology of Criticism and Theory 1900-2000*. Malden, MA: Blackwell. 362-78.

Berensmeyer, Ingo and Martin Spies. 2011. "Between Romance and Realism. 'Twice-Told' Urban Gothic in Herman Melville's 'Bartleby, the Scrivener' and Related Mid-19th-Century Narratives of Modern City Life." In: Michael Basseler and Ansgar Nünning (eds.), *A History of the American Short Story*. Trier: WVT. 109-22.

Bergmann, Ina. 2003. *And then the Child Becomes a Woman. Weibliche Initation in der amerikanischen Kurzgeschichte 1865-1970*. Heidelberg: Winter.

---. 2011. "Stories of Female Initiation. Flannery O'Connor's 'Good Country People' and Joyce Carol Oates's 'How I Contemplated the World From the Detroit House of Correction and Began My Life Over Again.'" In: Michael Basseler and Ansgar Nünning (eds.), *A History of the American Short Story: Genres - Developments - Model Interpretations*. Trier: WVT. 307-22.

Bies, Michael, Michael Gamper and Ingrid Kleeberg (eds.). 2013a. *Gattungs-Wissen. Wissenspoetologie und literarische Form*. Göttingen: Wallstein.

---. 2013b. "Einleitung." In: Bies et al.: *Gattungs-Wissen. Wissenspoetologie und literarische Form*. Göttingen: Wallstein. 7-18.

Birren, James E. 1996. "Foreword." In: James E. Birren et al. (eds.), *Aging and Biography. Explorations in Adult Development*. New York: Springer. ix-xi.

Bloom, Harold (ed.). 1985. *Willa Cather*. Broomall, PA: Chelsea House.

Bloom, Harold. 1999. *Shakespeare. The Invention of the Human*. New York: Riverhead Books.

--- (ed.). 2004. *John Cheever*. Broomall, PA: Chelsea House.

Boddy, Kasia. 2010. *The American Short Story Since 1950*. Edinburgh: Edinburgh UP.

Bogdal, Klaus-Michael. 2010. "Das Biologische und das Historische. Bewegungen im Grenzgebiet." In: Wolfgang Asholt and Ottmar Ette (eds.), *Literaturwissenschaft als Lebenswissenschaft. Programm - Projekte - Perspektiven*. Tübingen: Narr. 85-91.

Böhme, Hartmut. 2000. "Wer sagt, was Leben ist?" *Die Zeit* November 30, 41-42.

Bondurant, Mark. 2004. "Lucha Libre. The History of Mexican Pro-Wrestling." http://www.bongo.net/papers/lucha.htm. Last access: October 28, 2011.

Bonnet, Henri. 1979. "Dichotomy of Artistic Genres." In: Joseph P. Strelka (ed.), *Theories of Literary Genre*. University Park/London: Pennsylvania State UP. 3-16.

Borgards, Roland. 2007. "Wissen und Literatur. Eine Replik auf Tilmann Köppe." *Zeitschrift für Germanistik* 17.2: 425-28.

Bredella, Lothar. 1999. "How to Read and Teach Literary Texts. The Challenge of Neo-Pragmatism." In: Winfried Fluck (ed.), *Pragmatism and Literary Studies*. Tübingen: Narr. 181-206.

---. 2002. "John Dewey's Art as Experience." In: *Literarisches und interkulturelles Verstehen*. Tübingen: Narr. 164-75.

Breger, Claudia, Irmela Marei Krüger-Fürhoff and Tanja Nusser (eds.). 2008. *Engineering Life. Narrationen vom Menschen in Biomedizin, Kultur und Literatur*. Berlin: Kulturverlag Kadmos.

Brie, Steven and William Rossiter (eds.). 2011. *Literature and Ethics. From the Green Knight to the Dark Knight*. Cambridge: Cambridge Scholars Publisher.

Brosch, Renate. 2007. *Short Story. Textsorte und Leseerfahrung*. Trier: WVT.

Brown, James Robert. 1993 [1991]. *The Laboratory of the Mind. Thought Experiments in the Natural Sciences*. London/New York: Routledge.

Brown, Marshall. 1997. *Turning Points. Essays in the History of Cultural Expressions*. Stanford: Stanford UP.

Brown, Marshall and Joseph Luzzi (eds.). 2011. "Literary Value." Special Issue of *Modern Language Quarterly* 72.3.

Bruce, Donald and Anthony Purdy (eds.). 1994. *Literature and Science*. Amsterdam/Atlanta, GA: Rodopi.

Bruner, Jerome. 2004 [1987]. "Life as Narrative." In: *Social Research* 71.3: 691-710.

---. 1991. "The Narrative Construction of Reality." In: *Critical Inquiry* 18: 1-21.

Buchholz, Sabine. 2003. *Narrative Innovationen in der modernistischen britischen Short Story*. Trier: WVT.

Buell, Lawrence. 1982. "The Significance of Fantasy in Fitzgerald's Short Fiction." In: Jackson R. Bryer (ed.), *The Short Stories of F. Scott Fitzgerald. New Approaches in Criticism*. Madison: U of Wisconsin P. 23-38.

Bühler, Karl. 1999 [1934]. *Sprachtheorie. Die Darstellungsfunktion der Sprache*. 3rd ed. Stuttgart: G. Fischer.

Bühler, Jill and Antonia Eder (eds.). 2015. *Das unnütze Wissen in der Literatur*. Freiburg: Rombach.

Excerpt reprinted in *Short Story Criticism* 1: 46-50.

Burke, Kenneth. 1973. "Literature as Equipment for Living." *Philosophy of the Literary Form: Studies in Symbolic Action*. 3rd Edition. Berkeley: University of California Press. 293-304.

Burt, John. 2004. "Eudora Welty." In: Blanche Gelfant (ed.), *The Columbia Companion to the Twentieth-Century American Short Story*. New York: Columbia UP. 560-9.

Butler, R. N. 1963. "The Life Review: An Interpretation of Reminiscence in the Aged." In: *Psychiatry* 26: 65-75.

---. 1980. "The Life Review: An Unrecognized Bonanza." In: *International Journal of Aging and Human Development* 12: 35-38.

Calvino, Italo. 1986. *The Uses of Literature*. San Diego: Harcourt Brace.

Canguilhem, Georges. 2008. *Knowledge of Life*. Ed. Paola Marrati and Tood Meyers, transl. Stefanos Geroulanos and Daniela Ginsburg. New York: Fordham UP.

Carroll, Noel. 2002. "The Wheel of Virtue. Art, Literature, and Moral Knowledge." *The Journal of Aesthetics and Art Criticism* 60.1: 3-26.

Cather, Willa. 1992 [1931]. "Neighbour Rosicky." *Collected Stories*. New York: Random House. 231-61.

---. 2000 [1932]. "Old Mrs. Harris." *Collected Stories*. New York: Alfred Knopf. 262-314.

Cavell, Stanley. 1996 [1969]. "Knowing and Acknowledging." In: Stephen Mulhall (ed.), *The Stanley Cavell Reader*. Malden, MA: Blackwell. 46-71.

Charlton, Michael, Corinna Pette and Christina Burbaum. 2004. "Reading Strategies in Everyday Life. Different Ways of Reading a Novel Which Make a Difference." In: *Poetics Today* 25.2: 241-63.

Cheever, John. 2000. "The Country Husband." *The Stories of John Cheever*. New York: Alfred Knopf. 325-46.

Chialant, Maria Teresa and Marina Lops (eds.). 2012. *Time and the Short Story*. Bern: Peter Lang.

Cline, Ralph M. 1999. "Aging and the Public Schools. Visits of Charity – the Young Look at the Old." In: Sara Munson Deats and Lagretta Tallent Lenker (eds.), *Aging and Identity, A Humanities Perspective*. Westport, CT: Praeger. 169-80.

Cochran, Terry. 2007. "The Knowing of Literature." In: *New Literary History* 38.1: 127-43.

Coelsch-Foisner, Sabine. 2011. "Introduction. Life-Course Models in Literary Narratives." In: Sabine Coelsch-Foisner and Sarah Herbe (eds.), *From the Cradle to the Grave. Life-Course Models in Literary Genres*. Heidelberg: Winter. IX-XVII.

Cohen, Ralph. 2003. "Introduction. Notes Toward a Generic Reconstitution of Literary Study." In: *New Literary History* 34.3: v-xvi.

Cole, Thomas R. 2006 [1992]. *The Journey of Life. A Cultural History of Aging in America*. Cambridge: Cambridge UP.

Connor, Steven. 2006. "Against Life." In: Steven Connor, *Forensic Futures. Interrogating the Posthuman Subject*. London: Birkbeck College.

Conolly, Oliver and Bashar Haydar. 2007. "Literature, Knowledge, and Value." In: *Philosophy and Literature* 31.1: 111-24.

Conrad, Peter. 1999. *Modern Times and Modern Places. How Life and Art Were Transformed in a Century of Revolution, Innovation, and Radical Change*. New York: Knopf.

Cooke, Simon. 2011. "The Beginnings of the Modernist Short Story of Consciousness. Henry James's 'The Beast in the Jungle.'" In: Basseler/Nünning 2011. 171-186.

Copland, Sarah. 2014. "To Be Continued. The Story of Short Story Theory and Other Narrative Theory." *Narrative* 22.1: 132-49.

Crane, Stephen. 1977. [1897]. "The Open Boat." In: Joseph Katz (ed.), *The Portable Stephen Crane*. New York/London: Penguin. 360-86.

Cunningham, Hugh. 2006. *The Invention of Childhood*. London: BBC Books.

Davies, David. 2007. *Aesthetics and Literature*. Ann Arbor, MI: Continuum.

Davies, David and Carl Matheson. 2008. *Contemporary Readings in the Philosophy of Literature. An Analytic Approach*. Toronto: Broadview.

Davis, Charles E. 1972. "Welty's Old Mr. Marblehall." *The Explicator* 30. Item 40.

Dawson, Melanie. 2009. "Modern Maturity. Middle-Aged Anxiety in Modern American Fiction." In: *Literature Compass* 6.2: 253-73.

DeFalco, Amelia. 2010. *Uncanny Subjects. Aging in Contemporary Narrative*. Columbus: Ohio State UP.

Delaney Paul and Adrian Hunter (eds.). 2018. *The Edinburgh Companion to the Short Story in English*. Edinburgh: EUP.

Deleuze, Gilles. 1997. "Literature and Life." Transl. Daniel W. Smith and Michael A. Greco. In: *Critical Inquiry* 23.2: 225-30.

Deleuze, Gilles and Félix Guattari. 1986. *Kafka. Toward a Minor Literature*. Minneapolis/London: U of Minnesota P.

De Roche, Linda. 2006. *Student Companion to Willa Cather*. Westport, CT: Greenwood Press.

Devenport, Edward. 1981. "Literature as Thought Experiment." In: *The Literary Criterion* 16.2: 43-55.

Dewey, John. 2008 [1925]. *Experience and Nature*. McCutchen Press.

---. 2005 [1934]. *Art as Experience*. New York: Penguin.

Díaz, Junot. 1996. "Ysrael." *Drown*. London: Faber & Faber.

Dimock, Wai Chee. 2007. "Introduction: Genres as Fields of Knowledge." In: *PMLA* 122.5: 1377-88.

Dittrich, Andreas. 2007. "Ein Lob der Bescheidenheit. Zum Konflikt zwischen Erkenntnistheorie und Wissensgeschichte." *Zeitschrift für Germanistik* 3: 631-37.

Doerr, Anthony. 2010a. *Memory Wall. Stories*. New York: Scribner.

---. 2010b. "Afterworld." In *Doerr* 2010a, 187-242.

Dolezel, Lubomir. 1998. *Heterocosmica*. Baltimore: Johns Hopkins UP.

Donaldson, Scott. 1995. "Cheever's Shady Hill. A Suburban Sequence." In: Gerald Kennedy (ed.), *Modern American Short Story Sequences. Composite Fictions and Fictive Communities*. Cambridge: Cambridge UP. 133-50.

Donaldson, Scott. 2002 [1988]. *John Cheever. A Biography*. Lincoln, NE: iUniverse.

Douglass, Paul. 1986. *Bergson, Eliot, and American Literature*. Lexington: Kentucky UP.

Dünne, Jörg. 2011. "Von Listen und Lasten der Philologie für das Leben. Nicht mehr ganz zeitgemäße Betrachtungen zu der von Ottmar Ette initiierten Debatte um Literaturwissenschaft als Lebenswissenschaft." *Philologie im Netz* 57: 72-84.

Eagleton, Terry. 2008 [1983]. *Literary Theory. An Introduction*. Minneapolis: U of Minnesota P.

---. 2007. *The Meaning of Life*. Oxford: Oxford UP.

Eakin, Paul John. 1999. *How Our Lives Become Stories. Making Selves*. Ithaca/London: Cornell University Press.

Easterlin, Nancy. 2012. *A Biocultural Approach to Literary Theory and Interpretation*. Baltimore, MD: Johns Hopkins UP.

Easthope, Anthony. 1990. "The Question of Literary Value." *Textual Practice Winter* 4 (3): 376-89.

Eldridge, Richard. 2008. *Literature, Life, and Modernity*. New York: Columbia UP.

---. 2009. "What Writers Do. The Value of Literary Imagination." In: *JLT* 3.1: 1-18.

Elgin, Catherine Z. 2007. "The Laboratory of the Mind." In: John Gibson, Wolfgang Huemer and Luca Pocci (eds.), *A Sense of the World. Essays on Narrative, Fiction, and Knowledge*. London: Routledge. 43-54.

--- and Nelson Goodman (eds.). 1988. *Reconceptions in Philosophy and Other Arts and Sciences*. Indianapolis: Hackett.

Engelberg, Edward. 1989. *Elegiac Fictions. The Motif of the Unlived Life*. University Park/London: Pennsylvania State U.

Eppers, Arne. 2003. "Lesen. Literatur. Leben. Wie Literatur Wissen schafft." In: Arne Eppers and Hans-Peter Klemme (eds.), *Perspektiven einer anderen Moderne. Literatur und Interkulturalität. Festschrift für Leo Kreutzer*. Hannover: Revonnah. 27-39.

Erll, Astrid. 2004. "Reading Literature as Collective Texts: German and English War Novels of the 1920s as Media of Cultural and Communicative Memory." In: Christoph Bode, Sebastian Domsch and Hans Sauer (eds.), *Anglistentag München 2003: Proceedings*. Trier: WVT. 335-354.

Erll, Astrid, Herbert Grabes and Ansgar Nünning (eds.). 2008. *Ethics in Culture. The Dissemination of Values Through Literature and Other Media*. Berlin/New York: De Gruyter.

Ette, Ottmar. 2004. *ÜberLebenswissen. Die Aufgabe der Philologie*. Berlin: Kadmos.

---. 2007. "Literaturwissenschaft als Lebenswissenschaft. Eine Programmschrift im Jahr der Geisteswissenschaften." In: *Lendemains*: 7-32.

---. 2008a. "Epistemologie der écriture courte - écriture courte der Epistemologie. Versuch einer Antwort auf die Frage 'Was ist Nanophilologie?'" In: Ottmar Ette (ed.), *Nanophilologie: Literarische Kurz- und Kürzestformen in der Romania*. Tübingen: Niemeyer. 167-86.

---. 2008b. "Zur Einführung - Nanophilologie und Mikrotextualität." In: Ottmar Ette (ed.), *Nanophilologie. Literarische Kurz- und Kürzestformen in der Romania*. Tübingen: Niemeyer. 1-5.

---. 2009. "ÜberLebensWissen und ZusammenLebensWissen. Von Schiffbrüchen mit Überlebenden in Zeiten beschleunigter Globalisierung." In: Günter Butzer and Hubert Zapf (eds.), *Theorien der Literatur. Grundlagen und Perspektiven*. Vol. IV. Tübingen/Basel: Francke. 7-36.

---. 2010a. "Literature as Knowledge for Living, Literary Studies as Science for Living." In: *PMLA* 125.4: 977-93.

---. 2010b. *ZusammenLebensWissen. List, Last und Lust literarischer Konvivenz im globalen Maßstab*. Berlin: Kadmos.

Fagin, Nathan B. 1927. *The Phenomenon of Sherwood Anderson*. Baltimore: Johns Hopkins UP.

Farrell, Frank B. 2004. *Why Does Literature Matter?* Ithaca/London: Cornell UP.

Faulkner, William. "A Rose for Emily." *William Faulkner. Selected Short Stories*. New York: Random House. 47-59.

Felski, Rita. 2008. *Uses of Literature*. Malden, MA: Blackwell.

Fenner, Dagmar. 2007. *Das gute Leben*. Berlin/New York: De Gruyter.

Fireman, Gary D., Ted E. McVay, Jr. and Owen J. Flanagan. 2003. "Introduction." In: Gary D. Fireman, Ted E. McVay, Jr. and Owen J. Flanagan (eds.), *Narrative and Consciousness. Literature, Psychology, and the Brain*. Oxford/New York: Oxford UP. 3-16.

Fischer, David H. 1978. *Growing Old in America*. Expanded edition. Oxford: Oxford UP.

Fitzgerald, F. Scott. 2010 [1922]. "The Curious Case of Benjamin Button." *Tales of the Jazz Age*. Vol. 176-205. New York: Vintage.

Fluck, Winfried. 1997. *Das kulturelle Imaginäre. Funktionsgeschichte des amerikanischen Romans, 1790-1900*. Frankfurt a.M.: Suhrkamp.

---. 1999a. "The Legacy of Pragmatism. Pragmatist Approaches to Literary and Cultural Studies." In: Winfried Fluck (ed.), *Pragmatism and Literary Studies*. Tübingen: Narr. IX-XI.

---. 1999b. "Pragmatism and Aesthetic Experience." In: Winfried Fluck (ed.), *Pragmatism and Literary Studies*. Tübingen: Narr. 227-42.

----. 2009. "Why We Need Fiction. Reception Aesthetics, Literary Anthropology, Funktionsgeschichte." In: Laura Bieger and Johannes Voelz (eds.), *Romance With America? Essays on Culture, Literature, and American Studies*. Heidelberg: Winter. 365-84.

Fludernik, Monika. 1996. *Towards a 'Natural' Narratology*. London/New York: Routledge.

Ford, Richard. 2007. "Introduction." In: Richard Ford (ed.): *The New Granta Book of the American Short Story*. London: Granta. vii-xxii.

Fowler, Alastair. 1982. *Kinds of Literature. An Introduction to the Theory of Genres and Modes*. Oxford: Clarendon P.

Franklin, Benjamin. 2011 [1791]. *Benjamin Franklin's Autobiography*. New York: W.W. Norton & Co.

Freese, Peter. 1999a. *Die amerikanische Kurzgeschichte/The American Short Story. Gesammelte Aufsätze/Collected Essays*. München: Langenscheid-Longman.

---. 1999b. "Washington Irving, *The Sketchbook of Geoffrey Crayon, Gent.*" In: Freese 1999a. 89-123.

--- 1999c. "'Rising in the World' and 'Wanting to Know Why'. The Socialization Process as Theme of the American Short Story." In: Freese 1999a. 176-94.

Frost, Robert. 2007 [1915]. "The Road Not Taken." In: Nina Baym (ed.), *The Norton Anthology of American Literature, Vol. D*. New York: W.W. Norton & Co. 1399-400.

Frow, John. 2010 [2006]. *Genre*. London: Routledge.

Gabriel, Gottfried. 2010. "Der Erkenntniswert der Literatur." In: Alexander Löck and Jan Urbich (eds.), *Begriff der Literatur. Transdisziplinäre Perspektiven*. Berlin/New York: De Gruyter. 247-62.

Gamper, Michael. 2010. "Nicht-Wissen und Literatur. Eine Poetik des Irrtums bei Bacon, Lichtenberg, Novalis, Goethe." In: *Internationales Archiv für Sozialgeschichte der deutschen Literatur* 34.2: 92-120.

Ganten, Detlev, et al. (eds.). 2008. *Was ist der Mensch?* Berlin/New York: De Gruyter.

Gaskill, Nicholas M. 2008. "Experience and Signs. Towards a Pragmatist Literary Criticism." In: *New Literary History* 39: 165-83.

George, Stephen K. (Ed.). 2005. *Ethics, Literature, Theory*. Oxford: Rowman & Littlefield.

Gerhardt, Volker. 2000. "Einführung: 'Sich orientieren.'" In: Jürgen Mittelstraß (ed.), *Die Zukunft des Wissens*. Berlin: Akademie Verlag. 335-39.

---. 2008. "Selbstbestimmung." In: Detlev Ganten et al. (eds.), *Was ist der Mensch? Humanprojekt Interdisziplinäre Anthropologie*. Berlin/New York: De Gruyter. 1-10.

Gibson, John. 2007a. *Fiction and the Weave of Life*. Oxford/New York: Oxford UP.

---. 2007b. "Introduction. The Prospects of Literary Cognitivism." In: John Gibson, Wolfgang Huemer and Luca Pocci (eds.), *A Sense of the World. Essays on Fiction, Narrative, and Knowledge*. New York: Routledge. 1-9.

---, Wolfgang Huemer and Luca Pocci (eds.). 2007. *A Sense of the World. Essays on Fiction, Narrative, and Knowledge*. New York: Routledge.

Giddens, Anthony and Christopher Pierson. 1998. *Making Sense of Modernity. Conversations With Anthony Giddens*. Stanford, CA: Stanford UP.

Ginsberg, Elaine. 1975. "The Female Initiation Theme in American Fiction." In: *Studies in American Fiction* 3: 27-38.

Glenn, Eunice. 1988 [1947]. "Fantasy in the Fiction of Eudora Welty." In: John W. Aldridge (ed.), *Critiques and Essays on Modern Fiction*. The Ronald Press Co. Excerpt repr. in *Short Story Criticism* 1: 470-73.

Goodheart, Eugene. 2003. "What May Knew in 'The Beast in the Jungle.'" In: *The Sewanee Review* 111.1: 116-27.

Goodman, Nelson. 1978. *Ways of Worldmaking*. Indianapolis: Hackett.

Gourgouris, Stathis. 2003. *Does Literature Think?* Stanford: Stanford University Press.

Gullette, Margaet Morganroth. 2004. *Aged By Culture*. Chicago/London: University of Chicago Press.

Gymnich, Marion and Birgit Neumann. 2007. “Vorschläge für eine Relationierung verschiedener Aspekte und Dimensionen des Gattungskonzepts. Der Kompaktbegriff Gattung.” In: Marion Gymnich, Birgit Neumann and Ansgar Nünning (eds.), *Gattungstheorie und Gattungsgeschichte*. Trier: WVT. 31-52.

Gymnich, Marion, Birgit Neumann and Ansgar Nünning (eds.). 2007. *Gattungstheorie und Gattungsgeschichte*. Trier: WVT.

Hanson, Clare. 1989. “Introduction.” In: Clare Hanson (ed.), *Re-Reading the Short Story*. New York: St. Martin's Press. 1-9.

Hart, Jeffrey. 2011. “The Unlived Life.” In: *Sewanee Review* 119.3: 395-407.

Harte, Bret. 1992 [1870]. “The Outcasts of Poker Flat.” *The Luck of Roaring Camp and Other Short Stories*. Mineola: Dover. 11-20.

Hartung, Heike and Rüdiger Kunow (eds.). 2011a. *Age Studies*. Special issue of *Amerikastudien/American Studies* 56.1: 15-22.

---. 2011b. “Introduction. Age Studies.” In: Hartung/Kunow 2011a. 15-22.

Hassan, Ihab. 1958. “The Idea of Adolescence in American Fiction.” In: *American Quarterly* 10.3: 312-23.

Hawthorne, Nathaniel. 2007 [1832]. “My Kinsman, Major Molineux.” In: Nina Baym (Ed.), *The Norton Anthology of American Literature*. Vol. B. New York: W.W. Norton & Co. 1276-88.

---. 2007 [1835]. “Wakefield.” In: Nina Baym et al. (eds.), *The Norton Anthology of American Literature*. Vol. B. New York/London: W.W. Norton and Co. 1298-1304.

Hebel, Udo. 2008. *Einführung in die Amerikanistik/American Studies*. Stuttgart: Metzler.

Heidbrink, Ludger and Harald Welzer. 2007. *Das Ende der Bescheidenheit: Zur Verbesserung der Geistes- und Kulturwissenschaften*. München: Beck.

Heinz, Walter R. and Helga Krüger. 2001. “Life Course: Innovations and Challenges for Social Research.” In: *Current Sociology* 49.2: 29-45.

Hemingway, Ernest. 1987 [1936]. “The Snows of Kilimanjaro.” In: John Hemingway, Patrick Hemingway and Gregory Hemingway (eds.): *The Complete Stories of Ernest Hemingway. The Finca Vigía Edition*. New York: Sribner. 39-56.

Herman, David. 2013. *Storytelling and the Sciences of the Mind*. Cambridge, MA: MIT Press.

Herring, Henry D. 1986. “Literature, Concepts, and Knowledge.” In: *New Literary History* 18.1: 171-90.

Heywood, Colin. 2001. *A History of Childhood*. Oxford/Malden, MA: Blackwell.

Höcker, Arne, Jeannie Moser and Philippe Weber (eds.). 2006. *Wissen. Erzählen. Narrative der Humanwissenschaften*. Bielefeld: transcript.

Höffe, Otfried. 2007. *Lebenskunst und Moral*. München: Beck.

Hörisch, Jochen. 2007. *Das Wissen der Literatur*. München: Fink.

Horn, András. 1998. *Theorie der literarischen Gattungen. Ein Handbuch für Studierende der Literaturwissenschaft*. Würzburg: Königshausen & Neumann.

Hornung, Alfred (ed.). 2013. *American Lives*. Heidelberg: Winter.

Howells, Coral Ann. 1998. *Alice Munro*. Manchester/New York: Manchester UP.

Huemer, Wolfgang. 2007. "Why Read Literature? The Cognitive Function of Form." In: John Gibson, Wolfgang Huemer and Luca Pocci (eds.), *A Sense of the World: Essays on Fiction, Narrative, and Knowledge*. New York: Routledge. 233-45.

Humphrey, Richard. 2005. "Literarische Gattung und Gedächtnis." In: Astrid Erll and Ansgar Nünning (eds.): *Gedächtniskonzepte der Literaturwissenschaft. Theoretische Grundlegung und Anwendungsperspektiven*. Berlin/New York: De Gruyter. 73-96.

Hunter, Adrian. 2007. *The Cambridge Introduction to the Short Story in English*. Cambridge: Cambridge UP.

Hunter, Lynette. 2001. *Literary Value/Cultural Power. Verbal Arts in the Twenty-First Century*. Manchester: Manchester UP.

Ibánez, José R., José Francisco Fernández and Carmen M. Bretones (eds.). 2007. *Contemporary Debates on the Short Story*. Bern: Peter Lang.

Iftekharuddin, Farhat, et al. (eds.). 2003. *Postmodern Approaches to the Short Story*. Westport: Praeger.

Ingarden, Roman. 1973. *The Cognition of the Literary Work of Art*. Transl. Ruth Ann Crowley and Kenneth R. Olson. Evanston: Northwestern UP.

Irving, Washington. 1994 [1819]. "Rip Van Winkle." In: Walton Litz (ed.): *Major American Short Stories*. Oxford/New York: Oxford University Press. 22-37.

Iser, Wolfgang. 1989. "Toward a Literary Anthropology." In: Ralph Cohen (ed.), *The Future of Literary Theory*. London: Routledge. 208-28.

Iser, Wolfgang. 1994. *Der Akt des Lesens. Theorie ästhetischer Wirkung*. 4th ed. München: Wilhelm Fink.

---. 2000. "What is Literary Anthropology? The Difference between Explanatory and Exploratory Fictions." In: Michael P. Clark (ed.), *Revenge of the Aesthetic. The Place of Literature in Theory Today*. Berkeley et al.: U of California P. 157-79.

Jacques, Elliott. 2006 [1965]. "Death and the Mid-Life Crisis." In: Gabriele Junkers (ed.), *Is it too Late? Key Papers on Psychoanalysis and Ageing*. London: Karnac. 1-26.

James, Henry. 1986 [1897]. *What Maisie Knew*. London: Penguin.

---. 1993 [1903]. "The Beast in the Jungle." *The Beast in the Jungle and Other Stories*. New York: Dover. 33-72.

---. 1996 [1900]. "The Tree of Knowledge." *Henry James: Complete Stories 1898-1910*. New York: Penguin. 220-34.

---. 2003 [1893]. "The Middle Years." In: Christof Wegelin and Henry B. Wonham (eds.), *Tales of Henry James*. New York: W.W. Norton & Co. 211-28.

---. 2008 [1902]. *The Wings of the Dove*. London: Penguin.

James, William. N.d. "Lecture VII. Pragmatism and Humanism." <http://ebooks.adelaide.edu.au/j/james/william/pragmatism/lecture7.html>. Last access: October 12, 2009.

Jannidis, Fotis et al. (eds.). 2003. *Regeln der Bedeutung*. Berlin/New York: De Gruyter.

Jannidis, Fotis. 2008. "Zuerst Collegium Logicum. Zu Tilmann Köppes Beitrag Vom Wissen in Literatur.'" *Zeitschrift für Germanistik* 18: 373-77.

John, Eileen and Dominic M. Lopes (eds.). 2004. *Philosophy of Literature. Contemporary and Classic Readings. An Anthology*. Oxford: Blackwell.

Joyce, James. 1974 [1944]. "Definition of 'Epiphany.'" In: Eugene Current-García and Walton R. Patrick (eds.), *What is the Short Story?* Glenview/Brighton: Scott, Formesman and Company. 99-101.

Kaylor, Noel Harold (ed.). 1997. *Creative and Critical Approaches to the Short Story*. Lewiston, NY: Edwin Mellen Press.

Kazin, Alfred. 1995 [1942]. *On Native Ground*. San Diego, CA: Harvest.

Keen, Suzanne. 2007. *Empathy and the Novel*. Oxford: Oxford UP.

Kersten, Holger. 2011. "The Rise of Local-Color Writing in the American West. Bret Harte's 'The Outcasts of Poker Flat' and Mark Twain's 'The Celebrated Jumping Frog of Calaveras County.'" In: Michael Basseler and Ansgar Nünning (eds.), *A History of the American Short Story. Genres – Developments – Model Interpretations*. Trier: WVT. 123-36.

Klausnitzer, Ralf. 2008. *Literatur und Wissen: Zugänge - Modelle - Analysen*. Berlin: De Gruyter.

Klein, Christian. 2013. "Erzählung." In: Roland Borgards et al. (eds.), *Literatur und Wissen. Ein interdisziplinäres Handbuch*. Stuttgart: Metzler. 17-21.

Klepper, Martin. 2011. *The Discovery of Point of View. Observation and Narration in the American Novel 1790-1910*. Heidelberg: Winter.

Klinkert, Thomas and Monika Neuhofer (eds.). 2008a. *Literatur, Wissenschaft und Wissen seit der Epochenschwelle um 1800. Theorie - Epistemologie - komparatistische Fallstudien*. Berlin/New York: De Gruyter.

Klinkert, Thomas and Monika Neuhofer. 2008b. "Vorwort." In: Klinkert/Neuhofer 2008a. 1-16.

Knorr Cetina, Karin. 2005. “The Rise of a Culture of Life.” *EMBO Reports* 6: 76-80.

Kohlroß, Christian. 2007. *Literaturtheorie und Pragmatismus oder die Frage nach den Gründen des philologischen Wissens*. Tübingen: Niemeyer.

Kohli, Martin. 1985. “Die Institutionalisierung des Lebenslaufs. Historische Befunde und theoretische Argumente.” In: *Kölner Zeitschrift für Soziologie und Sozialpsychologie* 1: 1-29.

---. 1986. “Gesellschaftszeit und Lebenszeit.” In: *Soziale Welt* 4: 183-208.

---. 1990. “Das Alter als Herausforderung für die Theorie sozialer Ungleichheit.” In: Berger and Hradil (eds.), *Lebenslagen, Lebensläufe, Lebensstile*. Soziale Welt, Sonderband 7. Göttingen: Schwartz. 387-406

Köppe, Tilmann. 2005. “Literatur als Sinnstiftung.” In: *KulturPoetik. Zeitschrift für Kulturgeschichtliche Literaturwissenschaft/Journal of Cultural Poetics* 5.1: 1-16.

---. 2007a. “Vom Wissen in Literatur.” In: *Zeitschrift für Germanistik* 17.7: 398-410.

---. 2007b. “Fiktionalität, Wissen, Wissenschaft. Eine Replik auf Roland Borgards und Andreas Dittrich.” *Zeitschrift für Germanistik* 17.3. 638-46.

---. 2008. *Literatur und Erkenntnis. Studien zur kognitiven Signifikanz fiktionaler literarischer Werke*. Paderborn: Mentis.

--- (ed.). 2011a. *Literatur und Wissen. Theoretisch-methodische Zugänge*. Berlin/New York: De Gruyter.

---. 2011b. “Literatur und Wissen. Zur Strukturierung des Forschungsfeldes und seiner Kontroversen.” In: Tilmann Köppe (ed.), *Literatur und Wissen. Theoretisch-methodische Zugänge.* Berlin/New York: De Gruyter. 1-28.

Korte, Barbara. 2003. *The Short Story in Britain. A Historical Sketch and Anthology*. Tübingen: A. Francke.

Koselleck, Reinhart. 1979. “Einleitung.” In: Otto Brunner, Werner Conzem and Reinhart Koselleck (eds.), *Geschichtliche Grundbegriffe. Historisches Lexikon zur politisch-sozialen Sprache in Deutschland.* Bd. 1. Stuttgart: Klett. 1972. XV.

Kreyling, Michael. 1999. *Understanding Eudora Welty*. Columbia: U of South Carolina P.

Kucharzewski, Jan D. 2011. *Propositions About Life. Reengaging Literature and Science*. Heidelberg: Winter.

Kuehl, John R. 1991. *F. Scott Fitzgerald. A Study of the Short Fiction*. Ann Arbor, MI: Twayne.

Kuiken, Don, David S. Miall and Shelley Sikora. 2004. “Forms of Self-Implication in Literary Reading.” In: *Poetics Today* 25.2: 171-203.

Küpper, Joachim and Christoph Menke. 2003. "Einleitung." In: Joachim Küpper and Christoph Menke (eds.), *Dimensionen ästhetischer Erfahrung*. Frankfurt a.M.: Suhrkamp. 7-15.

Lakoff, George and Mark Johnson. 2003 [1980]. *Metaphors We Live By*. Chicago/London: U of Chicago P.

Lakoff, George and Mark Turner. 1989. *More than Cool Reason. A Field Guide to Poetic Metaphor*. Chicago/London: U of Chicago P.

Lamarque, Peter. 2007. "Aesthetics and Literature. A Problematic Relation?" In: *Philosophical Studies* 135.1: 27-40.

----. 2009. *The Philosophy of Literature*. Oxford: Blackwell.

Lamarque, Peter and Stein Haugom Olsen. 1996 [1994]. *Truth, Fiction and Literature. A Philosophical Perspective*. Oxford: Clarendon.

Latour, Bruno. 2004. "Why Has Critique Run Out of Steam? From Matters of Fact to Matters of Concern." *Critical Inquiry* 30.2: 225-48.

Leavitt, David. 2008. "David Leavitt on 'What Do You Want to Know For?' by Alice Munro." In: Laura Furman (ed.), *The O. Henry Prize Stories. The Best Stories of the Year*. New York: Anchor Books. 319-22.

Lecercle, Jean-Jacques. 2008. "Fiction, Science and Truth." In: Angela Locatelli (ed.), *La conocscenza della letteratura/The Knowledge of Literature*. Vol. 7. Bergamo: Bergamo UP. 13-28.

Leitch, Thomas M. 1989. "The Debunking Rhythm of the American Short Story." In: Susan Lohafer and Jo Ellen Clarey (eds.), *Short Story Theory at a Crossroads*. Baton Rouge: Louisiana State UP. 130-47.

---. 1997. "The New Yorker School." In: Jr. Noel Harold Kaylor (ed.), *Creative and Critical Approaches to the Short Story*. Lewiston: Edwin Mellen Press. 123-50.

Levine, Caroline. 2015. *Forms. Whole, Rhythm, Hierarchy, Network*. Princeton: Princeton UP.

Levy, Andrew. 1993. *The Culture and Commerce of the American Short Story*. Cambridge: Cambridge UP.

Leypoldt, Günter. 2008. "Uses of Metaphor. Richard Rorty's Literary Criticism and the Poetics of World-Making." In: *New Literary History* 39.1: 145-63.

Liska, Vivian. 2004. "Was weiß die Literatur?" In: *KulturPoetik. Zeitschrift für Kulturgeschichtliche Literaturwissenschaft/Journal of Cultural Poetics* 4.1: 1-18.

Livingston, Paisley. 1992. "Literature and Knowledge." In: Jonathan Dancey and Ernest Sosa (eds.), *A Companion to Epistemology*. London: Blackwell. 497-500.

Locatelli, Angela (ed.). 2002-2010. *La conoscenza della letteratura/The Knowledge of Literature*. 8 vols. Bergamo: Bergamo UP.

Löffler, Arno and Eberhard Späth (eds.). 2005. *Geschichte der englischen Kurzgeschichte*. Tübingen: Narr.

Löschnigg, Martin. 2011. "Short Story Cycles as Media of Life-Writing in Contemporary Canadian Literature." In: Sabine Coelsch-Foisner and Sarah Herbe (eds.), *From the Cradle to the Grave, Life-Course Models in Literary Genres*. Heidelberg: Winter. 107-17.

Löschnigg, Maria. 2014. *The Contemporary Canadian Short Story in English. Continuity and Change*. Trier: WVT.

Lohafer, Susan. 1994. "A Cognitive Approach to Storyness." In: Charles May (ed.), *New Short Story Theories*. Athens: Ohio UP. 301-11.

--- and Jo Ellyn Clarey (eds.). 1989. *Short Story Theory at a Crossroads*. Baton Rouge/London: Lousiana State UP.

Lombardy, Anthony. 2005. "Allen Tate and the Metaphysics of Metaphor." In: *The Southern Literary Journal* 37.2: 62-80.

Loughman, Celeste. 1980. "Eros and the Elderly. A Literary View." In: *The Gerontologist* 20.2: 182-87.

Lubbers, Klaus. 1977. *Typologie der Short Story*. Darmstadt: Wissenschaftliche Buchgesellschaft.

Lundblad, Michael. 2013. *The Birth of a Jungle. Animality in Progressive-Era U.S. Literature and Culture*. Oxford: OUP.

Lynch, Gerald and Angela Arnold Robbeson (eds.). 1999. *Dominant Impressions. Essays on the Canadian Short Story*. Ottawa: U of Ottawa P.

Malcolm, David. 2011. "The Short or the Long of It. How Can Short Stories Do Human Life?" In: Sabine Coelsch-Foisner and Sarah Herbe (eds.), *From the Cradle to the Grave. Life-Course Models in Literary Genres*. Heidelberg: Winter. 97-105.

March-Russell, Paul. 2009. *The Short Story. An Introduction*. Edinburgh: Edinburgh University Press.

Marcus, Mordecai. 1960. "What is an Initiation Story?" In: *Journal of Aesthetics and Art Criticism* 14: 221-27.

Matthews, Brander. 1901 [1885]. *The Philosophy of the Short-story*. New York: Longmans, Green & Co.

May, Charles. 1984. "The Nature of Knowledge in Short Fiction." In: *Studies in Short Fiction* 21.4: 327-38.

--- (ed.). 1997. *The New Short Story Theories*. Athens: Ohio State UP.

---. 2002. *The Short Story. The Reality of Artifice*. New York/London: Routledge.

---. 2004. "Why Short Stories are Essential and Why They are Seldom Read." In: Per Winther, Jakob Lothe and Hans H. Skei (eds.), *The Art of Brevity. Excursions in Short Fiction Theory and Analysis*. Columbia: University of South Carolina Press. 14-25.

McAdams, Dan P. 2006. *The Redemptive Self. Stories Americans Live By*. Oxford: OUP.

Means, David. 2008. "David Means on 'Folie à Deux' by William Trevor." In: Laura Furman (ed.), *The O. Henry Prize Stories 2008*. New York: Anchor Books. 322-25.

Melville, Herman. 2007 [1853]. "Bartleby, the Scrivener." In: Nina Baym (ed.), *The Norton Anthology of American Literature*. Vol. B. New York: W.W. Norton & Co. 2363-89.

Meuter, Norbert. 2009. "Narratives in Various Disciplines." In: Peter Hühn et al. (eds.), *Handbook of Narratology*. Berlin/New York: De Gruyter. 242-61.

Mikics, David. 2013. *Slow Reading in a Hurried Age*. Cambridge, MA/London: Harvard UP.

Miller, Andrew. 2007. "Lives Unled in Realist Fiction." In: *Representations* 98.1: 118-34.

Modlin, Charles E. 1992. "Introduction." In: Charles E. Modlin (ed.), *Certain Things Last. The Selected Short Stories of Sherwood Anderson*. New York: Four Walls Eight Windows. vii-xxii.

Morrison, Toni. 2007 [1983]. "Recitatif." In: Nina Baym (ed.): *Norton Anthology of American Literature*. Vol. E. New York: W.W. Norton & Co. 2685-98.

Morson, Gary Saul. 2003. "The Aphorism. Fragments from the Breakdown of Reason." In: *New Literary History* 34.3: 409-29.

Moser, Walter. 1993. "Literature. A Storehouse of Knowledge?" In: *SubStance* 22.2/3: 126-40.

Munro, Alice. 1999. "The Bear Came Over the Mountain." In: *The New Yorker* December 27. <https://www.newyorker.com/magazine/2013/10/21/the-bear-came-over-the-mountain-2.> Last access: June 12, 2017.

---. 1999 [1989]. "Meneseteung." In: John Updike (ed.), *The Best American Short Stories of the Century*. Boston/New York: Houghton Mifflin. 633-51.

---. 2008. "What Do You Want to Know For?" In: Laura Furman (ed.), *The O. Henry Prize Stories 2008*. New York: Anchor Books. 91-108.

Munson Deats, Sara and Lagretta Tallent Lenker (eds.). 1999. *Aging and Identity. A Humanities Perspective*. Westport, CT: Praeger. 169-80.

Müntefering, Nicola. 2010. *Das Kurzprosawerk Willa Cathers. Eine erzähltheoretische Analyse*. Frankfurt a.M.: Peter Lang.

Murphy, Georgann. 2009. "The Art of Alice Munro. Memory, Identity, and the Aesthetics of Connection." In: Harold Bloom (ed.), *Alice Munro*. New York: Infobase. 41-56.

Nischik, Reingard M. 1993. "Nachwort." In: Reingard Nischik (ed.), *Short Short Stories Universal. Thirty Stories from the English-Speaking World.* Stuttgart: Reclam. 1991-229.

Nischik, Reingard M. (ed.). 2007. *The Canadian Short Story. Interpretations.* Rochester, NY: Camden House.

Nünning, Ansgar. 2007. "Sechs Thesen zu den Aufgaben und Perspektiven einer lebenswissenschaftlich orientierten Literaturwissenschaft." *Lendemains* 32.126/127: 212-220.

---. 2008. "'Experiments in Life'. Formen und Funktionen der narrativen Inszenierung von Lebenskunst und Lebenswissen in George Eliots Romanen aus der Sicht einer lebenswissenschaftlich orientierten Literaturwissenschaft." In: Stefan Horlacher and Anna-Margaretha Horatschek (eds.), *Das gute Leben. Reflexionen zur Lebenskunst im britischen Roman vom Viktorianismus zur Postmoderne*. Trier: WVT. 83-117.

---. 2010. "Lebensexperimente und Weisen literarischer Welterzeugung. Thesen zu den Aufgaben und Perspektiven einer lebenswissenschaftlich orientierten Literaturwissenschaft." In: Wolfgang Asholt and Ottmar Ette (eds.), *Literaturwissenschaft als Lebenswissenschaft*. Vol. 45-64. Tübingen: Narr.

---. 2009b. "Steps Toward a Metaphorology (and Narratology) of Crises. On the Functions of Metaphors as Figurative Knowledge and Mininarrations." In: Herbert Grabes, Ansgar Nünning and Sibylle Baumbach (eds.), *Metaphors Shaping Culture and Theory*. Tübingen: Narr. 232-64.

---. 2012. "'With the Benefit of Hindsight'. Features and Functions of Turning-Points as a Narratological Concept and as a Way of Self-Making." In: Ansgar Nünning and Kai Sicks (eds.), *Turning Points. Concepts and Narratives of Change in Literature and Other Media*. Berlin/New York: De Gruyter. 31-58.

--- and Kai Sicks. 2012. "Conceptualizing Turning Points. Interdisciplinary Approaches, Metaphorical Implications and New Horizons." In: Ansgar Nünning and Kai Sicks (eds.), *Turning Points. Concepts and Narratives of Change in Literature and Other Media*. Berlin/New York: De Gruyter. 1-28.

Nünning, Vera. 2010. "Literatur als Lebenswissen. Die Bedeutung von Literatur für menschliches Verstehen und Zusammenleben am Beispiel von Ian McEwans Roman Enduring Love (1998)." In: Wolfgang Asholt and Ottmar Ette (eds.), *Literaturwissenschaft als Lebenswissenschaft. Programm - Projekte - Perspektiven*. Vol. 145-68. Tübingen: Narr.

Nussbaum, Martha C. 1990. *Love's Knowledge. Essays on Philosophy and Literature*. Oxford/New York: Oxford UP.

O'Connor, Flannery. 2009 [1955]. "A Good Man is Hard to Find." In: Flannery O'Connor, *The Complete Stories*. London: Faber & Faber. 117-33.

O'Connor, Frank. 1963. *The Lonely Voice. A Study of the Short Story*. London: Macmillan.

O'Grady, John P. 2003. "How Sustainable is the Idea of Sustainability?" *ISLE. Interdisciplinary Studies in Literature & Environment* 10.1: 1-10.

Ohi, Kevin. 2008. "Forms of Initiation. 'The Tree of Knowledge.'" In: *The Henry James Review* 29.2: 118-31.

Ortolano, Guy. 2009. *The Two Cultures Controversy. Science, Literature and Cultural Politics in Postwar Britain*. Cambridge/New York: Cambridge UP.

Paulson, William. 1993. "Literature, Knowledge, and Cultural Ecology." In: *SubStance* 22.2/3: 27-37.

Perez, Richard. 2007. "Racial Spills and Disfigured Faces in Piri Thomas's *Down These Mean Streets* and Junot Díaz's 'Ysrael.'" In: Lyn Di Orio Sandín and Richard Perez (eds.), *Contemporary U.S. Latino/a Literary Criticism*. New York: Palgrave Macmillan. 93-112.

Pethes, Nicolas. 2003. "Literatur- und Wissenschaftsgeschichte. Ein Forschungsbericht." In: *Internationales Archiv für Sozialgeschichte der Literatur* 28.1: 181-231.

Petry, Alice Hall. 1989. *Fitzgerald's Craft of Short Fiction. The Collected Stories 1920-1935*. Tuscaloosa: U of Alabama P.

Pettersson, Bo. 2008. "Procrustean Beds and Strange Bedfellows. On Literary Value as Assigned by Literary Theories." In: *Journal of Literary Theory* 2.1: 19-34.

Pickering, Jean. 1989. "Time and the Short Story." In: Clare Hanson (ed.), *Re-Reading the Short Story*. New York: St. Martin's Press. 45-54.

Poetics Today. 2002. Issue 23.1.

Polanyi, Michael. 2009 [1966]. *The Tacit Dimension*. Chicago: Chicago UP.

Polkinghorne, D.E. 1996. "Narrative Knowing and the Study of Lives." In: James E. Birren et al. (eds.), *Aging and Biography. Explorations in Adult Development*. New York: Springer. 77-99.

Pollack, Harriet. 2008 [1997]. "Photographic Convention and Story Composition. Eudora Welty's Use of Detail, Plot, Genre, and Expectation from 'A Worn Path' through *The Bride of the Innisfallen*." In: *Short Story Criticism* 111: 258-68.

Porter, Katherine Anne. 1979 [1941]. "Introduction." In: Eudora Welty, *A Curtain of Green*. San Diego/New York/London: Harvest. xi-xxv.

Poulet, Georges. 1956. *Studies in Human Time*. Baltimore, MD: Johns Hopkins UP.

Pratt, Mary Louise. 1994. "The Short Story. The Long and the Short of it." In: Charles May (ed.), *The New Short Story Theories*. Athens: Ohio State UP. 91-113.

Ricœur, Paul. 1983-85. *Temps et récit.* 3 vols. Paris: Edition du Seuill.

Ricœur, Paul. 2002. "Narrative Time." In: Brian Richardson (ed.), *Narrative Dynamics. Essays on Time, Plot, Closure, and Frames*. Athens: Ohio State UP. 35-46.

Richter, Klaus. 2011. "The Biology of Aging." In: Sabine Coelsch-Foisner and Sarah Herbe (eds.), *From the Cradle to the Grage. Life-Course Models in Literary Genres*. Heidelberg: Winter. 1-6.

Rippl, Gabriele. 2011. "Feminist Voices Around 1900. Kate Chopin's 'Desirée's Baby' and Charlotte Perkins Gilman's 'The Yellow Wall-Paper.'" In: Michael Basseler and Ansgar Nünning (eds.), *A History of the American Short Story*. Trier: WVT. 157-70.

Rohr, Susanne. 2011. "New Directions in the Post-War American Short Story. J.D. Salinger's Gladwaller-Trilogy and Bernard Malamud's 'The Mourners.'" In: Michael Basseler and Ansgar Nünning (eds.), *A History of the American Short Story. Genres – Developments – Model Interpretations*. Trier: WVT. 273-88.

Rorty, Richard. 1998. "The Inspirational Value of Great Works of Literature." In: *Achieving Our Country. Leftist Thought in Twentieth-Century-America*. Cambridge/London: Harvard University Press. 125-40.

Rorty, Richard. 2008. "Texts and Lumps." *New Literary History* 39.1: 53-68.

Rosa, Hartmut. 2013. *Social Acceleration. A New Theory of Modernity*. New York: Columbia P. [translation of Rosa, Hartmut. 2005. *Beschleunigung. Die Veränderung der Zeitstrukturen in der Moderne*. Frankfurt a.M.: Suhrkamp.]

Rosowski, Susan J. 2002 [1986]. "*Obscure Destinies.* Unalterable Realities." In: *Short Story Criticism* 50: 126-32.

Ruland, Richard and Malcolm Bradbury. 1992 [1991]. *From Puritanism to Postmodernism. A History of American Literature*. New York/Harmondsworth: Penguin.

Rüsen, Jörn. 2007. "Orientierung, Bildung, Globalisierung. Plädoyer für einen geisteswissenschaftlichen Humanismus." In: Jörg-Dieter Gauger and Günther Rüther (eds.), *Warum die Geisteswissenschaften Zukunft haben. Ein Beitrag zum Wissenschaftsjahr 2007*. Freiburg: Herder. 399-404.

Russo, Mary. 1999. "Aging and the Scandal of Anachronism." In: Kathleen Woodward (ed.), *Figuring Age. Women, Bodies, Generations*. Bloomington/Indiana: Indiana UP. 20-33.

Ryan, Marie-Laure. 2005. "Tellability." In: David Herman et al. (eds), *Routledge Encyclopedia of Narrative Theory*. London: Routledge. 589-91.

---. 2009. "Space." In: Peter Hühn et al. (eds.), *Handbook of Narratology*. Berlin/New York: De Gruyter. 420-33.

Saake, Irmhild. 2008. "Lebensphase Alter." In: Heinz Abels *et al.* (eds.), *Lebensphasen. Eine Einführung*. Wiesbaden: VS Verlag. 235-84.

Salter, James. 2007. "Last Night." *Last Night. Stories*. New York: Vintage.

Sandín, Lyn di Iorio. 2007. "The Latino Scapegoat. Knowledge Through Death in Short Stories by Joyce Carol Oates and Junot Díaz." In: Lyn Di Orio Sandín and Richard Perez (eds.), *Contemporary U.S. Latino/a Literary Criticism*. New York: Palgrave Macmillan. 15-34.

Saroyan, William. 2000 [1935]. "Resurrection of a Life." In: John Updike and Katrina Kenison (eds.), *The Best American Short Stories of the Century*. Boston/New York: Houghton Mifflin. 159-68.

Saunders, George. "The Semplica Girl Diaries." In: *Tenth of December*. London: Bloomsbury. 209-168.

Schacter, Daniel L. 1996. *Searching for Memory. The Brain, the Mind, and the Past*. New York: Basic Books.

Scheffer, Bernd. 1992. *Interpretation und Lebensroman. Zu einer konstruktivistischen Literaturtheorie*. Frankfurt a.M.: Suhrkamp.

Scheiding, Oliver and Martin Seidl. 2015. "Introduction." *Worlding America. A Transnational Anthology of Short Narratives Before 1800.* Stanford: Stanford UP. 1-18.

Schlaffer, Heinz. 1990. *Poesie und Wissen. Die Entstehung des ästhetischen Bewußtseins und der philologischen Erkenntnis*. Frankfurt a.M.: Suhrkamp.

Schmid, Wilhelm. 2014 [2007]. *Mit sich selbst befreundet sein. Von der Lebenskunst im Umgang mit sich selbst*. Frankfurt a.M.: Suhrkamp.

Schmitz-Emans, Monika (ed.). 2008. *Literature and Science. Literatur und Wissenschaft*. Würzburg: Königshausen & Neumann.

Schneider, Ralf. 2004. "Rezeptionstheorien." In: Ralf Schneider (ed.), *Literaturwissenschaft in Theorie und Praxis*. Tübingen: Narr. 189-212.

Scofield, Martin. 2001. "Winging It. Realism and Invention in the Stories of Tobias Wolff." In: *The Yearbook of English Studies* 31: 93-108.

---. 2006. *The Cambridge Introduction to the American Short Story*. Cambridge: Cambridge UP.

Seidl, Martin and Oliver Scheiding. 2011. "Early American Short Narratives. The Art of Story-Telling Prior to Washington Irving." In: Michael Basseler and Ansgar Nünning (eds.), *A History of the American Short Story. Genres – Developments – Model Interpretations*. Trier: WVT. 67-80.

Shields, David. 2010. *Reality Hunger*. London: Penguin.

Shusterman, Ronald (ed.). 2007. *Literature, Epistemology and Science*. London: Routldege.

Silber, Joan. 2009. *The Art of Time in Fiction. As Long as it Takes*. Saint Paul, MI: Graywolf Press.

Sirridge, Marjorie. 2004. "Sharing Life Stories." <http://www.med.umkc.edu/somhb/pdfs/sharing_life_stories.pdf>. Last access: Dec 3, 2011. n.p.

Slade, Joseph W. and Judith Yaross Lee (eds.). 1990. *Beyond the Two Cultures. Essays on Science, Technology, and Literature*. Ames: Iowa State UP.

Slingerland, Edward. 2008. *What Science Offers the Humanities: Integrating Body and Culture*. Cambridge/New York: Cambridge University Press.

Sloterdijk, Peter. 2009. *Du mußt dein Leben ändern*. Frankfurt a.M.: Suhrkamp.

Sontag, Susan. 1999 [1987]. "The Way We Live Now." In: John Updike (ed.), *The Best American Short Stories of the Century*. Boston/New York: Houghton Mifflin. 600-15.

Stehr, Nico. 2000. "Wissen und Information als Problem in der modernen Gesellschaft." In: Jürgen Mittelstraß (ed.), *Die Zukunft des Wissens*. Berlin: Akademie Verlag. 92-102.

Strelka, Joseph P. (ed.). 1979. *Theories of Literary Genre*. University Park/London: Pennsylvania State UP.

Suckow, Ruth. 1927. "The Short Story." *The Saturday Review of Literature* IV.17: 317-18.

Sukenick, Ronald. 2003 [1969]. *The Death of the Novel and Other Stories*. Tallahassee, FL: FC2.

Swirski, Peter. 1998. "Literature and Literary Knowledge." In: *The Journal of the Midwest Modern Language Association* 31.2: 6-23.

---. 2007. *Of Literature and Knowledge: Explorations in Narrative Thought Experiments, Evolution and Game Theory*. London/New York: Routledge.

Thompson, Evan. 2007. *Mind in Life. Biology, Phenomenology, and the Sciences of the Mind*. Cambridge, MA: Harvard UP.

Thurber, James. 1945 [1939]. "The Secret Life of Walter Mitty." In: *The Thurber Carnival*. New York: Harper and Brothers. 34-37.

Tigges, Wim (ed.). 1999. *Moments of Moment. Aspects of the Literary Epiphany*. Amsterdam: Rodopi.

Trotter, David. 2010. "Dis-enablement. Subject and Method in the Modernist Short Story." In: *Critical Quarterly* 52.2: 4-13.

Turner, Mark. 1996. *The Literary Mind. The Origins of Thought and Language*. New York/Oxford: Oxford UP.

Twain, Mark. 1994 [1865]. "The Celebrated Jumping Frog of Calaveras County." In: A. Walton Litz (ed.), *Major American Short Stories*. Oxford/New York: Oxford UP. 232-37.

Valenza, Robin. 2009. "How Literature Becomes Knowledge. A Case Study." In: *ELH* 76.1: 215-45.

Van Gorp, Hendrik and Ulla Musarra-Schröder (eds.). 2000. *Genres as Repositories of Cultural Memory*. Amsterdam/New York: Rodopi.

Vogl, Joseph. 1999. "Einleitung." In: Joseph Vogl (ed.), *Poetologien des Wissens um 1800*. München: Wilhelm Fink. 7-16.

Vogt, Robert. 2012. "'If the Stranger Hadn't Been There! ... But He Was!' The Staging of Turning Points in Alternate Histories, Science-Fiction Stories and Multiverse Narratives." In: Ansgar Nünning and Kai Sicks (eds.), *Turning Points*. 107-24.

Walsh, Dorothy. 1969. *Literature and Knowledge*. Middletown, CT: Wesleyan University Press.

Warren, James. 2001. "John Cheever." In: Blanche H. Gelfant (ed.), *The Columbia Companion to the Twentieth-Century American Short Story*. New York: Columbia UP. 199-205.

Warren, Robert Penn. 1983 [1946]. "Blackberry Winter." In: *The Circus in the Attic and Other Stories*. Orlando, FL: Harvest Books. 63-87.

Wasserman, Loretta. 2002 [1991]. "Part I: The Short Fiction." In: *Short Story Criticism* 50: 228-60. (reprinted from *Willa Cather. A Study of the Short Fiction.* Boston: Twayne)

Weinrich, Harald. 2007. "Was kostet die Zeit?" In: Harald Weinrich, *Wie zivilisiert ist der Teufel? Kurze Besuche bei Gut und Böse*. München: Beck. 11-22.

Welty, Eudora. 1980 [1941]. "Death of a Travelling Salesman." *The Collected Stories of Eudora Welty*. Orlando, FL: Harcourt. 119-30.

---. 1980 [1941]. "A Curtain of Green." *The Collected Stories of Eudora Welty*. Orlando, FL: Harcourt. 107-12.

---. 1980 [1941]. "Old Mr. Marblehall." *The Collected Stories of Eudora Welty*. Orlando, FL: Harcourt. 91-97.

---. 1980 [1941]. "A Visit of Charity." *The Collected Stories of Eudora Welty*. Orlando, FL: Harcourt. 113-18.

---. 1980 [1941]. "A Memory." *The Collected Stories of Eudora Welty*. Orlando, FL: Harcourt. 75-80.

---. 1980 [1963]. “Where Is the Voice Coming From?” *The Collected Stories of Eudora Welty*. Orlando, FL: Harcourt. 603-7.

---. 2003 [1983]. *One Writer's Beginnings*. Cambridge, MA: Harvard UP.

Weston, Ruth D. 2010. “Eudora Welty and the Short Story. Theory and Practice.” In: Alfred Bendixen and James Nagel (eds.), *A Companion to the American Short Story*. Malden, MA: Blackwell. 277-94.

Weymann, Ansgar. 2008. “Lebensphase Erwachsenenalter. Sozialisation, Konstruktion und institutionelle Vermittlung.” In: Heinz Abels et al. (ed.), *Lebensphasen. Eine Einführung*. Wiesbaden: VS Verlag. 158-234.

Wharton, Edith. 1968. “A Journey.” In: R.W.B. Lewis (ed.), *The Collected Short Stories of Edith Wharton*. Vol. 1. New York: Scribner. 79-87.

---. 1968 [1897]. “The Fulness of Life.” In: R.W.B. Lewis (ed.), *The Collected Short Stories of Edith Wharton*. Vol. 1. New York: Scribner. 12-20.

White, Hayden. 2003. “Anomalies of Genre. The Utility of Theory and History for the Study of Literary Genres.” In: *New Literary History* 34.3: 597-615.

Wilson, Ross (ed.). 2009. *The Meaning of 'Life' in Romantic Poetry and Poetics*. New York: Routledge.

Wood, Michael. 2005. *Literature and the Taste of Knowledge*. Cambridge/New York: Cambridge University Press.

Woodward, Kathleen. 1991. *Aging and Its Discontents. Freud and Other Fictions*. Bloomington: Indiana UP.

Woolf, Linda. 1998. “Life Review.” <http://www.webster.edu/~woolflm/lifereview.html>. Last access: December 17, 2011.

Wübben, Yvonne. 2013 “Forschungsskizze. Literatur und Wissen nach 1945.” In: Roland Borgards et al. (eds.), *Literatur und Wissen. Ein interdisziplinäres Handbuch*. Darmstadt: Wissenschaftliche Buchgesellschaft. 5-16.

Wyatt-Brown, Anne M. 1993. “Introduction. Aging, Gender, and Creativity.” In: Anne M. Wyatt-Brown and Janice Rossen (eds.), *Aging and Gender in Literature. Studies in Creativity*. Charlottesville/London: UP of Virginia. 1-16.

Zapf, Hubert. 2002. *Literatur als kulturelle Ökologie*. Berlin/New York: De Gruyter.

---. 2003. “Zwischen Dekonstruktion und Regeneration. Literatur als kulturelle Okologie.” In: Vilmar Geppert and Hubert Zapf (eds.): *Theorien der Literatur I*. Tübingen: Francke. 271-90.

---. 2008a. “Kulturelle Ökologie und literarisches Wissen. Perspektiven einer kulturökologischen Literaturwissenschaft an Beispielen der American Renaissance.” In: *KulturPoetik. Zeitschrift für Kulturgeschichtliche Literaturwissenschaft/Journal of Cultural Poetics* 8.2: 251-66.

---. 2008b. "Literary Ecology and the Ethics of Texts." In: *New Literary History* 39.4: 847-68.

---. 2016. *Literature as Cultural Ecology. Sustainable Texts*. London: Bloomsbury.

Zumthor, Paul. 2016. "Brevity as Form." *Narrative* 24.1: 73-81.

Zunshine, Lisa. 2006. *Why We Read Fiction. Theory of Mind and the Novel*. Columbus: Ohio State UP.

Zymner, Rüdiger. 2013. "Das 'Wissen' der Lyrik." In: Michael Bies et al (eds.), *Gattungs-Wissen. Wissenspoetologie und literarische Form*. Göttingen: Wallstein. 109-20.